BEYOND
CONTROL

BEYOND CONTROL

ABC and the Fate of the Networks

Huntington Williams

New York ATHENEUM 1989

ATHENEUM
Macmillan Publishing Company
866 Third Avenue, New York, N.Y. 10022
Collier Macmillan Canada, Inc.

Library of Congress Cataloging-in-Publication Data
Williams, Huntington.
    Beyond control: ABC and the fate of the networks / Huntington Williams.
        p.   cm.
    Includes index.
    ISBN 0-689-11818-X
    1. American Broadcasting Company. 2. Television broadcasting—United States.
I. Title.
HE8700.8.W55   1989
384.55′06′573—dc20   89-6734   CIP

Macmillan books are available at special discounts for bulk purchases for sales promotions, premiums, fund-raising, or educational use. For details, contact:

    Special Sales Director
    Macmillan Publishing Company
    866 Third Avenue
    New York, N.Y. 10022

10 9 8 7 6 5 4 3 2

Printed in the United States of America

To the memory of T.G.,
Ross Cooper and David Malone,
and for "Y"

All the great enterprises of the world are run by a few smart men: their aides and associates run down by rapid stages to the level of sheer morons.

H. L. Mencken
Minority Report

Acknowledgments

This is a nonfiction book, in which all similarities to persons living and dead are meant to be exact, and the author gets to thank the people who helped make it so. Ann Rittenberg of Atheneum Publishers and Julian Bach were the midwives for the project. Dana Points and Susannah Gray conducted much of the early research. Vivien Steir, Kimberly Wozencraft, Barry Langford, Martha Richler, and Beth Gilinsky read various drafts of the manuscript, and Alfred Evans typed most of it. Kathy Robbins, Marion Roach, Jane Hall, and Delia Marshall helped editorially, and Andy Boose, Elizabeth Perle, and Kristine Dahl gave publishing and legal advice. Oliver R. Goodenough, my lawyer, was a good friend throughout. Robert Stewart of Charles Scribner's Sons edited, and Ann Finlayson and Barbara Campo copyedited, the final product.

To the many network people who, in consenting to be interviewed, helped me understand this story, I express my deepest thanks. Any remaining errors or inconsistencies are my responsibility.

H.W.
June 1989

Contents

CONTENTS

BEYOND CONTROL

Prologue

On blazing days in mid-June, when the outdoor cafés on Central Park South stretched out their awnings and the grim and sooty canyons of midtown Manhattan sparkled against a pristine sky, a street performer known as the Trivial Pursuit Man sometimes loped down Avenue of the Americas to No. 1330 and installed himself on the newspaper vending machine in front of Hard Rock, the headquarters of ABC.

"Who's the Prime Minister of Australia?" he barked out.

The network mail-room boys, who sat on the front stoop by the ABC logo and watched pretty girls walk by, rapidly joined in the game.

"Ian Fraser!" one cried.

The Trivial Pursuit Man paused and brushed back a mop of red hair. A small crowd had formed on the sidewalk around him.

"Malcolm Fraser!" another amended.

"Right!" he shouted back. Then he shuffled the pack of index cards in his hand, and went on to the next question.

Like Alex Trebek on "Jeopardy," the Trivial Pursuit Man knew how to pace his material, and there was method to his madness. A graduate of Exeter and Harvard, he wanted to be a TV game-show host. His speaker's corner routine, which often lasted a half hour or more, was an impromptu network TV audition.

This was Broadcasting Row, the central nervous system of American television. An American flag fluttered at the corner outside Hard Rock, the network building where Leonard Goldenson ruled supreme. It was one block from Black Rock, the home of CBS and William Paley, and four blocks from 30 Rockefeller Plaza, the corporate headquarters of David Sarnoff and NBC.

In June 1981, two jobs at ABC were available—one as the editor of *Wide World,* the network's in-house magazine for employees, the other as a speechwriter for Leonard Goldenson, Elton Rule, and Fred Pierce, who were then ABC's chairman, president, and executive vice president. I spent nine months in the first job and more than three years in the second. The posts were not grand, but they offered a small foothold on a high network ledge, putting me in contact with everyone from the mail room to the corporate suite. After being handed a pair of binoculars, I didn't have to be told to watch.

During those four years at ABC I would witness the most extraordinary revolution in broadcasting since the beginning of network radio and network TV. In the short span of a few months, beginning with the $3.5 billion takeover of ABC in 1985, all three networks were shaken to the core. Sixty years of industry growth was swallowed up in an orgy of Wall Street greed. An ethic of million-dollar commercial minutes, gargantuan entertainment budgets, and outlandish network behavior, was suddenly put into the deep freeze.

When I arrived at ABC, the last days of the Big Three network empires were already at hand. The two personalities who had ruled the broadcasting industry from its early days had already fallen by the wayside—or were about to. David Sarnoff, the founder of RCA and NBC, laid out the map for broadcasting between 1928 and 1948, when network radio was king. He had died in 1971. William Paley, the founder of CBS, had worked alongside Sarnoff since 1928 and inherited his industry mantle during the first two decades of network TV. Paley, though he would later be resurrected by

4

the CBS takeover artist Laurence Tisch, was slowly receding from the scene. Tom Wyman, Paley's would-be successor, and the CBS board of directors were planning his ouster, just two years away.

But in the final decade, 1975 to 1985, Leonard Goldenson, ABC's founder, was still very much in charge, and his network, recently arrived, was still the Number One network in America. A remarkable cast of characters strutted larger-than-life on the stage: Fred Silverman, Roone Arledge, the young Barry Diller, and Michael Eisner.

Goldenson, unlike his two broadcasting peers, had spent the first twenty years of his career in the movies—in Hollywood. In the decade that led up to networks' demise he presided over a marriage between Hollywood and broadcasting that revolutionized both industries. It was the period when ABC shone like a super-nova. Fred Silverman reigned over network entertainment and promotion. Roone Arledge had turned TV sports into an overheated arena of multimillion-dollar contracts and athlete-stars. During the jackpot years, only news, the last leg of the network programming triangle, remained to be conquered—and Leonard Goldenson had his sights set on it too. He and his associates were turning the airwaves into a supercharged "show business" forum.

ABC's triumph came at an uneasy time. The network glowed with incandescent energy, but the bedrock of the broadcasting industry was slowly being eroded. In Hollywood, in Washington, and on Broadcasting Row, a real-life train of events was in progress. Radio and television had come of age far from the froth and glitter of Hollywood. But broadcasting, like the public that it was required to serve, became enamored with profits, and with the Hollywood programming that making profits entailed. And TV executives, enamored with images of sex and violence on the small screen, became picaresque actors in their own network soap operas.

While the industry was still young, while ABC was fighting its way to the top, its extravagance in programming was grist for the industry's mill. But when the network achieved success, the airwaves themselves were beyond control.

Working at ABC at the height of its power was a little bit like watching an old Hapsburg monarchy. The company's empire encompassed far-flung feudal dominions, yet its inner circle was rent by personal bickering and executive discord. Deep cracks were coming to the surface in the outlying Hollywood territories. In the corridors of Washington, ABC and its sister networks had lost their once-steady grip on the public policy-making process.

Despite their enormous influence and wealth, ABC, NBC, and CBS were vulnerable creatures, and the mind set that allowed them to prosper led ultimately to their demise. ABC, the last of the Big Three networks to triumph, was the first to fall in the broadcasting takeover wars. The $3.5 billion deal between Leonard Goldenson and Tom Murphy, his Capital Cities counterpart, was the "shot heard 'round the world" in a communications revolution that, as more recent events at Time, Warner, and Paramount bear out, is still ongoing today.

It's always hard to predict what the future may bring, but one thing is certain: The good, the bad, and the ugly in American television will never be the same.

The last time I looked, the Trivial Pursuit Man was on TV. His soap box made the midnight time slot on Manhattan public access cable and he was playing the same game.

1

25th Anniversary Party

"**G**ood evening, and welcome to ABC's fabulous, four-hour twenty-fifth birthday celebration."

On January 11, 1978, while the rest of America lay cold under a midwinter sky, Leonard Goldenson's TV network basked in the radiant Hollywood sun.

Southern California that evening was permeated by a fresh, limpid light, and the ABC Television Center—at the corner of Prospect and Talmadge, the site of the old Vitagraph studio, where *The Jazz Singer*, America's first talkie, was filmed in 1926—was a beehive of activity. The Lone Ranger galloped up on a horse. Batman and Robin appeared in hood and cape, and John Wayne wore black tie. Henry Winkler, Marlo Thomas, John Ritter, Jaclyn Smith, Olivia Newton-John—three hundred Hollywood stars altogether—were convening to help ABC celebrate its silver anniversary jubilee.

A convoy of sleek black limousines carrying the network's top brass pulled away from the Beverly Hills, the Bel Air, and the Century Plaza hotels across town, where the visitors from New York were staying. Upon arriving, all the guests walked up the sidewalk on a royal-red carpet, past the temporary green shrubbery that had been installed for the occasion. The spotlights were on. The cameras were waiting. This was no ordinary party. ABC's Silver Anniversary dinner would be taped, edited, and presented as a profit-making network "special" during the February sweeps ratings period, underwritten by Freshen-Up Gum, Excedrin, Hall's Mentho-Lyptus, and other advertising sponsors.

Penny Marshall and Cindy Williams, the stars of "Laverne and Shirley," set history in motion by blowing the dust from the cover of a Biblelike tome. Cindy Williams opened the book and read. "In 1953 . . . " She got no farther. Penny Marshall pressed the "silver anniversary plunger" on the lectern, and Act I, Scene 1 dissolved into a nighttime display of fireworks over the "Hollywood" sign in the hills above Los Angeles.

Barry Manilow sang "It's a Miracle."

On stage, Fred MacMurray introduced the party's formal theme. The network was all about a family, the star of "My Three Sons" told the studio audience. "As the years went by that family kept growing up.

"You folks at home are part of it too," MacMurray added for the camera, "because you are who we did it for."

Kristy McNichol, the star of the TV show "Family," was standing next to him on stage.

"Do you remember 'My Three Sons'?" MacMurray asked her. McNichol pretended she didn't.

"But you are old enough to remember the story of *Rocky*?" he persisted.

"Oh sure," McNichol replied. The year before *Rocky* had won the Oscar for Best Picture, beating out *Network*. "Sylvester Stallone plays a boxer who starts out a loser and works his way to the top."

"What happened to Rocky is exactly what happened to ABC," MacMurray explained.

That was the way it began—a four-hour museum of broadcasting, beginning with a montage of scenes from favorite family shows. Sparkling images from "Ozzie and Harriet" ("the Grandma and Grandpa of all family shows") and other highlights from the network's past filled the TV screen above the stage. There were programming vignettes from children's shows, Westerns, network comedy, action-adventure dramas, movies, and sports, all narrated by the stars who had appeared in them.

After the guests had polished off their lobsters and were making headway on a fresh case of champagne, comedian Alan King took the stage.

"We're gathered here after twenty-five years, and this is the first celebration," he began. "Because *this* is the first thing they ever had to celebrate!" King pointed to a large tripod display of ABC's prime-time schedule for 1977–78.

"The success of a TV network is its programs and schedule. And there it is! The reason for all this celebration! ABC is the Number One network!

"That's great until you consider there are only three networks, all competing in the great ratings race. That's comparable to running the Indianapolis 500 with a Hudson, a DeSoto, and an Edsel!"

The comedian turned to a second cardboard display showing ABC's prime-time schedule for the 1953–54 season, and went on to say, "The only way we can enjoy the thrill of victory is to go back to the agony of defeat."

He stripped off the layers of cardboard one-by-one, season-by-season, peeling away the years and exulting in the misery of the past. King called out the names of the programming disasters— "Boxing from Eastern Parkway," "Ozark Jubilee," "Jukebox Jury." Building to a climax, he hurled all of the schedules to the floor.

"Canceled! Canceled! Canceled!" he shouted.

The seasons were scattered around him on stage.

"There's a lot of lives on that floor," King observed quietly.

The Hollywood audience, meanwhile, had risen to its feet and was giving him wild, drunken applause.

There were a lot of important actors at the ABC Television Center that night—stars who could command big audiences and big-show business dollars, Hollywood personalities like John Ritter

9

of "Three's Company" and Henry Winkler of "Happy Days," who at the height of their popularity were worth more than $100,000 per thirty-second commercial to ABC. But Fred Silverman, then network TV's wunderkind programmer, outshone them all.

Silverman, the only larger-than-life TV executive in the audience, was a Daddy Bear among the network Goldilockses. He had turned the swooning frog-network into a prince. After magically transforming third-place ABC into the Number One network in America, he was widely hailed as the leading entertainment impresario in all of television.

In the Green Room, there were unhappier stars. Cliff Robertson—reeling from his discovery that a Hollywood executive named David Begelman had forged his name on two checks—was drinking heavily. Dressed in a bottle-green velvet suit, Robertson looked clammy and unsteady on his feet as he appeared on stage to present the montage of network drama specials.

Vince Edwards, the star of "Ben Casey," suffered a different kind of mishap. When he went up on stage at the end of the party, the stage collapsed under him and injured his leg; Edwards later sued ABC for damages.

Vic Morrow, the sergeant on "Combat," was sitting at one of the tables putting away bottles of champagne with Chuck Connors, star of "The Rifleman." (Morrow would later be decapitated by a helicopter rotor blade during the filming of *Twilight Zone: The Movie*.) And Ricky Nelson (who would later burn to death in an airplane crash) was helping a tipsy Harriet Nelson, his mother, back to her seat after her cameo stage appearance.

No TV pictures of these untoward incidents ever made it to air. They would have spoiled the celebration. This twenty-fifth anniversary birthday party was about a national treasure—America's communications airwaves—and the Medici prince who stood behind them. Toward the end of the evening Peter Strauss, the star of the ABC miniseries "Rich Man, Poor Man," appeared on stage.

"There is one person we must single out," Strauss announced.

As the TV cameras swung around to one of the candlelit tables, Leonard Goldenson's head glowed with ruddy health and a winter Florida tan. He was the person who had made it possible for this Hollywood galaxy to glitter. Goldenson was an island of abstinence in a sea of drunkenness, an updated television incarnation of the New York movie tycoon portrayed in F. Scott Fitzgerald's unfinished Hollywood novel, *The Last Tycoon*. At seventy-two, still functioning with disquieting resilience, he could make or break the careers of his younger colleagues by merely nodding or shaking his head. It was *Goldenson*'s birthday that the party was celebrating. It was almost twenty-five years to the day since he had taken control of a moribund ABC.

As he stood up, the TV executives and Hollywood actors in the audience, from John Wayne to Henry Winkler, gave Goldenson a sustained ovation.

"What you've seen tonight," "Good Morning America"'s David Hartman told the viewers at home, "is twenty-five years of us trying to please you. Like many parts of our lives, television is very competitive. But tonight we at ABC would like to put aside the competitive aspects."

The former star of "The Virginian" lifted his champagne glass, and an eerie hush fell over the suddenly tranquil crowd.

"Since we have been given the most powerful communications tool in the history of mankind," Hartman proposed, "may the next twenty-five years find us using it to the best of our ability, for the benefit of mankind, to inform and to educate, to entertain and delight, and thus enrich all of our lives."

As the guests drained their glasses, the trumpets sounded a coronation theme and John Forsythe's Michelob-smooth voice announced the party finale: "Ladies and Gentlemen, the ABC Super Singers."

The band segued into the theme song from *Rocky,* and a chorus of TV divas—Toni Tennille, Lola Falana, Leslie Uggams, Annette Funicello—entered stage left in evening gowns and started singing, "ABC's gonna fly, flying high, flying free and easy as ABC."

11

Toni Tennille stretched out her hands to the audience, and the dinner tables slowly emptied. The guests clambered forward, linking arms, rocking and swaying, singing to the beat of the *Rocky* song.

In January 1978, the old order in American broadcasting had reached its all-time historical peak. More than 73 million homes had TV sets. Every American household watched an average of six hours and seventeen minutes of TV each day. Almost $4 billion in advertising revenues went into the coffers of ABC, NBC, and CBS. And while the Big Three networks still had a monopoly on viewing, no network had more viewers than ABC.

No one was more pleasantly aware of these facts than Fred Pierce, the president of ABC Television, who had lured the famous programmer Fred Silverman away from CBS and overseen ABC's sudden rise to prominence.

Pierce, an obdurate, imposing man, was the network's most powerful in-the-trenches executive. He had spent his childhood in straitened circumstances in Bensonhurst, a working-class section of Brooklyn, where his father had managed a candy store and driven a cab. Pierce's two network nicknames were "The Jaw" and "The Great Stone Face." But Eddie Byrd, the network shoeshine man, called him "No Shine"—that was what Byrd heard every time he passed Pierce's office door; Pierce was always too busy to have his shoes polished.

But at forty-four, with the network riding high, Pierce was ready to try on for size the prerogatives of a Hollywood mogul. An impetuous streak lay hidden behind his stonelike mien. In the months preceding ABC's anniversary bash, he had become infatuated with a starlet in one of ABC's new prime-time shows, "Operation Petticoat." The starlet's name was Mindy Naud.

Naud, who had lived in Los Angeles since childhood, had grown up in TV. Her father produced daytime TV game shows, from which he derived a profitable living. Naud's girlhood neighbor in Toluca Lake, a prosperous section of town, was Garry Marshall, who had created the comedy series "Happy Days" for ABC. In "Mork and Mindy," a new comedy that Marshall was developing that year for ABC, Naud's name would be used for the Pam Dawber role.

During her student days at UCLA, Naud appeared as a model in one of her father's daytime shows. The experience so excited her that she promptly switched her major from Spanish to drama studies, signed with Universal Television, and began appearing on ABC shows like "Marcus Welby, M.D.," "The Six Million Dollar Man," and "Happy Days." On "Happy Days" she portrayed Paula Petralunga, the Fonz's first girlfriend.

A sparkling young actress, Naud knew how to tease, and her performance in a bit part on "McMillan" led to her role on "Operation Petticoat." Rock Hudson, the star of the show, played a police commissioner, and during one episode the script called for him to get a medical exam. Mindy Naud, playing the nurse, helped Hudson put on his coat after the examination.

"Gee, Commissioner, you look just great," Naud said.

"You don't look so bad yourself," Hudson replied. As he was leaving the doctor's office, he asked, "What are you doing this week?"

"Getting married."

"Oh?" Hudson reached the door.

"How about next week?" Naud teased.

Leonard Stern, the executive producer of the pilot for "Operation Petticoat," observed her performance in "McMillan." This new show was a Silverman spin-off from Blake Edwards' 1959 movie of the same title, which had starred Cary Grant and Tony Curtis—a wartime comedy about a Navy crew and five Army nurses aboard America's only pink-painted submarine.

Naud certainly had the right physical qualifications for the part of an "Operation Petticoat" nurse. "Its rich humor," the network drily explained in its publicity for the show, "derives from the highly charged presence of women where only men were meant to be." She looked every inch the "squeeze"—a tall, leggy, statuesque girl with green eyes and honey-blonde hair. Naud was also a quick study and highly intelligent. She auditioned and got the part, and when ABC decided to sign the pilot she found herself playing a key role in a regularly scheduled prime-time show.

The official biography of the actress furnished by the network spoke of Mindy Naud's "dancing eyes, fun-loving smile and warm, outgoing presence." Pierce's infatuation with her had not gone unnoticed either. "After she had left the room on a recent social occasion," her press kit said, "a suddenly dispirited gentleman inquired after a moment, 'Is somebody turning out the lights?' "

"Operation Petticoat" soon became a standing in-house joke at ABC. The show's real title, it was said, was not "Operation Petticoat" but "The Beverly Hills Navy." Several other amply proportioned nurses appeared in the series, including Jamie Lee Curtis, Tony Curtis' daughter, in her first major role. Colleagues envious of Pierce's presumed prerogatives took it for granted that his increasingly frequent trips to the West Coast involved late-night, off-the-set liaisons with leading ladies at the Beverly Hills Hotel. In fact, Pierce's attraction for Mindy Naud had not yet been consummated—and when it was, the consummation would come in a most unexpected way.

Shortly before the New Year in 1978, Fred Pierce, visiting the West Coast during the holidays, called up Mindy Naud and invited her out to dinner. He told his starlet-friend that Tony Thomopoulos, his network friend and colleague, was traveling with him. Naud asked a girlfriend along to make up a foursome.

After the group had gone to dinner, Naud suggested, "Why don't we go over to my friend Beverlee's for a nightcap?"

A well-known secret of ABC's success in the Silverman years was the network's reliance on "jiggle" (more crudely, "tits and ass") in prime time. The genre plunked down attractive, well-endowed women like Mindy Naud in zany settings, and then let the fur fly. That night Fred Pierce and Tony Thomopoulos, Silverman's overseers, were about to have the tables turned on them.

Beverlee Dean, Naud's friend, was a psychic.

Short and shaped like a dumpling, Dean had migrated to Hollywood from Wisconsin several years earlier in the hopes of establishing herself as a producer. Her specialty was game shows. Dean had pitched two new concepts—one called "Monte Carlo," the other "Disorder in the Court"—to big-time network producers. Neither had been bought. So she had started a sideline career, eking out a livelihood with star predictions.

There was plenty of work for Beverlee Dean as a psychic. Actors hoping to become stars were always anxious to hear what the future held in store for them. Among the celebrities whose success she had predicted were Suzanne Somers and Farah Fawcett-Majors, both of whom eventually appeared on ABC. *Los Angeles* magazine, which the network's publishing division had purchased in 1977, called Dean the "best psychic in the greater Los Angeles area."

Dean still dreamed of becoming a full-fledged member of mainstream Hollywood, someone like her friend Mindy Naud, who was beginning to be taken seriously as a show-biz professional. Privately, she practiced her psychic craft through handwriting analysis. Dean's clients were asked to write a sample sentence: "I am three feet taller than Tiny Tim." It happened to have the right letters for a "reading."

"Hey, Bev, I've got a couple of friends for you," Mindy Naud said over the telephone from the restaurant where she and her girlfriend and Pierce and Thomopoulos were having dinner.

Dean was at her home in Encino. Although it was the holiday season, she was not in good spirits. The prospect of giving two late-night readings on short notice did not improve her mood.

"These will be two of the most important readings you've ever done," Naud told her, and Dean quickly changed her mind.

A half-hour later, when the foursome showed up, Dean and her roommate, Theresa Fulbert, were deeply impressed. "Both looked really important," Fulbert recalled. Dean thought Thomopoulos "looked like a Greek god," and Pierce like "the nicest man you'd ever want to meet."

She asked who wanted to go first.

15

Thomopoulos, a dapper, fastidious man, seemed repulsed by the idea of having his fortune told. Like Pierce, his boss, he came from a lower-class background. Thomopoulos had spent much of his childhood in his father's Greek restaurant in the Bronx. His parents spoke little English. But after earning a B.S. in diplomacy from Georgetown, briefly considering the Foreign Service, and embarking on a career in network TV, Thomopoulos had left that background behind. As Pierce's all-purpose "liaison" man, however, it occasionally fell to him to perform ceremonial or distasteful tasks, and this evening he dutifully went upstairs and tested out Beverlee Dean's psychic skills.

The gist of his future, Dean told Thomopoulos, was that he was destined to become a "president" at ABC.

As Dean recalled the encounter, Thomopoulos scoffed at the prediction. "That's impossible," he said.

She pulled out a medallion of Saint Anthony, her patron saint, a supply of which she kept in a box by her bed. The medallion carried a special inscription on the back: "Love. Pass the Word. Beverlee Dean."

"Keep this with you, she told Thomopoulos, handing it to him. Since "Tony," his Christian name, stood for "Anthony," she thought the gift was particularly appropriate for him.

Before Thomopoulos left, he asked Dean not to tell Pierce what she had predicted for him.

Pierce was much more enthusiastic than Thomopoulos about having his fortune told. He wrote out, "I am three feet taller than Tiny Tim," on the scrap of paper that Dean provided, scrawled his initials, and added his birth date: "4/8/33."

The highly intuitive Dean latched onto Pierce right away. "I saw a lot of money," she remembered. "I loved this man instantly."

But when Dean discovered that Fred Silverman worked for Pierce, she gave him some bad news: "Do you think he's your friend?"

"I do," Pierce replied confidently.

"Well, you're in for a terrible upset." Silverman would be

leaving for NBC before his three-year contract with ABC was up, she told Pierce.

Pierce too scoffed that this prediction was out of the question, that Silverman had given his word of honor that he would not go to another network, but Dean continued unperturbed. Pierce could trust only two men, she said—"the man downstairs, Tony, and someone named Mark."

"Mark Cohen," Pierce echoed, referring to his top numbers cruncher (financial adviser) in New York.

Sensing that her predictions had struck home, Dean switched like a chameleon from her "psychic" self to her game-show self. She believed that she had helped Pierce professionally. She now wanted him to return the favor. When he proved unreceptive, the late-night session ended on an unresolved note.

Downstairs, Mindy Naud had been playing a guitar and singing. The readings had lasted more than two hours, and both Pierce and Thomopoulos were subdued. When the group left Beverlee Dean's, it was past midnight.

It had been one of the strangest nights in network television history. Pierce had started out thinking he would enjoy the company of a beautiful TV starlet; he had ended up spending most of the evening with a less-than beautiful network TV seer. On the way back to their hotel, Pierce and Thomopoulos talked quietly, not sharing with Naud and her girlfriend what Beverlee Dean had told them. They hadn't yet decided whether Beverlee Dean was for real. In a sense, they had just entered the Twilight Zone.

The meeting in New York in which Fred Silverman informed Fred Pierce that he had signed a new contract with NBC was not a pleasant one. It took place at about four o'clock in the afternoon on January 19, a few weeks after Pierce's late-night encounter with Beverlee Dean. Outside network headquarters the sky was rapidly growing leaden. An unforeseen storm, the first blizzard of the winter season, was approaching New York.

17

Silverman arrived at the door of Pierce's thirty-eighth floor network office looking nervous and agitated. The two remained closeted for about ten minutes. And when Silverman came out, in the words of one bystander, "He looked like somebody had just told him he was going to die."

Pierce emerged a few moments later.

"Is Fred leaving?" his secretary asked.

Pierce gave a curt nod. He was so furious that he could not open his mouth. After allowing network people to speculate for months about his plans, Silverman was reneging on a personal promise to Pierce that he would *not* go to NBC. But NBC had offered him a major promotion: He would not be just a chief programmer, as he had been at CBS and ABC; he would hold the title "corporate president," like Elton Rule at ABC, and wield the power of chief executive, like Leonard Goldenson. The only question still to be decided was whether or not Pierce would release him from his ABC contract so that he could start immediately at the competing network.

When Pierce recovered his poise, he went to the thirty-ninth floor, where Goldenson and Rule had offices, and told them about Silverman's conduct. The three men divided up the task of informing key network directors and employees before the news was publicly released.

When Pierce returned to his office it was getting late. Tony Thomopoulos arrived to help him place calls to Silverman's former colleagues at ABC Entertainment.

"That's funny," said one of them on being informed of the news. "I just had lunch with him today. He didn't say anything about leaving."

Pierce's voice immediately darkened. He was worried that Silverman might be stealing network trade secrets, and wanted to hear the details of the programmer's conversation. Then he changed his mind.

"Give me a full report tomorrow," he said abruptly. "I'm going one on one with that cocksucker, and I'm going to take his ass."

Pierce, his competitive juices afire, had decided to use the

one weapon left in his arsenal: forcing Silverman to fulfill his contract at ABC by keeping him on the network payroll, but to boot
him out of the building. The locks on Silverman's office were
changed. His files were sealed. The chief programmer was persona
non grata at ABC.

Later that same evening, when most network employees had
already left for the day, another colleague of Silverman's heard
that Pierce had tried to call him at home and went in person to
Pierce's thirty-eighth floor office. He wanted to make a pitch for
Silverman's job, the official title of which was "president" of ABC
Entertainment.

Pierce cut his sales talk short.

"I've already made my decision," he said, pointing to Tony
Thomopoulos.

Outside network headquarters, the blinding snowstorm raged.
The telephone calls and meetings went on into the night, while
New York was being transformed into a white wonderland. And
Beverlee Dean was batting two for two.

It had all happened within days of the twenty-fifth anniversary
birthday party in Hollywood.

2

Portrait of the Patriarch

Leonard Goldenson's network aerie was a hushed world far above the honking taxis and crowded sidewalks of street-level New York, a set of corner offices on the thirty-ninth floor of ABC headquarters that offered dramatic views—west to the Hudson River, and north across the treetops of Central Park, toward the George Washington Bridge and the New Jersey Palisades.

Getting up to see the old man was not hard for a newcomer with the right bona fides. ABC affected warm and friendly airs. Virginia Gerard, the lobby receptionist, greeted all guests with a quick, welcoming smile. Hill Miller, a rotund black clergyman's son in charge of lobby security, escorted you to the elevator bank leading upstairs.

The modest trappings of the thirty-ninth floor revealed Goldenson's utilitarian, spartan leanings. A simple yellow carpet covered the floor. The walls were modular and painted plain white. Even the art was unpretentious. A sculpture fragment in the reception area had the label "Sepik River Canoe—New Guinea" pasted next to its ABC I.D. number.

Sandy Merkel, who sat in the anteroom outside Goldenson's

office, acted as his personal gatekeeper. "He'll see you now," she said when he was ready.

And there, rising from behind his desk, was Goldenson—a compact, well-built man of youthful proportions. In his late seventies, at the height of his power, he did not make a striking physical impression. Eddie Byrd, the building bootblack, called Goldenson "Shorty" because of his diminutive size. But his shining eyes were still quietly observing everything around him. And for more than half a century, they had been first-hand witnesses to the history of Hollywood and network TV.

In 1905, when Goldenson was born, large portions of the United States were still isolated, backward, and rural, and the whole country was dominated by big-city capital and extortionist trusts. Henry Ford's model T, the telephone, and electricity were only beginning to replace implements of preindustrial labor like the horse-drawn plow.

Scottdale, Pennsylvania, Goldenson's home town, was a microcosm of Middle America. The close-knit community in the hills of western Pennsylvania managed to straddle two worlds. Salaried workers, the nascent middle class, worked at factories in town owned by U.S. Steel, H. C. Frick, and U.S. Pipe and Foundry. Family farms dotted the surrounding countryside.

His father was an upstanding Jewish citizen and the proprietor of Marks & Goldenson, one of two department stores in town. His mother Esther, a young Polish immigrant, had worked as a bookkeeper in Pittsburgh, forty miles distant, before marrying. Leonard was their first child and only son.

As a young boy, the chairman of ABC grew up in an age of Edwardian optimism, World's Fairs, and technological delight. Practical application followed quickly on the heels of invention. Little boys grew up imbued with ideas of Progress.

As Goldenson described it later, his boyhood and small-town upbringing imparted a lifelong ideal of "clean living." His mother— a "dynamo of energy" in her son's eyes—would be a kind of second ego throughout his adult life. She taught him the meaning of mitzvoth, the 613 commandments that guide the ethical Jewish life. The emphasis in Goldenson's childhood was on good deeds and direct action. Overt displays of sentiment did not belong in his emotional vocabulary.

But there was never any lack of enthusiasm or passion. In 1912, when Goldenson was seven, an immigrant showman named Adolph Zukor imported and released the country's first full-length feature film. It was called *Queen Elizabeth* and starred the actress Sarah Bernhardt. D. W. Griffith's *Birth of a Nation,* America's first home-grown film classic, was released in 1915, when he was ten. In addition to his department store, Goldenson's father owned a financial interest in one of Scottdale's two movie theaters. On Saturdays, when the son was expected to lend a hand at the store, he stole away to the theater instead.

Les Mots, the autobiography of Jean-Paul Sartre, an exact contemporary of Goldenson's in France, describes the magical effect that silent movies had on the first generation of children to experience them:

> A shaft of light crossed the hall; one could see dust and vapor dancing in it. A piano whinnied away the overture to *Fingal's Cave* and everyone understood that the criminal was about to appear. This new art was mine, just as it was everyone else's. We had the same mental age: I was seven and knew how to read; it was twelve and did not know how to talk. People said that it was in its early stage, that it had progress to make; I thought that we would grow up together.

When Goldenson was seventeen, he turned down a letter of admission to the Wharton School of Business in Philadelphia and a commission to West Point, in order to attend Harvard College. America's most celebrated institution of higher learning had a new quota system in 1923, which, while it restricted the number of Jewish admissions from big cities like New York and Chicago (where immigrants were still mostly unassimilated), made spaces available to minority students from the heartland. Harvard's Jewish system, which was later adopted by other Ivy League universities, worked in Goldenson's favor, and at his mother's urging, he left provincial Scottdale for the elite world of Cambridge.

In his first autumn at Harvard, Goldenson tried to join in college life by the most traditional route of all: He went out for freshman football. He weighed only 135, but he was a good athlete, and had started at quarterback for four years at the public high school in Scottdale. At Harvard, he ended up sitting on the bench, failed his first midterm exams too, and came close to flunking out.

Unwilling to return home a failure, he stayed over in Cambridge over the Christmas holidays, and in the next round of exams made dean's list. In 1927, he graduated early with a bachelor's degree in economics.

Goldenson was ambitious and persistent, and he also knew how to pick the right opening and when to say no. After Harvard, his father arranged a job for him at a leading Pittsburgh brokerage firm. One of his father's friends was a partner in the firm. Goldenson had worked summers there during college. At the time, the opportunity must have seemed ideal. Wall Street prices were rising, and a smart young man with good contacts could make money.

But Goldenson turned the job down. He wanted to get into the movie business, he told his father, not sell securities. Buying time, he went back to Cambridge for three years at Harvard Law School.

In the spring of 1930, he stopped off in New York, hoping that his new law degree would impress movie theater companies there. Manhattan was still the center of America's entertainment. Hollywood had consolidated after World War I, and a handful of New York distributors—Adolph Zukor at Paramount and Marcus Loew, whose theaters would later control Metro-Goldwyn-Mayer—dominated the industry. Zukor and Loew were the kingpins of theater chains that reached all across the country. Opulent New York movie halls—"cathedrals of kitsch," Hollywood historian Neal Gabler has fondly termed them—were their crown jewels. Movie hall spectacles were the quintessential melting-pot experience for big-city arrivals.

Goldenson, who wanted to break into the industry at the top, could not have arrived in New York at a worse time. October 1929 ushered in the Great Depression. "Wall Street Lays An Egg," announced the famous *Variety* headline. Between the building of movie theater chains and the ongoing Hollywood conversion from silent pictures to talkies (which had begun in 1927), the big movie producers and distributors were financially overextended, and cutting back on personnel instead of hiring. There was no room for a Harvard novice on the payroll.

So Goldenson returned to Scottdale and studied for the Pennsylvania bar that summer. He wasn't particularly happy at the prospect of working as a lawyer in Pittsburgh. It meant giving up his dream of a career in the movies. But when he learned that two other law school graduates, both judges' sons, were scheduled to start at the same Pittsburgh law firm as himself in the autumn, adding unexpected competition in that career line, he took advantage of the news to confer again with his parents.

"You should go to the biggest city in this country," Esther Goldenson told him.

With this recommendation from his mother, and financial backing from his father, Goldenson left for Manhattan for good. He was twenty-four.

"To youthful address all doors are open," Emerson once said, and the early careers of America's three top broadcasters bore him out.

David Sarnoff, the master builder of network radio, started his broadcasting career more than two decades before William Paley and Leonard Goldenson. The wireless, the maritime forebear of radio, came to America from England in 1899 in the hands of Guglielmo Marconi, its young Italian inventor. Sarnoff, a child immigrant trained in Talmud, arrived from Russia one year later. He hawked Yiddish-language newspapers in the Lower East Side as a boy, and began working at American Marconi, a subsidiary of the parent Marconi firm in Britain, when he was fifteen.

In 1912, Sarnoff was in charge of American Marconi's wireless booth at the Wanamaker's department store in Brooklyn when a faint electronic signal came pulsing more than a thousand miles across the North Atlantic:

"*S.S. Titanic* ran into iceberg. Sinking fast."

The twenty-one-year-old Sarnoff had cultivated a reputation as a diligent wireless operator by volunteering for duty at a lonely maritime station on Nantucket Island, and by spending a freezing winter aboard a seal-hunting ship in the Arctic. He was well versed in the skills of his profession, and had a great "fist": He could tap out his Morse code signals so rhythmically that the message sounded like a personal signature.

In his own account of the *Titanic* story, Sarnoff was the person who transmitted the first news of the tragedy to government authorities and to the press. President Taft ordered all other wireless stations off the air to clear the frequency for him. For three days he punched the signal key, alerting nearby ships, compiling lists, and passing on the names of the living and the dead to worried next-of-kin. Sarnoff worked nonstop until all the passengers were accounted for, and the *Carpathia* limped into New York harbor with the survivors. Then he took a Turkish bath, went home to bed, and returned to work the next day.

It was a colorful broadcasting founder's myth—"boy wonder of wireless saves mankind!"—and Sarnoff virtually wrote it himself. He spun the story first to a biographer, and confirmed it before a national TV audience in an interview with Edward R. Murrow on "Person to Person." Because there were few eyewitnesses to the goings-on at American Marconi in 1912, and because Sarnoff was later so instrumental in the real birth of early American broadcasting, it seeped into the lore of the industry as gospel truth. In fact, the tale was concocted.

The facts that matter were somewhat less grand. After World War I, when the wireless assets of American Marconi were still under wartime military seal, General Electric, with the connivance of the U.S. Navy, President Woodrow Wilson, and Congress, transferred them to a consortium of leading radio manufacturers that included Westinghouse and AT&T. American Marconi was re-named the Radio Corporation of America, or RCA for short. RCA was a shell company at first, a patent pool organized jointly by these major manufacturing interests. But Sarnoff, who by then was American Marconi's general manager, came to RCA as part of the deal. He played no role whatsoever in the *Titanic* disaster.

The events that established American broadcasting in its present pattern took place before anyone knew what radio or TV might turn into. In a now-famous 1915 memo, Sarnoff had presented to his American Marconi superiors the idea of building a "radio music box," but the memo gathered dust until the early 1920s. Only when AT&T used its intercity Long Lines to link up local radio stations that had sprung up independently after the war did network broadcasting begin to take shape. At RCA, where he had muscled his way into a senior-level post, Sarnoff started a second network that competed with AT&T's.

Then, in 1926, he engineered a top-secret deal that brought both networks under the umbrella of the newly created National Broadcasting Company. NBC called them the Red Network and the Blue Network. AT&T agreed to lease its Long Lines, making possible network transmission, but it exited the radio field. RCA, which owned NBC and controlled most of the patents required to manufacture radio sets, was now the major force in American broadcasting. And Sarnoff, who was thirty-six, controlled both companies.

NBC was almost America's *only* network company, but in 1928, when a talent agent named Arthur Judson visited Sarnoff's office in New York and offered to supply his two networks with classical music programming, Sarnoff turned him down cold. He saw broadcasting primarily as a means of spurring sales of radio sets. His only real programming achievement was to arrange for Arturo Toscanini to leave Fascist Italy ahead of World War II, and to put him in charge of his own NBC Symphony Orchestra; the gesture would be commercial broadcasting's last sustained bow to unsponsored programming.

"Then we will organize our own chain," Judson challenged.

According to historian Erik Barnouw, Sarnoff looked at Judson, leaned back in his chair, and roared with laughter.

"You can't do it!" he gloated.

When Judson started United Independent Broadcasters, a new network, it almost went bankrupt in its first year. Then William Paley stepped in.

Paley, like Sarnoff, was a son of Russian Jewish immigrants, but the two were opposites in almost every other respect. Sarnoff's boyhood was spent in Lower East Side poverty; Paley was raised in Philadelphia in a milieu of privilege and wealth. Sarnoff grasped the technology of broadcasting; Paley intuited currents of popular taste.

In the spring of 1928, when Paley was twenty-five and enjoying the life of a young dandy, he visited Paris with his parents after the tobacco auctions in Amsterdam that were an annual part of the family's cigar-manufacturing business. Paley went with a friend to the automobile design shop of Hibbard and Darrin, where an elegant Hispano-Suiza convertible caught his eye.

"It's too damn expensive," his friend said.

Paley impulsively wired his stockbroker in Philadelphia for $16,000 and had the convertible delivered to him in Paris at the Ritz, where he was staying.

"I engaged a chauffeur in Paris for a couple of weeks to drive me and my friend on our daily round of pleasure spots," he recalled in *As It Happened*, his memoir. "In Philadelphia, I didn't like driving it. It was so unusual that it drew crowds of people whenever it was parked on the street. I wanted an attention-getting object without the attention."

Arthur Judson's money-losing network fit this ambition perfectly. Six months after his insouciant purchase of the automobile, Paley paid $400,000—nearly half his million-dollar inheritance—for a controlling interest in United Independent Broadcasters, which would shortly be renamed the Columbia Broadcasting System. He moved from Philadelphia to New York, upgraded the network's lineup of local affiliates, and with a keen ear for what would attract listeners and advertisers, shifted its programming focus away from classical music. NBC introduced "Amos 'n Andy," breaking new ground in popular radio entertainment, in 1928. Paley signed up Bing Crosby, Will Rogers, the singer Kate Smith, and the big-band jazz orchestra of Paul Whiteman. Along with popular entertainment, advertising jingles began to inundate the airwaves.

Radio was still an infant industry. The going price for a weekly show on CBS and NBC in 1930 was $3,000. Sponsors like George Washington Hill of the American Tobacco Company, which produced Lucky Strike cigarettes and Cremo cigars, and Liggett & Myers Tobacco Company, the makers of Chesterfields, *owned* their time periods.

But broadcasting's growth during the Depression was nothing short of phenomenal. In 1930 there were 13 million radio sets in American homes; by 1940 the number of receiving sets had reached 40 million. Network radio's total revenues in 1930 were $27 million, up from $3.8 million just three years earlier; in 1940, they were $113 million.

And by 1931, when Paley turned thirty, his hunch that broadcasting could support more than one network company had paid off in spades. CBS took in more than $2.2 million that year in profits.

In 1933, as the industry of network radio took shape around Sarnoff and Paley, Goldenson's career was just getting started. He rented bachelor's quarters in the Chalfonte Hotel, at Broadway and 70th Street, on arriving in New York, and started looking for a job. Goldenson's sights were set on Hollywood, not broadcasting. If he had wanted to make his career in network radio, that door was already closed to him. The Blue Network, which would eventually become ABC, belonged to Sarnoff's domain at RCA and NBC.

At the end of a nine-month job search, Goldenson landed in the one-man office of Charles Franklin, the former general counsel to the Southern Pacific Railroad. For the next two-and-a-half years, frustrated by his inability to break into Hollywood, he worked mainly on railroad industry cases.

Then, one day, a Harvard Law School classmate telephoned with the news that Paramount Pictures, Adolph Zukor's motion picture theater-and-studio company, had filed for bankruptcy. Paramount's creditors were pressing it to reorganize in the depths of the Depression. One of the law firms assigned to act as a trustee while the studio got back on its feet was looking for a young lawyer with Goldenson's qualifications. Did he want the job?

Yes, he did.

David Sarnoff was network broadcasting's immigrant-founder, the Thomas Edison among his peers. He used his powers at RCA to drive the industry technologically from the age of the wireless forward into the age of color TV.

William Paley was network broadcasting's aristocrat-founder, a paradoxical combination of noblesse-oblige elitism and mass-culture profits. He endowed the Museum of Modern Art with his high-society friends in New York while showing "The Beverly Hillbillies" and "Petticoat Junction" to the rest of America.

Leonard Goldenson was network broadcasting's Hollywood-founder, the unknown soldier of television. After spending the first half of his career at Paramount, he gambled his way to the top at ABC.

Gambling was the side of Goldenson that few people who visited his thirty-ninth-floor office ever saw, the side of his personality that looked out the window and dreamed. During his years at Paramount he played poker, which his mother had taught him from books borrowed from the local library in Scottdale, with big studio heads in Hollywood from Jack Warner on down. At ABC he played the tables at the resort hotel casinos where the network held its divisional meetings. Craps was his favorite game, and his specialty in craps was what professionals call "pressing the bet"—leaving his winnings on the table for the next roll of the dice. When Goldenson came home from gambling trips to his home in

Mamaroneck, in Westchester County, associates said, he liked to lay his winnings on the kitchen table and say to his wife, "You spend it."

During one 1970s trip to the Dorado Beach Hotel in Puerto Rico, which had a big casino and which the network visited regularly each winter, Goldenson struck up a conversation with the employee sitting next to him on the plane and invited him to gamble. "You just bring along $100 and follow my moves," Goldenson said.

The employee, a vice president in personnel, had never gambled before. Goldenson smiled and said, "Do you trust me enough to do it?"

In one-and-a-half hours that night, the $100 turned into $7,000, which the vice president brought home on the plane ride back and used to buy a new car for his wife at Christmas. Goldenson, who started with a larger pile of chips, left the tables with an estimated $150,000.

Goldenson's high-stakes gambling career began in 1933, when he arrived in Paramount. Adolph Zukor's movie studio had gone bankrupt from a gamble that had gone wrong.

Before the Depression, the reigning dean of the motion picture industry had amassed a vast "network" of more than 1,500 local movie theaters, which by the late 1920s covered the entire country. Jesse Lasky and B. P. Schulberg were Zukor's leading studio partners on the West Coast. Their production expertise and his theaters had made Paramount the biggest movie combine in America. Zukor had perfected the art of distributing pictures through an industry practice known as block booking. He distributed top-quality and B-grade movies in a single package. Since local theaters had to exhibit both, all his product was seen by audiences. Although block booking tended to strangle independent producers, it was a cornerstone of the old studio system. The "golden age" of Hollywood was just beginning.

Zukor's business acumen and showman's talent almost led him to dominate broadcasting as well. Except for his streak of bad luck, he almost brought Hollywood and broadcasting together. In the late 1920s, when network radio burst on the scene, Zukor foresaw that TV would develop from it. He knew that Hollywood had to control broadcasting or would be controlled by it, and he purchased 50 percent of Paley's network in early 1929, a few months before the Wall Street crash.

Then the stock market caved in.

Through the 1920s, Zukor had financed his purchase of local movie theaters and of CBS with a high-risk pyramid scheme. He paid almost no cash upfront, offering the theater owners options on Paramount shares instead. If Paramount stock happened to be trading at $45, say, as it did before the Depression, he promised that it would rise in value to $65, or Paramount would redeem the difference in cash.

While stock prices were rising, Zukor built up the Paramount theater chain and expended little cash. After the 1929 crash, when the price fell to $3, Paramount's many creditors began calling in his chits. It was the most spectacular Depression-era bankruptcy in Hollywood, and among Zukor's principal creditors only Paley escaped scot-free. His lawyers had insisted on an "escape" clause in the sale agreement. If CBS reported $2 million in profits and Paramount's stock did not rise to the promised level at the end of two years, Paley had the option of buying back Zukor's half-interest in the network for the same amount of money that Paramount owed him. In 1932, he did so, enriching himself considerably in the bargain.

Many local theater owners around the country, however, were not as lucky, and their misfortune gave Goldenson his first career break. In 1933, when the twenty-seven-year-old Harvard graduate reported to 1501 Broadway, Paramount's headquarters in New York, he was introduced to S. A. Lynch. Lynch, an Atlanta-based movie theater owner, was another leading Zukor creditor. Instead of having a buyout clause, like Paley, he had taken over responsibility for reorganizing all of Paramount's theaters.

Lynch gave Goldenson his marching orders.

"I understand you're a very smart young fellow," he said.

"We're going to send you up to New England to straighten out our theaters there. I have some rules. Every week you'll report to me. I'll want to know what you're doing, and why you're doing it. And I'll want to know exactly what your recommendations are."

Lynch offered Goldenson two pieces of advice about deal making and working with stars.

"Don't crap on your own threshold," he said. Goldenson interpreted this as a warning not to become infatuated with Hollywood glamour—showgirls and vaudeville still shared the billing with movies at the bigger local theaters—and never to forget that money came first.

"And never slam the door."

In New England, Goldenson had the opportunity to put Lynch's deal-making advice into practice right away. As the point man for restructuring two hundred movie theaters, he moved to Boston and began investigating the four large circuits that covered the region. Performing due diligence for the studio's creditors, he interviewed bookers and buyers and collected financial data from Paramount's local co-owners, concerning how well their theaters were doing. Every weekend, he traveled by train to New York and delivered his findings to Lynch and to Y. Frank Freeman—another Zukor creditor from below the Mason-Dixon line, who was now working as a Paramount executive—who had to decide which theaters the studio should keep and which it should sell to best regain its fiscal health. It was a crash course in fine-tuning the Hollywood engine of local theater distribution.

For the young man from Scottdale, the New England reorganization was a heady movie industry experience. In 1933, W. C. Fields and Bing Crosby were Paramount's biggest money-earners. The studio had just released *Alice in Wonderland* and *Duck Soup*. Mae West was starring in *She Done Him Wrong*, and Cecil B. DeMille's *Cleopatra* and *The Plainsman*, with Gary Cooper, were in production, alongside *Hopalong Cassidy*.

Goldenson adapted to this new business environment with cocky enthusiasm. Ever since he had spent his childhood Saturdays in his father's movie theater, it had been his ambition to get in on the Hollywood action. Now he had the challenge of a lifetime.

Goldenson's bookkeeping skills were not yet on a par with his lawyerly self-assurance. During one of his many weekend visits to New York, he asked a young Paramount accountant named Simon B. Siegel to write up the balance sheet from one of the local theaters in New England. Examining the finished product, Goldenson exclaimed naively, "Look! The figures match to the penny!"

Siegel might have laughed. Instead he merely replied that they were supposed to.

Goldenson promptly commandeered Siegel from the Paramount comptroller's office to work with him for the duration of the New England reorganization. It was the beginning of a long working relationship between the two men.

By 1937, the New England theaters were reorganized, and Paramount was out of its court-ordered receivership and financially back on its feet. Zukor, who had been in exile on the West Coast during the bankruptcy workout, was back in the saddle in an honorary but still influential studio chairman's role. S. A. Lynch, his assets secured, had stepped out of the picture. Y. Frank Freeman, Goldenson's boss, was in charge of the Paramount theater division. And Barney Balaban, a vaudeville showman and theater owner from Chicago, was Paramount's new chief executive. The son of a Russian immigrant grocer, he typified the distribution-led Hollywood of the thirties and forties. Before taking the helm at the studio, Balaban had operated Chicago movie halls with exotic names like the Valencia, the Oriental, the Tivoli, and the Granada.

The owners of the New England theaters wanted Goldenson to remain in Boston, but Balaban took him under his wing. Goldenson returned to New York, gave up the regular practice of law, and started working as Freeman's personal assistant. At thirty-one, he began to court a Manhattan department-store heiress named Isabelle Weinstein.

The following year, when the head of studio production on the West Coast fell ill and Y. Frank Freeman moved to Hollywood to replace him, Goldenson took his place as president of the theater division. Eight years after leaving Scottdale, still just thirty-two years old, in charge of the world's largest chain of movie theaters, Goldenson had joined the charmed inner circle of movie-industry chieftains.

Goldenson did not have the most glamorous job at Paramount—far from it. The creative side of the movie business—deciding whether Joel McCrea could act in Preston Sturges' script, or Billy Wilder should direct Barbara Stanwyck, or Bing Crosby would jell with Bob Hope and Dorothy Lamour—was left to the studio heads on the West Coast, where a Hollywood genius like Irving Thalberg at MGM could reign supreme. But Goldenson was the hard-working executive behind the scenes, ensuring that the revenues from local theater coffers flowed into the corporate offices in New York. At every big Hollywood studio, local theaters provided the financial wherewithal that fueled the creative system and allowed screens across the country to flicker with such Paramount classics as *Double Indemnity, The Lost Weekend, The Blue Dahlia, Sullivan's Travels*, and *Road to Rio*.

During this period of his career, 1938 to 1948, Goldenson patented his probing style as a businessman. It was a life of perpetual movement. He traveled from California to the Carolinas, asking questions and checking up on regional theater operations. Wherever he saw problems, he fixed them, always with the aim of maximizing the flow of cash back to the Paramount office. In the process, Goldenson usually managed to make friends instead of enemies, but he never departed from strict business priorities. His colleagues at ABC would later describe the cold-blooded side of his personality by saying, "Leonard pisses ice water," or, "Leonard never made a deal he didn't make money at, including his marriage."

Goldenson did, in fact, marry Isabelle Weinstein, improving on his own family background. But it was a love match, as executives who observed them together over the years could attest. Years later, he confided to the manager of one of ABC's local affiliates, "Isabelle and I are more loving than any couple we know."

Beneath his puritan exterior Goldenson was a warm, sensitive, full-blooded animal, and while he ran Paramount's theaters he was certainly stirred by the spectacle of American movie entertainment. He had a front-row seat during the motion picture industry's best years. More than 75 million people visited movie houses each week in 1937. At the height of the Depression, the industry ranked fourteenth in revenues and eleventh in total assets among all American businesses. Goldenson was an unknown to the viewing public. He pursued his apprenticeship quietly. But he was a key cog in the Hollywood wheel. Like Sim Rosedale in Edith Wharton's *The House of Mirth*, he "was sensitive to shades of difference which Miss Bart would never have credited him with perceiving, because he had no corresponding variations of manner."

Paramount's first opportunity to reinvolve itself in broadcasting arose in 1938 when John Balaban, Barney Balaban's brother, called Goldenson to ask whether the theater division should apply for an experimental TV license that was up for grabs in Chicago. On Goldenson's recommendation, Paramount applied for and was granted the license. In 1939, David Sarnoff unveiled television technology publicly in the opening NBC broadcast at the World's Fair in New York, and Goldenson saw the new medium in action for the first time.

If Goldenson had inherited control of Paramount, for which Barney Balaban groomed him during World War II, Hollywood and network TV might have had a very different history. By 1948 Paramount had acquired a second TV license in Los Angeles, in addition to its Chicago station, and owned 25 percent of the company of Allen B. Dumont, a TV inventor, which owned TV stations in New York, Washington, and Pittsburgh. Dumont was planning to mount a network of his own, alongside CBS and NBC, and his resources in TV distribution, combined with Paramount's in programming, might have turned the studio into an entertainment monopoly capable of fulfilling Zukor's fondest block-booking dreams.

But shortly before Pearl Harbor, the Federal Communications Commission, which regulated the broadcasting, telephone, and telegraph industries, rendered an antitrust decision that changed the landscape of modern television. The FCC forced Sarnoff to spin off one of NBC's two radio networks. In 1943, after a ferocious legal battle, the Blue Network, the weaker of the two chains, was sold for $8 million to Edward J. Noble, an irascible entrepreneur who had made a personal fortune in Life Savers. Noble renamed the network the American Broadcasting Company.

Then, in 1948, the Supreme Court ended a two-decade-old legal fight over block booking and forced all the major Hollywood studios to spin off their theater divisions. The famous case of U.S. v. Paramount et al., more widely known as the divorcement decree, curbed Hollywood's monopoly on visual entertainment just as network TV arrived on the scene.

Most Hollywood studio heads tried to put off the implications of this second decision for as long as possible. But not Goldenson. For him, the divorcement decree offered another opportunity of a lifetime. The Supreme Court, in effect, had ordered that Paramount's theater division should become an independent company.

Goldenson asked the Paramount board of directors, of which he was a member, for permission to negotiate a consent decree with the Justice Department. This was the preliminary step toward obtaining his corporate independence. Because no other executive had the stomach for it, the board gave him the green light.

Goldenson spent the better part of a year negotiating the document that set the new Hollywood standard for antitrust compliance in Washington. The Paramount Theatre Division became United Paramount Theatres, with Goldenson as the chief executive. He assumed the lion's share of the studio's outstanding debt and inherited its TV station in Chicago. Under the terms of the

37

consent decree, he also agreed to sell more than half of his remaining movie theaters before 1957.

His company, shedding assets, was primed for acquisitions. Goldenson immediately began to seek out new opportunities in network television.

The years between 1948 and 1955 for network TV were a period of industry transition like the mid-1920s for network radio. The rules of the game were being decided in Washington, about 100 local TV stations were on the air, and NBC and CBS both had TV networks up and running. But until the FCC developed a comprehensive plan for allocating TV frequencies, the transition from radio was incomplete.

A key factor complicating the situation was the running battle between David Sarnoff and William Paley over whose technology would be chosen as the manufacturing standard for color TV. The FCC, when it selected Sarnoff's system (Paley's was nonelectronic), made a second, Solomonlike decision with long-term implications for TV. It divided the broadcast spectrum into "very high" and "ultra high" frequencies (VHF and UHF). One result, which few people foresaw at the time, was that during the first twenty years of the industry's development there were only enough local VHF-TV stations for two-and-a-half national TV networks.

While the industry ground rules for TV were still being decided, Goldenson's impulse was to buy local stations in New York and Los Angeles, combine them with his station in Chicago, and create the nucleus for his network from major-market stations.

The only problem was, there were no sellers. Anyone lucky enough to have secured a license before 1948 was unwilling to give it up. There was just one exception—ABC.

ABC owned five TV stations on Channel 7, in the preferred VHF band, in New York, Chicago, Los Angeles, San Francisco, and Detroit, and the cost of putting all of them on the air was causing Edward J. Noble all sorts of headaches. The strategy of Sarnoff and Paley during this period was to divert their profits from radio into TV. Noble's network, the weak sister of the Big Three, was overextended and pressed for cash. Banks would not lend him money unless he cosigned the notes personally.

A battle for ABC ensued, with three companies having a vital stake in the outcome. CBS wanted to buy the network, keeping its five TV stations and disbanding the ABC network itself; thus Paley would do away with a potential rival and acquire assets he needed. United Paramount Theatres wanted to buy the network, combine it with Paramount's Chicago station, and make it a full-fledged third network; this would put Goldenson into the television business, where he wanted to be. Dumont, of which Paramount still owned 25 percent, hoped to benefit from Paley's purchase and the expected demise of ABC; with Paramount's backing, it would then become America's third TV network.

Goldenson made the first move. During an hour-long conversation at the Waldorf Towers in early 1951, he elicited from Noble the asking price of $25 million for ABC, a hefty sum at the time, especially for a firm with a shaky outlook. ABC's losses in TV were almost $2 million a year and mounting. The company's five owned TV stations covered 20 percent of the country, but the network as a whole covered only 35 percent. Initially, Goldenson backed away from the deal.

Then he learned that Noble was talking with Paley, who had different reasons for being interested in ABC. Paley's network had plenty of performing talent; in 1948, thanks to an ingenious capital-gains tax dodge that company lawyers had devised, it had stolen NBC's Sunday night lineup of radio stars: Jack Benny, Edgar Bergen and Charlie McCarthy, Red Skelton, Burns and Allen, and "Amos 'n Andy."

Paley also had plenty of local TV affiliates. Although only 100 stations were on the air, his network, like NBC, covered most of America's heavily populated areas.

What Paley did *not* have—and what he wanted from ABC—was *owned* TV stations. In the battle with Sarnoff over color manufacturing standards, CBS had delayed applying for local TV station licenses. In 1951 it owned just one local TV station, in New York.

"You'll never get a deal with Paley past the FCC," Goldenson warned Noble—and with that the merger negotiations resumed between United Paramount Theatres and ABC, but Noble would not budge on his $25 million asking price. Goldenson finally agreed.

Goldenson met with the executive committee of United Paramount Theatres one afternoon in May 1951 to discuss the deal he had struck. Noble was still ABC's largest shareholder, and had promised Paley that, if he merged with Goldenson's company, CBS could buy one of the two TV stations that the new company would own in Chicago—ABC's and UPT's. He insisted that Goldenson's station should be the one sold.

As discussions progressed, Goldenson discovered that he was the only member of his own board of directors strongly in favor of the deal. Everyone else expressed serious doubts about Noble's intransigence and ABC's imminent bankruptcy. Goldenson himself was not entirely sure about the deal. He had asked his personal friends at Lehman Brothers, a prominent firm of investment bankers, for an informal opinion; they told him that NBC and CBS were too entrenched for a third network to succeed. But he kept his reservations to himself.

By evening, the meeting was deadlocked. An outsider's opinion was needed. John Coleman, a former Stock Exchange chairman and a key member of the executive committee, suggested Harry Hagerty, the vice chairman of Metropolitan Life Insurance. Hagerty's company was a leading creditor of United Paramount Theatres, and had lent money to CBS and RCA in the past. It was past nine o'clock in the evening when Coleman placed the call to Hagerty's apartment, rousing him from bed. The meeting moved from the Carlyle to Coleman's Upper East Side apartment. There, after listening to all the other directors, Hagerty turned to Goldenson.

"Leonard, what is your feeling?"

"Right now, I doubt there is room for more than two-and-a-quarter networks," Goldenson replied, "but I feel there will be three networks in our time. I'm willing to take the gamble."

Hagerty agreed and added that he would back the new company with loans if necessary.

On that note, a new force in American broadcasting was born. Another two years would pass before the FCC gave the final approval to the merger, but not long after the deal was announced, the newest network founder got a call from David Sarnoff.

"What are you going to do for programming?" Sarnoff asked. The wily old fox of RCA brazenly suggested that Goldenson fill his schedule with NBC and CBS reruns.

"Mr. Sarnoff, I didn't buy ABC to be a second-run network," Goldenson replied. "You and CBS give me no choice. I'm going to bring in Hollywood."

The modern era in American broadcasting was beginning. The silver screen was about to enter the home.

3

New Boys' Network

Bringing in Hollywood wasn't all that easy at first. Not long after the deal that gave him control of ABC was announced, Goldenson had lunch with Nicholas Schenck, the head of Loew's Theaters, which distributed the films of Metro-Goldwyn-Mayer. Schenck, a Hollywood eminence grise, was probably the most powerful and feared man in motion pictures during the 1930s and 1940s. And he wasn't very happy with Goldenson.

"Leonard, you're a traitor to the motion picture industry," he accused him bitterly.

In 1953, most of Hollywood shared Schenck's opinion. Without their captive theater chains, the movie studios were hopelessly inefficient. Moreover, TV was luring audiences away from the theaters altogether. Goldenson, once a member of the old movie-studio world, had jumped ship and gone over to television. To the people at ABC, on the other hand, he was an outsider. Goldenson found himself in no-man's-land: a turncoat to Hollywood and an *arriviste* to broadcasters.

"Mr. Schenck," he replied, "let's assume you could put a

trailer for your next Clark Gable picture into every American home. How much would you pay?"

"A lot," Schenck admitted.

"I rest my case," said Goldenson.

As soon as the FCC approved his ABC deal, Goldenson traveled to the West Coast to try to crack what amounted to a studio boycott of television. He started at William Morris, the talent agency, where his friend Abe Lastfogel was in charge.

"Abe, I need plenty of help," he said. "Who can you give me?"

The studios were cutting back on production, but talent agencies welcomed any source of new work for their clients, and Lastfogel supplied ABC with Danny Thomas for "Make Room for Daddy," and Ray Bolger, Georgie Jessel, and Sammy Davis, Jr., for network comedy and variety shows.

Goldenson went next to Jack Warner. The head of Warner Brothers was renowned as a Hollywood "heller," a gambler and womanizer. He liked the prospect of producing TV shows even less than Schenck, but Goldenson had played poker with Warner in the past, and thought he might bluff him into changing his mind.

"Leonard, I know you want to talk about television," Warner said when the two men sat down to dinner, "but I don't want to waste valuable time on that lousy subject. I'll talk about anything else—pictures, women, horses, money, you name it."

Goldenson let Warner start talking, smoothly switched the conversation over to television, and in several additional meetings persuaded him to establish Warner Brothers Television, a new Hollywood subsidiary, with his son-in-law, William Orr, in charge. Everything was done in the family way—Hollywood's way. Goldenson looked over the Warner Brothers film library, picked three movie properties, including *King's Row*, starring Ronald Reagan, and *Casablanca*, as properties suitable for less-grand television adaptation, and the shows began airing in rotation on the weekly "Warner Brothers Presents" in the fall of 1955. They were the first prime-time series produced by a major studio. And

"Cheyenne," the least-known property, turned into a network hit.

It was a Hollywood programming watershed. All across the country, the prewar movie palaces and the live vaudeville acts that had sustained their show business tradition were dying. Movie theaters gave away free flatware on Tuesday nights, when Milton Berle's show was broadcast on CBS. No outlandish attempt to keep the audience's patronage was left untried. Movie attendance fell off from 78 million tickets sold per week to 58 million in 1950, and would plummet to 25 million by 1960. Of the great New York movie palaces, only Radio City Music Hall managed to keep its brass bathroom fixtures and Art Deco trim from being sold at auction or destroyed. Radio City kept its doors open—barely.

Cheyenne, on the other hand, starred an unknown Hollywood actor named Clint Walker, whose previous movie exposure had been as a spear carrier in B-grade properties shot on Warner's back lot. The programming trend in adult TV westerns, which *Cheyenne* started, made the studios realize that they could shift production over to TV without sacrificing marquee-name stars. Most of Hollywood began producing prime-time shows for television (with the notable exception of Paramount, which stuck its head firmly in the sand). And the old radio tradition of live broadcast shows, controlled by their sponsors, vanished overnight.

Goldenson had made his point. He had proved to Hollywood that network TV was a viable buyer of studio product. He had proved to advertisers that ABC did not need big radio stars, like Jack Benny and Milton Berle, to attract a big audience.

"After 'Cheyenne' it was like shooting craps," he recalled.

In 1954 Goldenson received a visit in New York from Walt and Roy Disney. The studio they controlled did not rank among the Hollywood "majors," because it had never owned movie theaters. The Disneys wanted to build a new theme park in California and needed financing to do so, and as part of the deal, they offered to supply Goldenson with new programming. Although Goldenson didn't know it at the time, Sarnoff and Paley had both said no. He lent the brothers $15 million in return for 35 percent of Disneyland,

and committed the network to pay $35 million in license fees over seven years for a new Walt Disney TV series.

By the following year schoolchildren all across America were wearing Davy Crockett hats and Mickey Mouse ears and singing, "See you real soon. Why? Because we *like* you!" "Disneyland," which premiered in the fall of 1954, was the network's first Nielsen Top Ten Hit.

Goldenson was on a programming roll, and he had to be, for the network he had bought was a lemon. In 1952, when the FCC had split the TV spectrum into VHF stations on channels 2–13 and UHF stations on channels 14–83, big cities like New York, Los Angeles, and Chicago received allocations for at least three local TV stations to broadcast over preferred VHF frequencies. ABC, NBC, and CBS competed on equal terms there. But in smaller towns and cities, like Charlotte, Baton Rouge, Knoxville, and Dayton, there was no third VHF station available to carry the signal of the third TV network. The magnitude of this deficiency in ABC's distribution system dawned on Goldenson only *after* he had bought the network. During this period the Dumont Network was still vying with ABC for the honor of being America's third network. Scores of UHF stations, carrying the signal of one or the other, came on the air, flared like fireflies, and died. In 1955 Dumont followed suit.

Goldenson remained in his United Paramount Theatre offices at 1501 Broadway until 1956. From Edward J. Noble he had inherited a top network manager named Robert Kintner, who, for the first three years of the merger, worked badly with almost every new executive Goldenson placed under him. Kintner was a brusque, intelligent ex-journalist with a taste for hard liquor, and he was Noble's man. In 1956, as soon as his Hollywood deal making bore fruit, Goldenson sacked him and moved north to a run-down converted riding stable at 7 West 66th Street that was his headquarters for the next ten years.

Many network old-timers still fondly recall 1956–1966—an era of tenacity, hardship and woe—as ABC's go-go years. The network operated in black-and-white, and was still a tiny company, usually just one step ahead of the bill collectors. Three city blocks were all that separated the converted building where Goldenson worked from the rat-infested loft above the A&P at 68th and Broadway, where young staffers, earning $58 a week in 1956, kept track of station clearances and weekly ratings.

Everyone who worked at the network in this period was viscerally interested in seeing it grow and thrive. It was common knowledge among employees that Goldenson had installed a private movie theater at his home in Mamaroneck in order to watch new films before their public release; he did this in order to stay abreast of new programming trends. They knew that on Friday evenings he often walked to the bank with a shopping bag of United Paramount Theatre receipts, the money that kept network payroll checks from bouncing. They personally witnessed the Goldenson strategy of squeezing the last drams of cash from his fading theater business and diverting them into the rapidly growing but still unprofitable network.

After Kintner left, Goldenson promoted a research and sales wizard named Oliver ("Ollie") Treyz into his old job. The new network president was a workaholic, can-do executive who looked like Edward G. Robinson and liked to smoke big cigars. Goldenson treated Treyz like a surrogate son, and gave him carte blanche to run the network as he saw fit. In his six years at the helm, Treyz repaid the compliment by building it into a viable industry competitor.

ABC's first hit after "Cheyenne" was "Maverick," which starred the young James Garner and premiered in 1957. By then enough local TV stations were on the air for the network to cobble together a patchwork system of national coverage. "Leave it to Beaver" and "Ozzie and Harriet" were playing to family audiences. The "Lawrence Welk Show" was still relatively young. And before the fad in TV westerns ended—in 1959, twenty-seven shows in this vein aired in prime time on ABC, NBC, and CBS—Treyz and Warner Brothers Television developed a new programming genre: the hour-long action-adventure show.

"77 Sunset Strip," which premiered on ABC in 1958, started the new trend, and series like "Hawaiian Eye," "Naked City," "Bus Stop," and "The Untouchables" carried it forward into the 1960s. They were gritty, realistic dramas long on violence and geared to big-city audiences. "Untouchables" featured Robert Stack in the role of Eliot Ness, and turned a real-life Treasury agent from the Prohibition era into an unforgettable TV character. "Naked City" gave the young Robert Redford, Dustin Hoffman, Peter Fonda, and Jon Voight their TV acting debuts. "There are eight million stories in the naked city, and this is one of them," the famous tagline of "Naked City," epitomized the realistic, Philip Marlowe qualities of the early action-adventure genre.

Ollie Treyz was an energetic president who brooked no interference at ABC. Television was expanding at a madcap pace. The number of TV sets in American homes had gone from 4 million in 1950 to 52 million in 1960. Network TV advertising revenues were $550 million in 1955; they were nearly $1 billion in 1962. ABC, NBC, and CBS were truly becoming the Big Three, and ABC, because its network had started so far behind, was growing the fastest of all. Treyz tripled its sales figures during six years, but he sometimes sold the same inventory three times over. His tactics alienated Madison Avenue buyers.

"They're all whores," Treyz liked to say of network advertisers.

In 1962, Treyz's insouciant attitude caught up with him. Goldenson summoned the troubled executive to network headquarters and fired him. A job was arranged for Treyz at Warner Brothers, but he never recovered professionally. Treyz had given ABC his all.

"I told Ollie he was going to get in a wringer one of these days if he kept double-talking everybody," said Tom Moore to a network colleague.

Moore, Treyz's successor, had a knack for maintaining amicable relations with Madison Avenue. He was a courtly, old-line Southerner who looked like a clean-shaven Santa Claus. He had started his career at the Forest Lawn Cemetery in Los Angeles, selling funeral lots. One day he spotted a camera truck, there to televise an Easter Sunday service. He looked inside the truck, saw the TV monitors, and experienced something akin to an Easter epiphany. What impressed Moore most, he later told his colleagues, were the cables. They seemed to stretch far into the distance, past Forest Lawn into infinity.

"It's the greatest thing since sliced bread," Moore liked to say to network advertisers, "and here are the numbers to prove it."

Audience numbers were the basis for Madison Avenue transactions and the key to all network revenues. An audience had to be quantified before it could be sold, and Nielsen provided only the raw data. The person who provided sales numbers to Ollie Treyz was a polymath named Julius Barnathan, who ran the old research department above the A&P. The person who provided them to Tom Moore was Fred Pierce.

When Pierce had arrived in 1956, a baby-faced twenty-three-year-old graduate of City College of New York, Barnathan greeted him with a sheaf of papers.

"What's that?" Pierce asked.

"It's a ratings book," Barnathan gruffly replied.

Barnathan ran the research department like a master class in methods of network TV sales. Broadcasting's structure had changed from radio days. Instead of turning entire time periods over to advertisers, who had owned most radio shows, Goldenson had inserted ABC as the middleman between Hollywood and sponsors. Network TV typically *licensed* its entertainment programming. The Hollywood studio owned the copyright to its product, plus any revenues that came in after ABC, NBC, or CBS had aired the show twice. But the networks were free to ask as much for minute-long commercials inserted into the show (and later for thirty-second and fifteen-second spots) as the Madison Avenue market would bear.

49

There were two immediate benefits from this new industry practice. As a purely practical matter, Goldenson's licensing strategy kept CBS and NBC from stealing ABC programs. Advertisers had no network loyalties, and could move shows that they owned from one network to another, as had happened to ABC with "The U.S. Steel Hour." Second, program licensing opened up the network TV airwaves to new advertisers who could not afford half-hour or hour-long time periods entirely on their own.

Before coming to ABC, Barnathan had written a master's thesis at Columbia on statistical probability in games of chance, and his brain processed research data and sales figures like a finely tuned machine. At the end of each workday he conducted informal seminars peppered with profanity for Fred Pierce, Leonard Goldberg, Seymour Amlen, Jerry Zucker and other impressionable recruits whose network careers hinged on Goldenson's success.

Each new season brought a fresh crop of pilots and a new round of sales. When the pilot for "Ben Casey" reached New York in the spring of 1961, Edgar Scherick, then the head of network sales, told Goldenson that he thought the actor in the lead role had star potential. Vince Edwards, like Clint Walker in "Cheyenne," was a complete unknown, and a minimum of six commercial minutes had to be sold for "Ben Casey" to turn a profit. Goldenson had to decide whether or not to pick up the pilot before any sales commitments were in. He decided to press the bet.

"If you can sell two minutes, we'll go with it," Goldenson told Scherick. He called him every day for the next two weeks to find out if the availabilities had been sold.

When "Ben Casey" premiered in the fall, it was ABC's biggest new hit since "Maverick." Along with Richard Chamberlain on "Dr. Kildare," Vince Edwards and "Ben Casey" started the trend in TV medical shows.

Goldenson's programming vision relied on serendipity, intuition, and guts. One day while driving into work with Spyros Skouros, the head of Twentieth Century-Fox, he had a brainstorm. Goldenson had watched *Imitation of Life*, a 1959 Universal release starring Lana Turner, in his home theater over the weekend. The ripe, middle-aged Turner had made such an impression on him that he asked Skouros if Twentieth Century-Fox had a movie property with her in it in its movie vaults. Skouros said yes, another Lana Turner movie could be arranged. "Peyton Place," the adapted series, premiered in the fall of 1964. It was network TV's first prime-time adult melodrama.

"Peyton Place" joined three new comedies—"Bewitched," "The Addams Family," and "No Time for Sergeants"—on the schedule in the fall of 1964. The successful returning series that year were "McHale's Navy," "Combat," and "My Three Sons." For a few weeks, ABC won the Nielsen ratings in the fifty biggest U.S. markets. The American broadcasting economy, after a decade of steady growth, finally seemed capable of supporting three equal networks.

An architect's model for a new network headquarters building had sat in the lobby of 7 West 66th Street, waiting to be built. But when a skyscraper leasehold at 1330 Avenue of the Americas came on the New York real estate market, Goldenson scrapped the model and moved there instead. His network had joined the big leagues, next door to CBS and four blocks from NBC in midtown Manhattan.

The excitement of being Number One did not last long. Before fall 1964 was over, ABC's built-in distribution handicap had taken its toll, and the network slipped back to Number Three. The network's programming story was then eclipsed by a very different industry development. Leonard Goldenson embarked on a plan of merger with Harold Geneen's International Telephone and Telegraph Company.

In late 1965, when the ITT deal was struck, the old business trusts of early in the century were being modernized in publicly owned business conglomerates. ABC was beset by outside suitors— in addition to Geneen, Norton Simon and Howard Hughes made buyout offers—just as the networks changed over to color television technology. For the first time since he took control of ABC, Goldenson decided to fashion his network in NBC's image, not

CBS's, and accepted Geneen's merger offer of $350 million in ITT stock, plus $25 million in loans for conversion to NBC's color system. The catch in the deal was that ABC could *not* borrow money from any other source until the buyout was approved in Washington.

For two years the ITT merger was deliberated in the nation's capital. The FCC approved the buyout twice, but the Justice Department refused to sanction it. On New Year's Day, 1968, after Washington had made its overall intentions clear, Geneen canceled his offer, and Goldenson had to start all over.

This was not the best period in the network's history. By 1968, both ABC and its founder were the butt of industry jokes. One punchline referred to the Loft's candy store at the corner of 53rd Street in New York, in the network's new midtown headquarters building. Network visitors didn't have to enter 1330 Avenue of the Americas, the joke went; all they had to do was shout, "Hey, Leonard!" to the thirty-ninth floor, and he would come down. The network was still his, in other words, but it was just a "candy store."

"Do you want to know how to end the Vietnam War?" a second joke went. "Just put it on ABC, it'll be over in thirteen weeks."

In 1968 Lyndon B. Johnson wearily announced, "I will not seek, nor will I accept, the nomination of my party." Robert Kennedy and Eugene McCarthy battled each other for Don Quixote's crown. Hubert Humphrey threw his hat into the ring. Richard Nixon and Spiro Agnew linked arms and signaled V for victory.

For a generation of baby boomers, poised on the cusp of adolescence, the preceding decade had been an extended pleasure cruise, a childhood trip to Disneyland, to "Gilligan's Island," to television Utopia. Actors shot dead on one show reappeared on another—until Martin Luther King and Bobby Kennedy were assassinated, Mayor Daley snarled, and race riots tore up downtown Detroit, Newark, and Washington. The living dead were resurrected instead. Richard Nixon was elected President, promising "law and order" and a "secret plan" to end the Vietnam War.

There was no going back to the stately black-and-white images of President Kennedy's funeral procession. The American public saw it all, in living color. And as the baby boom generation came of age, flailing with pent-up energy, Leonard Goldenson saw new opportunity. His audience was growing up, and his network was bursting at the seams with energy. All he needed was someone to harness the energy and pull his company together.

And so, a few days after his ITT deal fell through, Goldenson chose Elton Rule as ABC's new network president.

Goldenson had been eyeing the general manager of KABC-TV in Los Angeles for some time, but whenever he had inquired about the possibility of his coming to New York in a local station job in the past, Rule had put him off.

"If there should ever be an opportunity to run the network," Rule had said, "just let me know."

And after watching his predecessors lose the job one by one, Rule had a healthy skepticism about the network responsibilities he was inheriting. But more than Kintner, Treyz, or Moore, he succeeded in putting his own personal stamp on them. On the day he arrived in New York, one mid-level network executive greeted him in the elevator with a hearty, "Congratulations!"

"For what?" Rule replied in an easygoing voice. He was sporting a crew cut, blue serge suit, and winter California tan.

"I hear you're going to be with us awhile."

Rule just smiled and shook his head, pooh-poohing his new appointment.

At his first staff meeting, he gave a pep talk. He outlined all the problem areas: The network was still unprofitable. Most of its local affiliates were the weakest stations in their markets. Ratings were poor. Because the ratings were poor, ABC had less money than it needed to buy programming in Hollywood. The television business was all too simple. To be profitable, a network had to operate with equilateral efficiency, balancing the programming cost point, the advertising demand revenue point, and the local affiliate clearance distribution point. When it was operating at peak efficiency, a network's affiliate lineup reached 99 percent of all viewers, its programs earned better than a one-third audience share, and its inventory sold in a "demand" Madison Avenue marketplace. When the three points balanced, the money poured out like coins from a Las Vegas slot machine. But one lemon unbalanced the one-armed bandit, and ABC's weak affiliate lineup skewed its entire network triangle.

Rule's message was that the problems could be solved.

"We're going to do it," he said.

He paused and grinned at the men in coats and ties at the table.

"And we're going to have a lot of *fun* doing it."

Rule was one of the most colorful and uninhibited of the executives who were about to transform the network TV business. A third-generation Californian, he had Gold Rush roots. His grandfather, after migrating West, had worked the Argonaut and Kennedy mines in the Mother Lode region, near Sutter Creek. His father died when Rule was one-and-a half, and he started work as a boy, delivering the *Saturday Evening Post* and *Country Gentleman* in Stockton. He was working as a jack-of-all-trades at KROY-AM, a radio station in Sacramento, just before World War II, and received an officer's commission in the National Guard. Landing in the Aleutians as a second lieutenant with the 7th Infantry Division, he later fought at Kwajalein, Leyte, and Okinawa in the South Pacific. By the time his regiment entered Korea, ahead of the task force which would later accept the Japanese surrender, he was a commanding major.

It was easy for most of Rule's network colleagues to like him. He brought something new to the network: the confidence, look, and feel of a winner. At fifty-one, he was over six feet tall, slim and rugged. He created space for the people around him.

A few members of the network old guard, resentful that a California station manager had invaded their New York territory, viewed Goldenson's new WASP as someone brought in to appease Wall Street after the ITT fiasco. But such sentiments were motivated mostly by jealousy. It was the norm in broadcasting for Jewish industry leaders—Sarnoff, Paley, and Goldenson—to hire Anglo-Saxons as network presidents. Treyz and Moore had both been gentiles. Rule simply outshone them. He had Paul Newman eyes, a never-say-die smile, and a reputation as a lady's man. "Never fly under false flags" was one of his mottoes.

Rule drew on the remarkable group of maverick programmers that Goldenson had cultivated, while trying to make ABC Number One. In 1968 the most influential among them by far was the thirty-eight-year-old president of ABC Sports, Roone Arledge.

In 1951, Arledge had spent the summer before his senior year at Columbia College waiting on tables at an inn on Cape Cod. One night, when a family stopped by for a meal after the dining room closed, the hostess turned them away.

"I can't let you be disappointed," Arledge said. "Come on in. I'll wait on you."

After his graduation from Columbia, Arledge worked his way up through channels to an interview with the vice president in charge of programming at the Dumont Network. As he walked into the executive's office, the interviewer looked up, seemed to recognize him, and asked, "How's everything at the Wayside Inn in Chatham?" Arledge's Good Samaritan instincts had helped him get his first job in TV.

Arledge served a two-year stint as an army radio producer, won an Emmy at NBC for a children's TV series called "Hi, Mom!," and in 1960 was working at the station in New York when Edgar Scherick walked into the studio. Goldenson had just bought Scherick's TV sports-production company to produce ABC's coverage of NCAA football games. Arledge had just put together a new pilot of a magazine show called "For Men Only," which was playing on a monitor.

"Who produced that?" Scherick asked.

Someone pointed at Arledge, on the other side of the room, and Scherick hired him to staff-produce the NCAA games. In 1961, when Scherick moved up to network sales, and then to the chief entertainment programmer's job, Arledge took over sports.

ABC Sports was hardly a powerhouse at the time, but at the end of the first NCAA season, Arledge proposed the anthology series, "Wide World of Sports," that would help make it one. The show was almost canceled after six weeks because no advertisers were buying it. Only a good word from Scherick and Tom Moore, and the financial backing of Goldenson, who was impressed by Arledge's energy and wanted to give the show more than the usual latitude to succeed, saved it. "Wide World of Sports" went on to become *the* seedbed for modern sports television.

Working with a handful of production and technical assistants, Arledge introduced one innovation after another—instant replay, slow motion, split screens, hand-held cameras—that allowed him to narrate sports events as compelling stories. Jim McKay was his principal on-air commentator. Don Ohlmeyer, John Martin, Jim Spence, Chet Forte, Chuck Simmons, and Dennis Lewin formed the cadre of producers. Julius Barnathan, who moved through several high-level positions before landing at Broadcast Operations and Engineering, provided the technical support.

During the mid-1960s, while most of ABC's entertainment programs were lucky to clear 150 local affiliates, "Wide World of Sports" cleared 200. Affiliates loved "the thrill of victory, the agony of defeat." There was nothing like it on the air anywhere. Arledge and his sports colleagues had given ABC an exclusive.

In 1964 he adapted the "Wide World of Sports" format to the Olympics, beaming the Winter Games via satellite from Innsbruck to the United States. In 1968, with technical resources of ever greater sophistication, Arledge's coverage of the Winter Games in Grenoble caused an international sensation. Peggy Fleming twirled. Jean-Claude Killy schussed. Arledge fastened a mini-camera to the belt of a downhill racer and soundtracked the footage with Pete Townshend's guitar solo from *Tommy*. As the mountains rushed by, the screen invited viewers into a new, adrenaline-charged world.

To current viewers jaded by the surfeit of TV sports, Arledge's early Olympic success may matter little, but in 1968 he was breaking this ground for the very first time. Later that year, in Mexico City, he captured the timely, unsettling image of medal winners Tommie Smith and John Carlos, unsmiling, heads bowed, saluting the American flag with clenched Black Power fists as the national anthem played.

Arledge's programming was worth millions to the network, and in 1968, on the heels of the canceled ITT merger, it gave ABC a much-needed morale boost. Goldenson named him president of ABC Sports that same year.

In 1970 came Howard Cosell. Arledge was the TV industry's most esteemed sports producer, but even he had not been able to break the hold of CBS and NBC on NFL football and major league baseball. Network TV's two biggest money sports had always belonged to the two largest networks. In 1970, when the NFL scheduled regular-season league games on Monday night, ABC Sports went big-time—broadcasting during the prime-time hours normally reserved for Hollywood show business.

"I saw that program last night with Howard Cosell and Don Meredith yakking away," Henry Ford, a major sponsor of "Monday Night Football," told Goldenson after the first broadcast. "I couldn't even enjoy the game. Can we take them off?"

Goldenson called Arledge and asked for his opinion.

"I'd like to have five weeks," Arledge replied. "If Cosell hogs the mike, I'll pull the string on him."

Goldenson stalled Ford, and three weeks later he got a call back.

"You know Leonard, I apologize," Ford said. "I like that yakking as much as the football."

"Monday Night Football" was the beginning of Arledge's virtual withdrawal from the rest of the network. At a time when ABC was still struggling, he was its biggest celebrity. At times he seemed to be running a network of his own. Each time viewers heard the phrase, "The executive producer of ABC Sports is Roone Arledge" at the end of a broadcast, he took home a residual payment. No one else at ABC had the kind of "talent" deal that Arledge did (but eventually top sports producers and directors did). The per-broadcast fee was reportedly between $5,000 and $10,000, but no one knew for sure—network higher-ups kept the exact terms of the contract under lock and key. But Arledge himself began making himself scarce at company meetings, even when asked by Rule and Goldenson to attend. He had made ABC Sports his personal network fiefdom.

When ABC's board of affiliate governors met in Makaha, Hawaii, in late 1969, Arledge's plan for starting his broadcasts of NFL games live on the East Coast at 9 P.M. was the most controversial item on the agenda. West Coast affiliates would have to preempt their local news at 6 to accommodate the games. Arledge was supposed to defend the plan in person. His wife Ann traveled to Hawaii with all the other network executives, expecting him to show up. But Arledge, at the last minute, learned that President Nixon would be attending the Army-Navy football game, and stayed behind with him. He was courting real-world power; the rest of the network was just make-believe.

Hollywood in 1970 was in a state of barely controlled panic. The number of studio-produced films had dropped to less than 300 per year. Box-office receipts were $240 million *lower* in 1970 than the $1.6 billion culled in 1946. And while formula picture making with reliable stars like John Wayne, Kirk Douglas, and Robert Mitchum was almost dead, low-budget independent films were making counter-culture stars out of hippie actors like Dennis Hopper, Jack Nicholson, and Peter Fonda.

Hollywood's identity as charmed West Coast nation was fading fast with such developments. The 1960s merger wave had swept through the industry too, bringing in new studio owners with little or no sense of the movie past. Stephen Ross of Kinney Parking Systems was running Warner Brothers. Charles Bluhdorn of Gulf & Western had purchased Paramount. A Las Vegas financier named Kirk Kerkorian owned MGM. And the TransAmerica life insurance conglomerate had bought United Artists.

The financial swirl led operating studio heads, who had already lost confidence in their ability to produce hits, to begin to doubt their ability to recognize hits once they were made. Universal Pictures produced George Lucas' *American Graffiti* and nearly shelved it—until Francis Ford Coppola, fresh from his Oscar success with *The Godfather* and one of *American Graffiti*'s coproducers, asked to buy the distribution rights outright. The studio turned the offer down and distributed the film itself, and *American Graffiti* went on to gross more than $100 million in the United States and Canada alone. Universal also gave Dennis Hopper $2 million with the instructions, "Go make us another *Easy Rider*." Hopper tripped the light fantastic to Peru, sampled the local flora and fauna during the filming, and edited his picture in Taos. It was called *The Last Movie*, and attacked the culture of Hollywood movie making so explicitly that Universal quickly buried it.

Lew Wasserman, the chairman of MCA, was the new dean of Hollywood—his talent agency had purchased Universal, the West Coast's largest studio, in 1961—but even he was not immune to the creative anarchy of the period. One day Wasserman asked an aide to comb the studio ranks for production assistants under twenty-five with hair over their collars:

"Get me some crazies," was the way he put it.

Unlike most entertainment companies in town, Goldenson's network did not have to go looking for "crazies"; it already had them in-house. ABC was cultivating the two youngest, senior-level programmers in television—Barry Diller and Michael Eisner.

In 1966 Diller was an unemployed, prematurely balding twenty-four-year-old. His family had made lots of money in Southern California real estate, but he was a UCLA dropout. Diller was already close to the seat of power in Hollywood; while a junior agent at William Morris, he had worked as a driver for Abe Lastfogel, the monarch of the talent world. Lastfogel was one of the best-connected men in town. The only problem was that Diller was a bad driver.

One day, as Diller later told network colleagues, he hit the brakes too hard. Lastfogel landed on the floor of the limousine, and Diller wound up without a job.

Not without resources, he called Marlo Thomas, who had helped him get the job at William Morris in the first place. The daughter of Danny Thomas of "Make Room for Daddy," an old friend of his from high school, was starring in the ABC series "That Girl." On Marlo Thomas' recommendation, Barry Diller interviewed for the job. When Scherick left ABC to go into independent production a few months later, Goldberg, who succeeded him as chief programmer, invited Diller to work with him in New York. Diller started out as a glorified office boy.

In 1966 Michael Eisner was also twenty-two and looking for a job. He was a graduate of Lawrenceville School and Denison College whose father was a prosperous lawyer, but he started at the bottom too, working at NBC as a page during his college years. He then joined the management trainee program at CBS, and worked as a commercial coordinator in daytime programming, screening the advertisements the network inserted in its afternoon soap operas. It wasn't much of a job, and Eisner didn't stay in it long. Fred Silverman, only a few years older than he, was already running CBS's entire daytime schedule, and promotion prospects were slim. Eisner was a rich kid, while Silverman's father had been a TV repairman in Rego Park, Queens. Seeing the handwriting on the CBS wall, Eisner mailed out two hundred copies of his résumé. One of them landed on Diller's desk in New York.

Like Arledge before them, Diller and Eisner had the advantage of starting their careers in a programming department that had nowhere to go but up. ABC's lowly network status and unlikely Hollywood connections had fostered a renegade creativity and a hell-for-leather "We're number three, we've got nothing to lose" attitude among the programming staff. It was virtually an ABC tradition for ambitious young programmers to arrive, spend a few years, and leave. Goldenson could not afford to pay enough to keep his brightest staffers. Instead, he trained them and launched their careers.

Hollywood was slowly filling up with programmers from the third-place network. David Melnick, Doug Cramer, Harve Bennett, Paul Picard, Lawrence Gordon, and Aaron Spelling were among the now celebrated movie and TV producers who got their starts on the entertainment staff.

Diller and Eisner, ABC's youngest network programmers, stood out even as office boys. Diller had his mind set on proving himself as a "baby mogul" in the Irving Thalberg mold. Shortly after he arrived in New York, Goldenson and Leonard Goldberg gave him an opening.

Charles Bluhdorn, the Gulf & Western entrepreneur who had bought Paramount Pictures in 1965, was having trouble making the acquisition work. Under Barney Balaban, Paramount had blundered badly by selling its library of pre-1948 black-and-white movies to Lew Wasserman at MCA. Wasserman, one of the first Hollywood executives to recognize the upside potential of television, promptly licensed them to network TV. As a result, instead of taking money from the networks, Paramount was forced to subsist on the meager income from its new feature films.

Goldenson could help solve Bluhdorn's cash problems, and at the same time bring his old employer into the orbit of ABC, by licensing a package of Paramount's new color movies. It had always galled Goldenson that Paramount had never produced for television after he left the studio. In his own mind, he had never really left Hollywood.

Barry Diller was designated as the go-between in the negotiations with Bluhdorn. One industry account of this vital transaction portrays a cool Diller bringing Bluhdorn down in price while the two men sat eating sandwiches on the thirty-seventh floor of 1330 Avenue of the Americas. Bluhdorn, an Austrian Jew who had survived the Nazi death camps, was apparently not so cool.

"If you're going to scream, there's no reason to continue," Diller told him.

Bluhdorn did not like this insolent tone. "Do you know who you're talking to?"

"Are we here to make a deal or not?" Diller replied. They made a deal.

The film package that Diller bought for the network in 1966 actually turned into a ratings disaster.

"It was *dreck*," said Seymour Amlen, the research whiz who evaluated the package afterward. "Not just B movies—C and D movies. The network lost millions. We were told later that the only reason it went through was because Goldenson was willing to do Bluhdorn a favor."

Actually Goldenson had approved the deal because he wanted Paramount to become a regular supplier for ABC—and that part of the deal worked. In 1967, thanks in part to money from ABC's generous licensing fees, Bluhdorn bought Desilu Productions, and its television series backlist, with titles like "I Love Lucy" and "The Untouchables," gave the studio credibility and a revenue source to branch out into TV production. Diller was already playing in the big leagues.

In 1969, before Leonard Goldberg left ABC to run Screen Gems, Columbia Pictures' TV subsidiary, one of his last decisions was to put Diller in charge of "The ABC Movie of the Week." Diller considered all jobs in relation to whether they could advance or harm his career, and disliked the assignment at first. He was being asked to break new ground in an untested TV genre, for no network had ever produced made-for-TV movies before. ABC was doing so only because it could no longer pay the exorbitant licensing fees that Hollywood was charging for feature films. Diller thought "Movie of the Week" was a recipe for failure.

He chose "high concept" storylines, marquee actors, and young Hollywood directorial talent—and the ratings surprised everyone. The network's research department projected a 27 percent audience share the first season; it averaged 33. The next season the share figure jumped to 35, the next to 38. But it was hardly surprising that young viewers would watch; Diller gave the production go-ahead to films like *Duel*, Steven Spielberg's first feature-length directorial project.

Once he had mastered the made-for-TV movie genre, Diller grew more confident and began investigating newer and bolder ideas. If a network home-grown product could hold an audience's attention for ninety minutes, why not for two full evenings, or even three? Under Martin Starger, Goldberg's successor as the network's chief programmer, Diller put into development the literary properties *QB VII, Rich Man, Poor Man, Roots,* and later *The Winds of War,* which together formed the basis of the TV miniseries genre.

Eisner, who had started a rung below Diller in the programming department, was equally ambitious. After Diller had served as Goldberg's Mr. Fixit, Eisner played the same role for Martin Starger, apprenticing in series programming. In 1971 he went to Las Vegas, auditioned Michael Jackson, and turned the Jackson Five into animated TV characters. ABC promptly went from third to first in the children's programming ratings. The following year, when he was placed in charge of the daytime schedule, Eisner brought his wife Jane to the thirty-seventh-floor conference room and spent hours with her watching three-quarter-inch cassettes of daytime soaps, picking apart storylines to figure out what made them tick.

Eisner's infectious, gangly charm provided comic relief from Diller's blunt, driven intensity. Diller was shy and uncomfortable. He had a reputation for being an enthusiastic closet gay, with a penchant for young men and an "alternative" life-style. His way of reacting to the stories that circulated about him was to act prim and nervous on the job. Eisner, by contrast, was sloppy and vital, wore ill-fitting clothes, and rode to work with his wife perched on the pillion of his motorcycle. He had a Jimmy Stewart "gee whiz" quality, and seemed always to need a shave.

"I fight to keep my instincts clean," Diller once told *Broadcasting* magazine. "Instead of allowing our natural instincts to flow, we tend to relate to what we've learned. I try not to base future decisions on past success. I must judge in the abstract."

Eisner used a different set of terms for the programming proc-

63

ess. "Audiences are looking for anything that smells unique and new and stimulating and sensual," he said, "anything that will make them *feel*."

With programmers like Arledge, Diller, and Eisner working in the same building, it was only a matter of time before ABC threw off its third-place yoke and leaped ahead in the ratings.

4

Shaking the Dice

"**W**hat's new?" Goldenson asked Leonard Goldberg each spring when he was the chief programmer and the fresh crop of network pilots rolled in. "Remember, all we have to sell are flickering images on a screen."

Enthusiasm, youth, vigor—these were the qualities that Goldenson wanted his network to project. But he himself was growing older. Goldenson had turned sixty in 1965, and two years of protracted ITT deliberations since then had done nothing to rejuvenate him. One executive in the room with Goldenson when he learned that the Justice Department had filed suit against the merger plan remembered all the color draining from his face. In one instant Goldenson seemed to age twenty years.

In the spring of 1971, Goldenson's hectic work life caught up with him. After compressing two business trips to California and to Europe, the annual meeting of his shareholders, and a weekend tennis game into too short a span, he ended up in the intensive care unit of Columbia Presbyterian Hospital with a heart attack.

Goldenson had remarkable recuperative powers and re-covered quickly. After convalescing for several weeks on doctor's orders, he was eager to return to work. But while his prognosis was still unclear, an oddly unsettling feeling invaded 1330 Avenue of the Americas. For years, the question had been not *Would* the network lose money? but How *much?* Now that it was becoming profitable, a new question surfaced: Who would inherit Golden-son's founder's crown?

In 1971 there was not much doubt that it would be Elton Rule. Under his leadership, whose strategy he had presented at his first staff meeting, the network was yielding tangible results. One night at a time, 5–10 percent a year, ABC was steadily building strength. Rule's own local station, KABC-TV in Los Angeles, proved that incremental gains could work; it beat out KCBS and KNBC in the ratings with the same programming the network's affiliates aired in the rest of the country. It was only a matter of time before the network as a whole broke through.

The pieces of the puzzle fell into place fairly quickly. Monty Hall, the unctuous host of "Let's Make a Deal," had a contract dispute with NBC in 1969, and found *himself* searching for the prize behind "Door Number One, Door Number Two, or Door Number Three." He picked ABC, and "Let's Make a Deal" carried its ratings over to the network's daytime schedule. The show, leading a moribund slate of afternoon soaps, lifted ABC out of the daytime-programming cellar, ahead of NBC.

On Tuesday night "Cheyenne" and "Wyatt Earp" had once been a powerful combination for ABC, and "McHale's Navy" and "Combat" had later replaced them. But Red Skelton's comedy hour consistently won the night for CBS—until 1969, when Rule counter-programmed "The Mod Squad," made-for-TV movies, and "Marcus Welby, M.D." CBS and NBC both had documentary news—traditionally the lowest-rated kind of network program-ming—at 10 P.M. on Tuesday, so ABC's new lineup built ratings strength by default as the night progressed. "Welby," a new series that season, ranked eighth in 1969–70 and broke the long dry spell.

It was ABC's first prime-time Nielsen Top Ten hit since 1967. With the same lineup during the 1970–71 season, "Marcus Welby, M.D." was the Number One show in all of television.

It was time for a little celebration. Goldenson usually spent his birthday, December 7, in a warm, exotic locale, and the annual gathering of the affiliate board of governors, which was held around that date, provided the perfect excuse.

In December 1969, Goldenson, Rule, and a dozen other top ABC executives and their wives boarded a United Airlines stretch DC-8 bound for Hawaii. They sat in the coach section; the network was still far from rich, and even Goldenson and Rule did not fly first-class. But they were headed for Makaha, on the west coast of Oahu. Scores of *heiau* (shrines) dotted the sacred ground by the Pacific Ocean. In the shadow of Mount Kaala, the highest peak on the island, the Hawaiians worshipped the spirits of their ancient religion.

The New York arrivals and their affiliate guests were ferried by helicopter from the Honolulu airport to the Makaha resort hotel for five days of dancing and drinking, golf and tennis, and talking.

"I had some prepared remarks," Rule began the business discussions, "but they were discarded in view of the tone of this meeting—complete informality."

The midyear report showed ABC still trailing NBC and CBS in the national Nielsens, with a 16.0 prime-time rating compared to 19.2 for CBS and 19.1 for NBC. But when the audience was measured in the seventy largest TV markets, which mattered most to network advertisers, ABC's ratings shot up. The network boasted seven of the top fifteen programs in this category. And in the arena of audience demographics—especially women and men 18–49, which had become the industry standard for Madison Avenue buys—the numbers were even higher.

The network overview that Rule presented in Hawaii seemed to fulfill the promises that he had made in New York. He radiated confidence and optimism, and the quality of his leadership was reflected in two favorite dinner toasts he made to his close colleagues.

"Deny yourselves nothing!" he said. And, "Kindness!"

Even the weather at Makaha was on the side of the arrivals. At the luau that was the main social event of the five-day meeting, ominous clouds gathered on the mountains, and a destructive tide began running on the beaches. But the Hawaiian natives beat a drum and blew a sacred conch. Auntie Hilo Hattie, Kahili, and Leimoni regaled the visitors with sword and hula dances. Penny Silva sang. Al Harrington, the star-to-be of "Hawaii Five-O," entertained. The storm withheld its force.

Only as the luau was ending, after the natives sang out "Aloha" and the guests began leaving, did the winds swirl down, blowing out all the lanterns. The visitors returned, flushed and excited, to the safety of the hotel.

Rule got the promotion that seemed to assure him of the network succession less than a year after Goldenson's heart attack. For almost two decades, ever since the 1953 merger, the chairman's seat at ABC had remained vacant. The job was Goldenson's escape valve. If one day he decided to step back from the ongoing operations of the company and enter semiretirement, he could take the title of chairman and yield his nominal authority while maintaining his founder's control.

In 1972 Goldenson did just that. He named Rule ABC's new president and chief operating officer, and appointed him simultaneously to the inner sanctum executive committee on the board of directors. It had taken Rule four years to rise from a station manager's job in Los Angeles to the presidency of the corporation. Simon B. Siegel, who had worked closely with Goldenson since Paramount days (and who, over the years, had come to look more and more like Isaac Bashevis Singer) decided to retire at the same time as Goldenson stepped up.

The appointment of Rule and the retirement of Siegel signaled a sea change in the network's operating climate. Siegel had been an advocate of tightly controlled spending; Rule, a wide-open work-and-play personality, believed in spending money to make money. And after conquering the TV network, he quickly set out to do the same with ABC as a whole.

A lot of egos, including Fred Pierce's, were wounded during Rule's rapid rise. With Goldenson's backing, Rule took advantage of his newfound authority to put his own stamp on the company. He selected I. Martin Pompadur, a close network aide, to run all of ABC's nonbroadcasting operations in records, theme parks, and publishing, which were slated to grow rapidly. He placed Walter Schwartz, a former radio executive, in a new job overseeing ABC Television, which comprised the TV network and the company's five owned TV stations.

But in the middle of the 1972–73 season, after four good seasons, the network suddenly began to stagnate. Rule's choice to run it was unable to coordinate the strong-willed executives who worked under him.

"I feel like an admiral in the middle of a group of battleships, each pushing in a different direction," Schwartz confided to Julius Barnathan a few months into his new job.

The other problem was industry competition. From the very beginning of network TV, there had been two ways of measuring the audience: total viewership and audience demographics. Total viewership was a purely quantitative measurement; in this category, the A.C. Nielsen Company measured how many eyes were watching a particular network show. Demographics was more qualitative; it isolated viewers according to age group and sex.

Because CBS had the most comprehensive system of local affiliates across the country, it had long prided itself on its ability to attract the largest number of viewers. As a result, CBS programming, not surprisingly, had tended toward rural audiences. "The Beverly Hillbillies" and "Petticoat Junction" were typical examples of CBS's programming approach. And throughout the

1950s and during most of the 1960s, Madison Avenue bought air time on a total viewership basis.

Since the earliest days of network radio, NBC's identity as a broadcaster had been associated with the big-city, clear-channel stations that allow Texas car drivers with AM radios to hear a Cincinnati signal at night. Because it had a weak affiliate system in rural areas, Goldenson's network had always tried hardest to please big-city audiences. The gritty realism of "Naked City," "The Untouchables," "77 Sunset Strip" didn't play well in Paducah County or the Bible Belt, but they attracted viewers where ABC had stations to reach them. While CBS was televising "The Andy Griffith Show" and NBC "The Jack Paar Program," ABC was airing "Bus Stop," a series so brutal and graphic that one episode had sparked the first Congressional inquiry into televised violence.

Unlike CBS and NBC during the sixties, ABC made demographics a conscious part of its sales strategy. While NBC and CBS continued to sell commercials on the basis of guaranteed total viewership, Pierce and the network sales staff would guarantee a certain number of women 18–49 or men 18–49. In this way ABC received 29 percent of Madison Avenue network TV advertising budgets at a time when it was averaging just 24 percent of the audience. First NBC and then CBS began to copy its programming and sales approach. By 1971, when "All in the Family" premiered, the sales edge had closed.

Curiously, ABC had financed the development of two pilots of "All in the Family." The Norman Lear show was almost signed to appear on its schedule. But Goldenson, in perhaps the worst programming decision of his career, decided that Lear's brand of realistic comedy would offend conservative affiliates in the Bible Belt and turned it down. "All in the Family" went to CBS, where, in effect, it replaced "The Beverly Hillbillies" as America's leading comedy, costing ABC dearly in younger, urban viewers. It was what Hollywood programmers call a "locomotive" hit—it pulled other CBS shows along. Fred Silverman, who had taken over as CBS's chief programmer, developed "Maude," "The Jeffersons," and other comedy spin-offs from "All in the Family" and planted

70

them in strategic spots on the schedule. The effect on ABC's ratings was disastrous. "Marcus Welby, M.D." dropped from first to thirteenth place in one year, and "ABC Movie of the Week" from fifth to seventeenth the next.

By the beginning of the 1974–1975 season the network was in a bind. Four prime-time series with the letter K in the title were on its schedule that year—"Kung Fu," "Kodiak," "Kolchak: The Night Stalker," and "Nakia"—and ABC's ratings fell to their lowest point in more than a decade. The network shuffled programs and time periods, but to no avail. The audience gains of the previous five years were being sliced away. Executives at CBS and NBC called it the "year of the K," and laughed, but at ABC there was no time for excuses or explanations. A solution was needed, fast. Heads would roll.

But whose? Barry Diller, who by this time was in charge of the entire prime-time schedule, was the primary culprit in the debacle, but he made one of the all-time-great Hollywood escapes from responsibility. Just before the 1974–75 season began, Frank Yablans, Paramount's president, insulted Charles Bluhdorn, its owner, in a *New York* magazine interview. (Yablans had the studio on a roll and was trying to take all the credit.) Bluhdorn telephoned Leonard Goldenson, asking if he could hire that nice young man who had negotiated the network's licensing arrangement with Paramount a few years before. Diller's success with made-for-TV movies made him a credible candidate for the job, and Goldenson released him from his network contract. In a move that shocked network colleagues and Hollywood insiders alike, Diller was named the studio's new chairman, Yablans' boss. Diller was only thirty-two, and the only other man to hold the title of chairman at Paramount before him was Adolph Zukor, who would die in 1976 at the age of 103.

Walter Schwartz was reassigned in the fall of 1974 from ABC Television to Leisure Group II, a makeshift division of dwindling movie theaters, three tourist parks, and a bottled water company.

Fred Pierce, who had been acting as Schwartz's deputy, was then called to Elton Rule's office. He had patiently bided his time, waiting for a chance to run ABC Television. When the network most needed him, it seemed, Pierce would get to run it.

Rule greeted him jovially. "Okay, hot shot," he told Pierce. "You wanted the job. Now you've got it."

Pierce's colleagues in research had always sensed that he had that special "something." His first job at ABC was supplying the A.C. Nielsen Co. with a daily listing of the local stations that carried the network's programming. The young ratings clerk was so single-minded about his work and devoted to numbers that Jerry Zucker, the friend who compiled Pierce's tax returns in those early days, once proposed investing $5,000 of his own money in return for 10 percent of Pierce's future earnings.

Pierce told Zucker he thought he was crazy, but such an expression of confidence made him smile.

While Arledge, Diller, and Eisner represented the network's creative side, developing sports and entertainment programs that attracted viewers to ABC, Pierce represented the financial side. His job was to translate the audience into numbers that could be sold to advertisers. Pierce first defined this role for himself in 1962, when he was promoted from network research into sales planning. He was not *in* sales or *in* programming. Salesmen tended to be gregarious hard-drinking men who schmoozed Madison Avenue advertisers at the 21 Club or in the American Bar and Grill. Programmers belonged mostly in Hollywood, concocting offbeat drama and comedy. Pierce's special forte was to work behind the scenes compiling all the sales arithmetic.

More than any of his colleagues, he had his finger on the revenue pulse. When a salesman needed network approval to shave prices in order to close a deal, they went to Pierce for the go-ahead. Even Leonard Goldenson called Pierce's office to find out what commercial inventory in the network's programs had sold for. Pierce successfully added a minute of commercials to "Wide World of Sports," and he failed to add another minute to "Batman." He spent most of the 1960s constantly plotting new ways for the network to increase revenues.

As soon as he was named president of ABC Television, he began plotting to woo Fred Silverman away from CBS.

Pierce and Silverman were old acquaintances. While writing a master's thesis at Ohio State on ABC's programming strategies in the 1950s, Silverman had contacted the network for data, and Pierce had been the researcher who supplied it. The two men had met briefly. Then their paths had diverged for the next fifteen years.

Silverman had started in programming at WGN, a local TV station in Chicago, not affiliated with a network. Its entire schedule had to be programmed locally. Silverman was more than equal to the task. He bought *Bomba the Jungle Boy* movies in syndication, edited them down to an hour, and added a jungle drum opening. Presto! "Zim Bomba," a WGN ratings success, was born. He bought *Robin Hood* and *Tom Sawyer* movies, retitled them as "Family Classics," and counterprogrammed them on Friday night against Bob Hope. WGN won the time period.

In 1962, just as Silverman was starting a new job at WPIX, WGN's sister station in New York, Michael Dann, CBS's chief programmer during the 1960s, read Silverman's Ohio State thesis. "I could see the kid had instincts that were unbelievable," Dann later recalled.

Dann was responsible for hiring the twenty-five-year-old Silverman at CBS. When Dann retired from the job, he also recommended that Silverman replace him as that network's chief programmer. When Silverman took over at the end of the 1969–70 season, CBS was in a dead heat with NBC for the top spot in the overall prime-time ratings. Silverman developed "M*A*S*H" and "The Mary Tyler Moore Show," picked up "All in the Family" and its comedy spin-offs. Four years later, CBS was airing nine shows out of the Nielsen Top Ten.

Pierce's first big decision during ABC's Year of the K was to promote Michael Eisner to become his second in command in network programming and to ask him to come up with six new programs for the 1974–75 "second season." Working on a tight deadline, Eisner delivered six new series in January and February, divided equally between comedy and action-adventure. Three new comedies premiered in January—"Barney Miller," from producer Danny Arnold, "Hot L Baltimore," adapted by Norman Lear from a Lanford Wilson off-Broadway play, and "Karen," a new show from Gene Reynolds and Larry Gelbart, the producers of "M*A*S*H," about a "progressive" Washington lobbyist. None of the comedies was an instant hit, but Eisner had consciously sought out the top producers in Hollywood. The fact that Pierce was willing to pay top dollar for programming did not go unnoticed there.

All three action-adventure series scored big in February. Here Pierce gave Eisner hard-boiled instructions to return to ABC's big-city, male-oriented roots. "Baretta," starring Robert Blake, came first; it was based on the real-life story of a Newark police detective. "Caribe," with Stacy Keach, came second; it involved a two-man Miami police squad operating in the Caribbean. "S.W.A.T.," starring Robert Urich, came third; it was a Spelling-Goldberg spin-off of "The Rookies," one of ABC's few established hits, and became one of the most violent shows ever to air on network TV.

ABC ended its second season on a turnaround note, but Michael Eisner had little time to savor his success. Although he had worked hard with Martin Starger all fall and winter, and was the person most responsible for the change, Pierce had already started negotiating with Silverman to take over Starger's chief programmer's job before the New Year.

Pierce and Silverman worked next-door to one another on Broadcasting Row in New York, but they had met only in passing after their first encounter in 1958. Pierce's secretary, using a social pretext to conduct network business, invited Silverman to her wedding reception in September 1974 so that Pierce might broach the topic of his coming on board. When Silverman arrived on the Upper East Side terrace where the reception was being held, he headed straight for Pierce. The two men talked happily in a corner, oblivious to the other guests.

That Christmas they met again when Pierce wandered into the 21 Club after a holiday party and bumped into Fred Silverman near the bar. As they drank, Silverman hinted that he was feeling restless and overworked at CBS. Pierce wasted no time offering him a new job. It was not an extended courtship. Like bears, they sniffed and shook paws.

Early that winter the terms of the contract were negotiated in secret in out-of-the-way Manhattan hotels. Silverman would receive a yearly salary of $250,000 (far above what ABC had paid chief programmers in the past), network stock options worth $1 million, free housing on East and West coasts, and regular use of a company limousine.

Much more important than the salary or perks, however, was the meeting of two minds. Pierce was the son of a taxicab driver from Brooklyn, Silverman that of a TV repairman in Queens. Both knew that between them they could transform American television.

Pierce asked Silverman to start as soon as the contract was ready, but Silverman demurred and continued at CBS through the end of the 1974–75 season, so that he could fulfill the terms of his contract. The news of his appointment was thus delayed for several months. While Michael Eisner put the network back into the prime-time picture that spring, Silverman was devising the CBS schedule that he, as ABC's new chief programmer, would compete against the following fall.

The announcement in May electrified Broadcasting Row and Hollywood. On Wall Street, ABC's stock rose two points in one day. (At the time, it seemed like a big leap.) Not only had the network rebounded that spring from a horrendous autumn start, it had stolen from the competition the leading programmer in all of network TV.

Only Michael Eisner, who had been eased out of his job at CBS by Silverman, was made glum by the news of his former boss's impending arrival.

"There goes my fucking job," Eisner told a colleague. "He's going to fire me again."

5

Jackpot

Silverman arrived at ABC like the gunslinger in a classic Western who ambles into the saloon, takes the one vacant chair at the poker table, and commands, "Deal me in." Most of the programming cards that ABC held for the coming season were already on the table. Others lay in sequence near the top of the deck. But when Silverman picked up the hand, he played it like a consummate gambler, spotting card combinations and betting angles that no one at ABC had noticed before.

Physically imposing yet strangely childlike, Silverman was a walking paradox. He wore finely tailored suits that crumpled around his rotund, bulky frame. Wreathing himself in wisps of smoke, he trailed cigarette ash around the conference room during meetings. He liked to dramatize the quicksilver quality of his quirky intelligence. At bottom a blue-collar worker, he exercised all his privileges to the nth degree and acted out the role of a network prima donna with a bulldozer style.

"He's a lox!" Silverman would say whenever anyone tried to block him.

In the fall of 1975 ABC, NBC, and CBS had all adopted a new self-censorship policy to ward off complaints in Washington, and at their local affiliates, about sex and violence and the use of offensive language in prime-time. Most Americans *liked* sex and violence—violence especially had a long and favored history in both Hollywood and network TV programming. In a typical evolution, Clint Eastwood had gone from playing the likable Rowdy Yates in "Rawhide" to the savage Dirty Harry. ABC played by the same rules: Out of "The Rifleman," "S.W.A.T." was born. But in 1974, after an NBC telecast of the made-for-TV movie *Born Innocent*, in which Linda Blair portrayed a fourteen-year-old girl raped with a broom handle by women in a female detention center, the barometer of public opinion swung hard against the depiction of gratuitous violence on the public airwaves. America was weary of political assassinations, protest, and the Vietnam War, and viewers and affiliates recoiled. To head off a full-scale programming review by Washington regulators, the big three networks voluntarily agreed to create a Family Viewing Hour, between 8 and 9 P.M., during which only programs of a nonviolent and wholesome nature would be aired. The measure, which was proposed by CBS, was designed to protect impressionable children and adolescents watching at that early evening hour. It left 9–11 P.M. (Eastern time) entirely open to network discretion.

In the hands of Fred Pierce and Fred Silverman, the Family Viewing Hour also proved to be a Faustian bargain for CBS and NBC, scrambling viewing patterns in the lead-off hour every night of the week.

Pierce scheduled his network's strongest action-adventure series—"S.W.A.T.," "Baretta," "The Rookies," and "The Streets of San Francisco," all dramas that depended heavily on relatively violent story lines—in a programming "ridgepole" at 9 P.M. The time period allowed their formats to remain unchanged.

At CBS, by contrast, "All in the Family" was scheduled at 8 P.M., in a lead-in time period; it had to be moved to 9 P.M. or have its "realistic" scripts censored. The network gave executive producer Norman Lear the option of rescheduling the show, and the scripts remained unexpurgated. But Lear filed the First Amendment lawsuit in Hollywood that led eventually to the court-ordered demise of the Family Viewing Hour. While "All in the Family" was top-rated for one final season, it lost its value to CBS as a lead-in comedy. The next fall season, the show dropped out of the Nielsen Top Ten.

Michael Eisner, meanwhile, was developing a new comedy at ABC—"Happy Days"—to take over the top spot from "All in the Family."

Instead of firing Eisner a second time, Silverman worked closely with him; "Happy Days" was their first important collaboration. The show had scored low-to-middling ratings during its first season-and-a-half on the air and was on the verge of being canceled when it went from canned laughter to live taping. Eisner noticed that the gruff, leather-jacketed character of "Fonzie" Fonzarelli, based on producer Garry Marshall's adolescent memories and portrayed by actor Henry Winkler, got almost all the studio applause. Eisner instructed Marshall henceforth to tailor his scripts to the part, and in the fall of 1975 the show's ratings caught fire.

Scheduled for the lead-off time period on Tuesdays, "Happy Days" became the network TV industry's newest "locomotive" comedy hit. At CBS, Silverman had coupled "Maude" and "The Jeffersons" to "All in the Family." At ABC, he and Eisner spun off "Laverne and Shirley," another Garry Marshall series, from "Happy Days" and slotted it in the time period directly following the parent show. The jokes got racier as the night progressed. The farcical "Three's Company," a sitcom ménage à trois with John Ritter, Joyce DeWitt, and Suzanne Somers, was the next comedy building block. By the 1977–78 season all three shows were the top-rated series in network TV.

The "Happy Days" strain of comedy was only one programming ingredient boosting ABC's ratings in Silverman's first season. Another was "Starsky and Hutch," a new cop show from Aaron Spelling and Leonard Goldberg, which premiered the same fall. Scheduled with "Baretta" on Wednesday night, it was Eisner's third big action-adventure hit since the second season of the year before. "Starsky and Hutch" helped lock up the audience for "adult" drama.

Pierce belatedly acknowledged Eisner's contributions as programmer by promoting him to senior vice president at ABC Entertainment when the 1975–76 season ended. Eisner and Silverman had been working side by side through the development cycle for 1976–77. Then Goldenson got another call from Paramount, this time from Barry Diller. Yablans, taking Charles Bluhdorn's cue, had moved on, and Diller wanted Eisner to fill the studio presidency. He needed Goldenson's permission to hire him.

"You can't keep someone against his will," Goldenson said. The network chairman, who released Eisner from his newly signed contract two-and-a-half years before it was due to expire, now had two top programming protégés—both rich Jewish boys—running his former studio. Their activity at Paramount in the coming eight years would keenly affect the destiny of ABC, and ultimately become a major factor in the reshaping of Hollywood and network TV.

Six months after Silverman's arrival, the power of ABC's lineup crystallized around two special events. Roone Arledge's Winter Olympics in Innsbruck lifted the network to first place in the ratings. The twelve-hour TV adaptation of Irwin Shaw's *Rich Man, Poor Man,* network TV's first big miniseries, kept it there.

Silverman, meanwhile, was just beginning to put his own personal stamp on the network. He pulled ABC's next big hit series out of the pile of pilots that had been headed for the dustbin before his move to ABC. The pilot had been poorly executed, and the series had not made the schedule—but it made Silverman jump up and down with excitement.

"It's a forty share!" he shouted in the screening room. "It's got forty share written all over it!"

Reworked to Silverman's specifications, "Charlie's Angels" premiered on ABC in the fall of 1976.

A month before the start of the new season, Roone Arledge broadcast the Summer Olympics from Montreal. Silverman adroitly used the sports coverage as a promotional platform for "Charlie's Angels" and other programming on his new 1976–77 schedule. That September the network shot out of the blocks, keeping its streak from the winter and spring intact. ABC was winning the prime-time ratings every single week.

Just as CBS and NBC were waking up to the uncomfortable fact that the era of two-and-a-half networks had definitely ended, a new winter miniseries sent the industry compass spinning once again. In January 1979, more than 130 million TV viewers watched the twelve-hour adaptation of Alex Haley's *Roots*. The miniseries scored the largest Nielsen ratings in broadcasting history.

Every program that ABC aired after "Roots" seemed to attract new viewers. The miniseries had raised the programming ante for network TV years to come. And Silverman, who had inherited a project already in progress before his arrival, got the credit for guiding it through to success at ABC. Silverman seemed to have borrowed a line from Captain James T. Kirk—"Beam us up, Scotty." He had transported the company into a brave new world.

Something quite strange began happening in American TV entertainment at about this very time, and a small scheduling shift at ABC at the end of the 1975–76 season pointed the way. To make room for his own development slate, Silverman jettisoned "S.W.A.T.," moving "Baretta" into its old time period. In "Baretta"'s he placed "Charlie's Angels," the leading edge of the new programming wave.

Broadly speaking, sex had replaced violence as the preferred "quick fix" of the American television audience. "Charlie's Angels" redrew the boundaries of the action-adventure programming genre. Instead of Philip Marlowe characters, "Charlie's Angels" starred Kate Jackson, Jaclyn Smith, and Farrah Fawcett-Majors as three female private eyes. Women were playing traditional men's roles. "Charlie's Angels" shied away from overt sexism—in the show, the women enjoyed a measure of on-the-job independence—but the stars were also Charlie's "girls," dependent servants of an absentee male boss, displaying plenty of flesh, and one or more of them usually fell into the malevolent clutches of "bad guys" in each weekly episode. Violence was present, but obliquely: It was a primal TV scene of bra-less beauty, bound, gagged, and squirming. The erotic suspense lay in the uncertainty about what might happen if the women *couldn't* untie themselves and escape.

Because there was lots of "jiggle" in "Charlie's Angels" and other similarly cast ABC series, executives at CBS and NBC were quick to label it "tits and ass" programming. But it was Silverman's specialty and the cornerstone of a new entertainment creed. America's Number One network had tapped into an unconscious shift in the boundaries of socially acceptable behavior on TV. While television violence had been indirectly banned in Washington, interest in sex was still unfettered. Herpes simplex was relatively unknown. AIDS had not yet become a major health problem. *Thy Neighbor's Wife*, a Gay Talese book about the sex industry, was on the *New York Times* best-seller list, and even a born-again peanut farmer from Georgia, campaigning for the White House, felt free to go on-the-record in *Playboy* and say, "I have lusted in my heart."

More acceptable in the regulatory arena than violence, sex was also more reliable as a vehicle for advertising. The number of American working women was steadily increasing. And women viewers, who earned more disposable income and were increasingly important to advertisers, were more interested in TV sex than in TV violence. As long as ABC offered the fig leaf of "independence" to its female characters and avoided sexist stereotyping, it could capture both male and female viewers.

The advertising dimension was the key. For four years beginning in 1975, national TV advertising demand went through the roof. The network marketplace grew 24 percent one year, 21 percent the next, and 15 percent the next. As the revenue base broadened and swelled, cumulative growth for the four-year period reached a staggering 100 percent. Advertisers spent $2.3 billion for network air time in 1975. By 1979, they were spending $4.6 billion.

While all network broadcasters gained from the expansion, Goldenson's network reaped a windfall. At ABC the surging Nielsen ratings met the flood of advertising demand head-on. The company's balance sheet entered regions of earnings that no network had ever experienced before. The network's profits before taxes for 1975 totaled more than $29 million. In 1976 they were $83 million. In 1977 they were $165 million. ABC's local TV stations in New York, Los Angeles, Chicago, San Francisco, and Detroit were earning similar amounts. Even in the glory days of CBS and NBC, there had never been such a confluence of financial rivers. ABC was literally awash with cash.

For many employees, it was as though the Long March had turned into a Gold Rush. Network departments began vying to see which could host the most extravagant end-of-the-year Christmas bash. The 21 Club, Tavern-on-the-Green, Studio 54—all shared in the profits. The heads of overbudgeted departments had the perfect incentive to party: They had to spend their extra funds or have them cut automatically from the department's budget allocation for the following calendar year.

The fleet of limousines that transported the seniormost network executives around town had license plates that proudly proclaimed their allegiance: "ABC-1," "ABC-2," "ABC-3." Every sidewalk pedestrian could guess who was in the car. A generation of network executives who had spent their formative years in the Depression found themselves caught up in the nouveau-riche euphoria. Network researchers who earned $72 a week in 1958 were making $1,300 a week twenty years later. Fred Pierce's annual salary in 1956 had been $3,016; in 1978, it was $784,000.

To many employees, the most satisfying feeling was luxuriating in the knowledge that a whole nation of viewers wanted to join the party. After "Roots," every young person in New York and Hollywood seemed to be trying to get a job at ABC. The wave of public adulation coincided with a ballooning growth of the network's work force. Jobs that had remained empty in the past were filled. New positions opened. When the personnel office put out an open call, the crowd of applicants overflowed the Hard Rock lobby, spilling out the front door and around the block. Just processing all the applicants added new personnel to the company rolls.

And now, for the first time, women had joined the network

work force in large numbers. As much as the free-flowing money, this was what changed ABC. It had formerly been company policy for every new hire to be personally approved by Simon B. Siegel. Under Elton Rule, department heads (who were all men) did their own hiring. Most of them, married or single, had Jimmy Carter lust in their hearts and were eager to take their places on the network casting couch.

As the profit spigots opened, an exuberant, free-spirited raunchiness percolated through the company. In 1976 ABC gave free air time to United Airlines, which owned the Plaza Hotel in New York, in exchange for long-term exclusive use of its most sumptuous seventeen-room triplex suite. The network's idea was to use the sixty-foot chandeliered living room, dining room, billiard room, and bedrooms to entertain celebrity guests and sales clients in the grandest style. But like other ABC hotel facilities elsewhere in the city, the Plaza suite also provided a trysting spot for randy executives. It was safer than the office and more luxurious than taking lunchtime "nooners" across the street at the Hilton.

Almost everyone participated in intrepid new sexual adventures. After one especially raucous Christmas party, a top-level network executive invited three colleagues to unwind with him in one of the network's hotel suites. A graying hippie, he worked hard and liked to party harder. When the foursome, two men and two women, arrived at the hotel stone drunk, he stepped into the bathroom and reappeared wearing a terrycloth bathrobe.

"Which one do you want?" he asked the other man as the bathrobe dropped to the floor.

Another scene took place on the fifteenth floor of the network headquarters building in New York. Fifteen was a warehouse floor, where maintenance and storage facilities were located; the elevator would not stop on fifteen without a special access key. But one day at lunchtime, an executive at CBS, whose windows faced ABC's directly across 53rd Street, called a friend at ABC.

"Do you want to know what I see?" the executive said, laughing. In the storage area, a naked couple—a middle-aged man and younger woman—lay sprawled over a vacant desk and were making feverish love.

The network had turned into a vast horny Babylon, an excuse for on-the-job mating, and an oasis of promiscuity. John Severino, who now ran KABC-TV in Los Angeles, liked to go on dates with blond viewers who called him up after his on-air editorials; the libido of the dark-haired Severino was so strong and indiscriminate that subordinates, borrowing Sylvester Stallone's much-publicized nickname, called him the Italian Stallion. Red-headed Roone Arledge seemed to like giving male renditions of the song "I'm Jist a Girl Who Cain't Say No." He had divorced his first wife and married his secretary, a former Miss Alabama; and during the network's expansive hiring phase, the ABC Sports predilection for attractive, college-educated female jocks turned into a standing joke at career advisory offices of Ivy League and other top universities around the country. One year it was a varsity tennis player from Princeton, a cheerleader from UNC the next. The likelihood that these women would be promoted from the entry-level production jobs for which they had been hired depended implicitly on their willingness to sleep with the men they worked for.

ABC was not unique in indulging in this casual corporate sex. The learned journals of the period, *Playboy* and *Penthouse*, ran articles describing how on-the-job sex could improve a person's work performance, conjuring up images of under-the-desk fellatio and conference-room head jobs as healthier and more stimulating than caffeine. Television, it is often said, mirrors reality. Maybe so. Working at ABC during the jackpot years was like making love in front of a mirror.

What would happen after the exhilarating ride was over, when the addiction set in? The end of the network's twenty-fifth anniversary birthday party in Hollywood (it wasn't televised until February 1978) provided a visual clue. After the last commercial came the closing fillip, a piece of black-and-white footage from the 1950s, when religious spokesmen still appeared on the networks in prime time.

The announcer's voice intoned: "And now, once again, Bishop Fulton J. Sheen."

Bishop Sheen had won an Emmy in 1952 as TV's "most outstanding personality." His "Life Is Worth Living" and "Mission to the World" had once aired on ABC. When Sheen's oversized image appeared on the birthday party TV screen, where the conclusion to one of his weekly talks was being projected, his demeanor was somber.

"Our subject next week will be," Sheen began—and then halted himself in midsentence, seemingly at a loss for words. He continued: "Do professional careers harden women?"

Bishop Sheen wiggled his bushy eyebrows up and down, as if to say, "And what do you think about *that* cockeyed topic?"

Then the birthday credits and the local news came on.

"What's this I hear about Silverman?" a Wall Street acquaintance asked Goldenson when the magnetic chief programmer showed up on the cover of *Time*. "I thought ABC was *your* company."

The photograph showed Silverman's arms outstretched, carving a space in front of him for the superimposed image of a TV set. The man and the television set seemed organically connected. Freddy Silverman, a.k.a. TV's Master Showman, had taken over network TV.

Rule, hearing of the remark from Goldenson, turned to a public-relations aide: "I think you've got a problem."

Everyone at ABC deserved credit for its newfound success, but at the start of the 1977–78 season, a newcomer was getting all the glory. When the network held its gala Christmas party at Tavern-on-the-Green in Central Park, Silverman decided to walk from the office to the restaurant instead of taking his limousine. Surrounded by a gaggle of network programmers, he conducted an impromptu business meeting during the stroll up Sixth Avenue. By the time the group arrived, the discussion had reached a crescendo, and the gaggle had turned into a crowd. All heads at Tavern-on-the-Green turned to watch the network Pied Piper arrive. Silverman did not just come to the party. He brought the party with him.

He was renowned for throwing temper tantrums whenever he was irked or depressed, but he compensated for this spoiled-brat behavior when he was in good humor. He lived and breathed television, and the television industry picked up and followed the rhythm. Two years before Silverman arrived at ABC, the A. C. Nielsen Co. had introduced overnight ratings, accelerating the pace of the business. In the fifties and sixties, network TV had resembled a sedate, two-handed game of cards between CBS and NBC, and ABC had simply tagged along. Now it resembled a furious game of seven-card stud, with ABC leading the pack.

Silverman pushed the ratings machine full tilt, reading every script of every series episode, often demanding desired changes from Hollywood producers—and always getting them. An inspired tactician, he was ruthlessly competitive, sapping CBS and NBC by enticing their on-air talent to sign exclusive ABC deals. Rob Reiner of "All in the Family," Redd Foxx of "Sanford and Son," and Harvey Korman of "The Carol Burnett Show" switched networks. Silverman lured away James L. Brooks, Ed Weinberger, Dave Davis, and Stan Daniels, key writers of "The Mary Tyler Moore Show," and turned them into independent producers on the Paramount lot.

On-air promotion and scheduling were perhaps his strongest programming gifts. Once he had developed a potential hit, he scheduled it carefully and promoted it to the hilt. He pounced on news of new CBS and NBC series or movie premieres, targeted the date, and hyped his programming alternative with a vengeance. Silverman personally scanned ABC's series for sound bites and snippets of visual "tease" before episodes aired. He often cleared the air time at the last minute, and dropped them in, three to four hundred spots a week, for maximum effect.

"It was saturation bombing," said Edwin Vane, a programmer who worked closely with him. "Eisenhower, Marshall, and Churchill all wrapped into one."

"The bionic Jew," Bill Cosby described Silverman during a comedy ad-lib in Hollywood.

Mercurial and moody, Silverman was pampered, overly protected, and difficult to work with. One day the personnel department was asked to meet with him to discuss secretarial needs. Alan Ross, a new vice president in personnel, took the elevator to the thirty-seventh floor and announced himself to Silverman's secretary.

"I won't deal with a lackey," said Silverman in a guttural voice from behind his office door.

The then head of personnel, Peter Cusack, was in Elton Rule's office at the moment, mapping out a new employee-benefit plan. The subaltern, insulted by the "lackey" label, went directly to Rule's office and interrupted the meeting.

Patient but firm, Rule telephoned Silverman: "Freddy, I'm in a meeting with Peter Cusack. Will you let Mr. Ross see to your needs?"

"You bastard," Silverman growled when Ross returned. "I want a cupcake. Got it? A cupcake. That's all I have time for. Now get out!"

Ross proceeded to the fortieth-floor network dining room, borrowed a silver platter, and bought three cupcakes from a midtown bakery—one with vanilla icing, one with chocolate, and one with half-and-half. He arranged them all neatly on the platter and sent them upstairs. A few minutes later his telephone rang. Ross trembled as he picked up the receiver.

"You're all right!" Silverman said, laughing. "Come on up."

For all his bluster, Silverman liked to work with women and worked well with them. During his tenure at ABC Entertainment, he redrew the programming department gender lines, putting more women in top-level positions than at any other department in the company. Barbara Gallagher, his personal assistant in New York, became vice president of specials and variety programs. He named Marcy Carsey, his protégé in development, head of comedy. Bridget Potter was another top development executive; she started on the West Coast and moved East. Silverman promoted Pam

Dixon in casting, hired Jackie Smith from CBS to run daytime programming, and helped appoint Esther Shapiro, the eventual creator of "Dynasty," to the senior vice presidency in made-for-TV movies and miniseries.

This brigade of talented women staffers was one of the things that distinguished Silverman from Pierce. Silverman and Pierce had worked together hand in glove since the contract negotiations that had brought Silverman to ABC. They were partners in the network's remarkable success and even shared an industry label— "the two Freds."

But Silverman, more voluble and more visible, appeared to almost everyone in the TV industry to be the more indispensable partner in the collaboration. He was a showman and programmer; Pierce worked in sales and research. Pierce dealt with numbers; Silverman supplied the magic. It did not seem to matter that Pierce had hired Silverman and was his boss, not vice versa. The core of their relationship had not changed since 1958: Pierce doled out the data; Silverman wrote the thesis.

By the middle of Silverman's third season at ABC, the two Freds were moving at full speed, like Formula One cars racing into a turn, and their egos were heading for a crash. For the first two years, Pierce had been content to let the chief programmer occupy the limelight, self-confident in the knowledge that he, Fred Pierce, had been the architect of ABC's turnaround. But after the network became firmly ensconced in the Number One spot, he hemmed in his *Wunderkind*.

Pierce liked to surround himself with a small clique of men. Mark Cohen, a senior vice president at ABC Television, kept a tight rein on finance; he had worked with Pierce in sales planning. A bristly street kid from the Bronx named Lew Erlicht was Pierce's programming protégé; Pierce had plucked Erlicht out of WLS-TV, ABC's owned station in Chicago, and promoted him into a senior vice presidency at ABC Entertainment. Erlicht was nominally responsible for late-night, daytime, feature-film acquisitions, and children's entertainment—all the network's programming, in fact, except prime-time series—but it was a job with training wheels. Silverman controlled prime-time series absolutely. Tony Thomopoulos, Pierce's closest insider, was his personal assistant at ABC Television and acted as a minister without portfolio. He attended Silverman's meetings as Pierce's representative, and then apprised Pierce of everything that went on there.

The loyalties of Pierce's clique were to him, not Silverman. Its members worked at the office and socialized in Westchester County together. They were a tight-knit unit that keyed off one man. Erlicht made Pierce laugh, Thomopoulos gave him a patina of self-assurance, and Cohen played his honest sidekick. All four marveled at the gulf between their backgrounds and past, and where the network was headed. They had no desire to bank the fire in their bellies.

Silverman, meanwhile, grew restless. He wanted a new challenge.

Silverman first asked Pierce for added responsibilities in mid-1977. Thanks to the profits from his entertainment programs, the network was finally going to make a start on upgrading its news division, long the poorest in the industry. Believing in his own infallibility, Silverman thought he deserved the job, but Pierce turned him down and named Roone Arledge to the post instead.

With little prospect of a big promotion, and with Pierce's hand-picked lieutenants circling around him, Silverman had nothing to do but maintain the network's Number One status.

"I'm so tired, my brains feel like jelly," he began telling colleagues.

When Pierce first raised the topic of Silverman's contract renewal, he hoped that a big salary increase might induce him to stay at ABC. Pierce desperately wanted to keep the chief programmer. Why kill the goose that was laying the golden eggs? Silverman said he wanted to keep his options open. The negotiations stalled for six months. Then Pierce, who realized that the prospect of Silverman working as an independent producer was not all bad, put the question a different way: If Silverman would not stay, would he promise not to work for another network?

When Silverman said yes, Pierce promptly relayed the promise to ABC's board of directors.

In the week before ABC's twenty-fifth anniversary, Silverman went on the record at a press conference in Los Angeles, denying publicly that he would be leaving for NBC. He claimed that his plans were not fixed, and scorned as "ridiculous" reports that he would leave for NBC. But even as he publicly denied it, Silverman was knee-deep in secret negotiations with NBC for a new job, one that would give him all that he had desired from Pierce and more.

Pierce would take the news as a terrible betrayal.

6

T.T. in Lotusland

As the falling snow of the January blizzard blanketed New York on the night of Fred Silverman's departure, Fred Pierce and Tony Thomopoulos walked the half-block from Pierce's office to a network suite at the Dorset Hotel, and rode out the storm together.

The next morning—with the New York metropolitan area paralyzed, most businesses shut down, and out-of-town commuters housebound—they sat in the hotel dining room having breakfast. Barbara Gallagher stopped by. Gallagher had been Silverman's closest associate at the network and was among the few employees who came to work that day. Like most people, she had heard the news about Silverman that morning on TV.

Pierce looked up at her and projected his hurt. "Are you with me?" he demanded aggressively.

Gallagher, taken aback by Pierce's either-him-or-me tone, replied quietly, "Yes, I am."

That was the way it went, not just the morning of Silverman's defection, but for weeks and months afterward. After Pierce and Thomopoulos got back to the office, a handful of top network executives straggled in, and the faithful few met for lunch on the

93

fortieth floor and assessed the damage. The public-relations staff quickly revised the story of the network's success.

"Teams win championships, not individual stars," Pierce told *Broadcasting* magazine. Translation: Contrary to public perception, Silverman had not done it all.

"There's no question that Freddy is very talented, but he was never very good at developing new shows," Pierce continued in the *New York Times*. "He's an expert at improving shows and scheduling them, but not at making them happen from scratch." Translation: At NBC, where Silverman was headed, he would not be getting help from the likes of Michael Eisner and other talented executives on ABC's West Coast programming staff.

Pierce was sitting on the richest programming legacy in network TV history, but he actively denigrated the achievements of his former collaborator. He also felt insecure enough to spy on him. While Silverman spent the five months remaining on his ABC contract on a minisabbatical in Hawaii, drawing a salary but unable to work, Pierce instructed his own staff in New York to monitor passenger lists on all commercial flights to and from the islands. Pierce knew from past experience how important the kind of "inside information" about ABC's upcoming fall schedule that Silverman would bring to NBC could be, and wanted to ensure that his former chief programmer had to wait as long as possible to make contact with his new employer.

The network had once sung a very different tune. When ABC's affiliates had convened at the 21 Club a few months before Silverman's departure, they presented him with a Steuben crystal, with a dedication that read, "To Fred Silverman, TV's real star, who made us Number One."

So the new era began. Tony Thomopoulos was the new man of the hour. As the news of his appointment spread, the West Coast programming staff buzzed with anticipation.

On the West Coast, ABC Entertainment had settled into a new satellite network headquarters in Century City at 2040 Avenue of the Stars. The luxurious modern office and shopping center that had grown up on the old Twentieth Century-Fox backlot was in perfect keeping with ABC's new Number One status. Large green plants drank in the sunshine that streamed through the cathedral ceiling on the fifth floor, where the network's top programmers worked. The corner offices offered commanding vistas of downtown Los Angeles and the Hollywood hills.

Thomopoulos was an unknown quantity on the West Coast compared to Fred Silverman. An eight-by-ten press photograph of the newcomer circulated around the fifth floor to help staffers who were unfamiliar with him to recognize the new boss. A few secretaries taped it in the spot above their desks reserved for pictures of their boyfriends and movie idols. Thomopoulos had soft lips, and his hair was cut in George Hamilton style. Some thought he had a cute smile.

At the cocktail reception at the Century Plaza Hotel where he formally introduced himself, Thomopoulos politely thanked the West Coast staff for its past and future efforts. Nattily dressed in a well-tailored suit, he was the picture of a successful executive.

His speech ended with an odd reference to his predecessor. Like Thomopoulos, Silverman had worn well-tailored suits, but they had never quite seemed to fit. Silverman's scruffy, blue-collar style, in fact, had led to a nickname, "the rumple-suited Silverman."

"I can guarantee you this," Thomopoulos said. "The press won't have another rumpled suit to kick around." Most of the women listening laughed and clapped.

"We'll give him that, he's better-looking than Silverman," Eisner said to the staffer who told him about the jibe. "But that's about it."

Nineteen seventy-eight, the year Fred Silverman left ABC, marked a watershed in American network television. The harbingers of change stood all around. It was the year that ABC, after two decades of weak national distribution, strengthened its affiliate lineup and stole local stations from CBS and NBC. Fred Silverman took over at NBC, sending that network into a tailspin that took it five years to correct. Roone Arledge began a blitzkrieg transformation of ABC News, which would eventually overtake its new competitors at CBS and NBC. In Hollywood, Barry Diller and Michael Eisner were releasing the first in what would become a long string of low-budget movie hits at Paramount Pictures. New networks from Home Box Office and Turner Broadcasting were surfacing too. For the first time since the Big Three networks had assumed control in 1948, the balance of power in American entertainment was shifting, this time in Hollywood's direction.

Another event, much less heralded, also took place in 1978. Fred Pierce put Beverlee Dean on the payroll.

Thomopoulos took over ABC Entertainment at the busiest time of the year in the program-development cycle. Between January and April, the new fall schedule had to be put together. Returning series were overhauled, new scripts scrutinized, and rough cuts of new pilots previewed.

The long-term fortunes of the network rode on the creative decisions that it made during this critical period, but in 1978 the network had the luxury of building on strength. During the season that had just ended, Lee Majors in "The Six Million Dollar Man" and "The ABC Sunday Night Movie" had been featured on Sunday night. Monday alternated between NFL games in the fall and made-for-TV movies in the winter and spring. On Tuesday, the comedies "Happy Days," "Laverne and Shirley," "Three's Company," and "Soap" were annihilating the competition. "Eight Is Enough," "Charlie's Angels," and "Baretta" aired on Wednesday, and "Welcome Back, Kotter" and "Barney Miller" were perennial favorites on Thursday. Friday was a movie night, and "The Love Boat," "Fantasy Island," and "Operation Petticoat" rounded out the schedule on Saturday. As H. L. Mencken once said, "No one ever went broke underestimating the taste of the American public."

From a business point of view, ABC's lineup at the end of the

1977–78 season was an awesome thing to behold. The network had twelve programs in the Nielsen Top Twenty, seven out of the top ten and four out of the top four. And the golden touch in new program development seemed to be concentrated in a particular office on the fifth floor of 2040 Avenue of the Stars—the "white office," where the vice president for prime-time series development took charge.

When Barry Diller held the job, he had requested the white office's stark, minimalist decor—white shutters, white oak floors, white rugs, and glass and chrome trimmings. Diller put his aesthetic stamp on the office while the network was building its Century City space, and left for Paramount before the construction was finished. Michael Eisner, his successor in the job, turned the white office into a Grand Central Station for the Hollywood staff.

The offices of the vice presidents and directors for comedy and drama development were clustered nearby. In an adjacent coffee nook, people congregated informally each morning. During the year and a half that Eisner was in charge of series development in Century City, the white office was a beehive for supplier pitches and meetings to refine new scripts and pilots. Eisner liked to work over meals, and in one month alone his bill for catered lunches came to $12,000.

Eisner left ABC Entertainment too, almost eighteen months before Silverman's departure. When Thomopoulos arrived, an easygoing Midwesterner named Steve Gentry was holding the Hollywood staff together. When he took over the white office, Gentry changed the decor, but the luck held. Gentry was the network's top-ranking West Coast official—"the Gary Cooper of the network," Barbara Gallagher called him. Laconic and handsome, he liked to help other people achieve results instead of taking the credit himself. The roster of young creative executives who had started out as his personal assistants reads like a Who's Who of Hollywood. Kim LeMasters, who eventually became the president of CBS Entertainment, and Bob Boyett, a leading comedy producer of "Perfect Strangers" and other network shows, were among those who got their early training from Gentry.

97

Pierce had handpicked Gentry for the top job after Eisner left for Paramount, and working under him in Hollywood was one of the most talented groups of creative executives ever assembled at one network. In the wake of Silverman's departure, Fred had called them his programming "team." Marcy Carsey and Tom Werner, who would later produce "The Cosby Show," ran comedy and variety development. Brandon Stoddard, who had briefly vied with Gentry for Eisner's job, was in charge of drama development, miniseries, and made-for-TV movies. Stoddard was a rare TV animal—an educated man of mass culture. From a rich family, he had gone to school at Deerfield and Yale before training in daytime and children's programming. His extensive work on "Roots" had made him Goldenson's favorite programmer. Esther Shapiro and Leonard Hill, his lieutenants in miniseries and made-for-TV movies, were, like Carsey and Werner, destined to become top independent producers in Hollywood, Shapiro as the producer of "Dynasty."

With so much talent on the West Coast programming staff, one up-and-coming young executive felt obliged to resign because the odds of getting a network promotion were so slim. In 1977, Brandon Tartikoff was languishing in current comedy, a maintenance area for existing shows at ABC. He wanted to develop original programs. A job opened up in the made-for-TV movies area while Silverman was still at ABC, and Silverman recommended him for the job.

"Hire this kid, he's smart," Silverman told Stoddard, who ran made-for-TV movies. But Stoddard was still piqued over Gentry's promotion, and did not push to hire Tartikoff. When another candidate got the job, a chagrined Tartikoff left for NBC. He was working there in a low-level job when Silverman arrived. Silverman, who was running the whole company, put Tartikoff in charge of NBC Entertainment.

While the West Coast programmers busily prepared that winter and spring for the upcoming prime-time season, another would-be network programmer sought admittance to the hallowed precincts of Century City. Beverlee Dean thought she possessed "the right stuff" to join Fred Pierce's team, and when she learned that her predictions about Silverman and Thomopoulos had come true, she wasted no time trying to exploit what she believed was her special relationship with the two executives. She began telephoning New York to offer them her services on an exclusive, ongoing basis.

"I called them up all the time," Dean recalled. "I just wouldn't give up.

"Do you want to know what I think about next season?" Dean asked Pierce.

"He would laugh at me, but he wouldn't hang up. I would say, 'I'm not a psychic, Fred, don't you understand? I'm very creative. I know what shows are going to make it.' He would get real uptight and say he would think about it."

Pierce was too busy coordinating the reams of data from the research and sales departments in New York with all the activity in Hollywood to pay attention to a would-be game-show producer in Encino. But Dean was just warming to her task. That winter she accompanied Mindy Naud to an invitation-only broadcast-industry dinner party in Las Vegas, and managed to cadge a seat right next to Pierce. Like an impertinent staffer, she offered him her opinions about which new pilots ABC should license for the upcoming season. "Taxi," "Mork & Mindy," and "Vega$" were her shows of choice.

Pierce was still distracted. Henry Winkler's contract with Paramount, for the role of the Fonz on "Happy Days," was up for renewal in early 1978, and the licensing rights for the show, which had to be negotiated separately by ABC, were too. The boilerplate guarantee of "first negotiation, first refusal," which usually gave the networks a lock on renewal negotiations for existing series, was missing from the "Happy Days" contract. Paramount was legally entitled to hold an auction and shop the show.

It was not likely that Diller and Eisner would move "Happy Days" to another network. "Mork & Mindy" and "Taxi," two fresh new comedies, were in development at Paramount for ABC Entertainment that spring. But the simple notion that the show *could* be shopped made Pierce unhappy. "Happy Days" was still the TV industry's biggest hit. Silverman was about to arrive at NBC. The implied threat gave Paramount enormous leverage in the licensing renewal.

Henry Winkler's attorney in Los Angeles, a well-regarded entertainment lawyer named Skip Brittenham, knew that Diller and Eisner would use Paramount's advantage to wring new commitments for new pilots, made-for-TV movies, and series out of ABC, and he wanted his client, the star of the show, to be in on the action. Instead of negotiating Winkler's new contract with Paramount, Brittenham contacted ABC and preemptively offered the network an exclusive on Winkler. "Happy Days" was worthless without the Fonz. Winkler was willing to stay on the show in return for a long-term production deal with ABC. The upshot was that ABC agreed to buy three new series, which Winkler, not Paramount, would own.

Eisner, who had turned "Happy Days" into a hit and Winkler into a star, was outraged.

"You've taken one of our stars without talking to us," he stormed. In his new role as president of Paramount, he took a very different view of Hollywood matters from the one he had taken at ABC. Eisner swore that the studio would never do business with ABC again.

A Mexican standoff of mutual threats and recriminations ensued. The three series that Pierce had promised Winkler would eventually launch the actor as a top-flight independent producer. But in a visit to Paramount's Melrose Avenue headquarters, Pierce also committed ABC to buying another batch of new series, made-for-TV movies, and pilots from the studio. "Happy Days," with Winkler as the Fonz, would stay on ABC in following seasons.

Paramount's lawyers marveled in the aftermath: "Isn't it wonderful the way Michael is all over Pierce!"

ABC, indeed, had promised to pay Paramount penalty points and options if it decided not to keep the new series on the schedule.

Eisner would roll the concessions forward profitably for years to come.

But at the time, Pierce and Thomopoulos had much to be pleased about too. The long-term deal they had signed seemed to assure a steady flow of product from Hollywood's top talent. Working with established suppliers was the key to maintaining Silverman's legacy, Pierce had told Goldenson and Rule; that had been his rationale in making the Thomopoulos appointment. The only missing ingredient in the deal was a guarantee that Garry Marshall and other Paramount producers, whose output had been critical to ABC's success, would continue to work in TV development at the studio.

When the "Happy Days" situation was resolved, Beverlee Dean cast her net around Pierce. Each spring, after the new fall schedule was set, ABC invited New York advertising agencies and the working press to a lavish show-and-tell in New York, for a preview of new and returning shows. Live appearances by Hollywood stars warmed up the crowd. A posh buffet capped the ceremony.

The day ABC Entertainment hosted this event in the Grand Ballroom of the Hilton Hotel, Roone Arledge planned to announce a coup of his own. ABC Sports had just acquired the live broadcast rights to Muhammad Ali's rematch with heavyweight champ Leon Spinks. The fight had reportedly cost the network a cool $5.5 million.

Meanwhile, out in Hollywood, a friend of Beverlee Dean's, a black woman named Nancy Carter who represented Ali in his capacity as a nonpugilist, had been trying to sell the network a docudrama project in which the great fighter would portray himself. The entertainment division was interested, and Carter had a handshake deal with Thomopoulos. "If we get the fight, you get to do the docudrama," Carter remembered Thomopoulos saying.

Dean suggested to Carter that she travel to New York for the Arledge press conference, since this might move the docudrama forward. Dean invited herself to the ceremony, too. ABC Entertainment's fall presentation was scheduled to take place in the morning at the Hilton Hotel. Ali, who was staying at the Americana Hotel, would appear at a separate press conference in the afternoon.

When Dean and Carter arrived at the Americana, Ali was surrounded by a herd of handlers. "Watch this," Carter said.

Carter was a beautiful woman. Standing at the back of the crowd, she waved, and Ali stopped dead in his tracks.

"My God, he's in love with you," Dean gasped.

Ali's infatuation with Nancy Carter, and Carter's friendship with Dean, gave Dean the power to act temporarily as Ali's personal agent. Dean called ahead to the advertiser presentation at the Hilton Hotel to say that the fighter would be making a special guest appearance there. Dean, Carter, and Ali arrived, and were made to wait.

"Do they know I'm here?" Ali asked impatiently.

"No, it's a surprise," Carter replied.

"A surprise! A surprise!" Ali cried gleefully. "Show me somewhere I can hide."

Ducking behind the curtain, he played with the folds in the fabric like a child. Then his name was called, the curtain was parted, and he made his entrance—to resounding applause. Ali was in the last stage of his boxing career, but he still meant big ratings to the Madison Avenue buyers and TV journalists in the audience.

Pierce and Thomopoulos were sitting in the front row. Suddenly Pierce's mouth dropped open with surprise. What was Beverlee Dean doing up on stage with Ali?

"Beverlee stood near Ali," recalled Carter. "She made sure that Pierce saw her."

When the presentation was over, Pierce went backstage, where Carter introduced him to Ali. "You de boss. You de boss, den," Ali said, playacting Uncle Tom for the big network boss.

Pierce seemed genuinely amused. He turned to Dean.

"I bought those programs you told me about," he told her. Indeed, "Taxi," "Mork & Mindy," and "Vega$" had all made the fall schedule.

Pierce then asked Dean to meet him for breakfast at the Dorset Hotel the next morning. There, over scrambled eggs, she quickly got down to business and asked Pierce for a network job. This time the answer was more hopeful! "He said I'd be hearing from him."

Beverlee Dean was going to join the team.

The next Big Event on the network's calendar was the affiliates' meeting in Los Angeles in May. This was the major event of the year, with wining, dining, gala fetes, live entertainment—all in Hollywood, the entertainment capital of the world. The network spent more than $1.5 million over three days to make its local affiliates feel like distinguished ambassadors of Middle America.

That spring in Los Angeles the mood was particularly exuberant. Carved ice swans adorned the evening dessert tables, and well-known stars from popular TV shows mingled with the crowd. Local station managers from Portland, Maine, to Portland, Oregon, got to meet in person the flickering images that they put on television. It helped that the network was doing so well. During the 1977–78 season ABC's overall prime-time ratings had averaged better than two Nielsen points above CBS's, better than three above NBC's. Such results translated into enormous profits at local stations across the country.

The lead-off session of the three-day meeting was the presentation of the upcoming fall schedule, and Steve Gentry was once again the keynote speaker. His speech was scheduled to begin on Monday morning, and a practice run-through was scheduled for Sunday afternoon.

On Sunday afternoon, Gentry was missing.

For several hours the staffers participating in the run-through waited at the Century Plaza Hotel, expecting Gentry to turn up. That morning he had gone flying with Bruce Geller, a Hollywood writer-friend who had created, among other popular TV shows, "Mission: Impossible." Gentry and Geller were qualified pilots; Gentry had spent four years as a Navy fighter pilot, seeing action in Vietnam before he began working in TV. Geller's twin engine

103

Cessna 237 Skymaster left the Santa Monica airport headed for Santa Barbara, ninety miles away—an easy, half-day trip up the coast.

But the coastal mountain range surrounding Santa Barbara is often shrouded in fog, and on that Sunday morning, the fog was especially thick. Residents near Santa Barbara recalled hearing sounds of a plane flying toward the mountains, and then the sounds abruptly stopped. At the Santa Barbara airport, a blip disappeared from the radar screen.

When the fog finally lifted that afternoon and the crash site was located, Gentry and Geller were found dead. When they heard the news, the members of the programming staff waiting for Gentry at Century City began weeping.

Fred Pierce released a statement saying that much of the network's programming strength had been made possible by Gentry's contributions. The affiliates' meeting opened the next morning with an official "minute of silence" to mark his death. But the party roared on. It was too much to expect an event planned months in advance to screech suddenly to a halt, and in any case, few local station heads realized what Gentry had meant to ABC.

Gentry's funeral, which most network officials attended, was just one sorrowful event sandwiched in between the festivities. On Monday morning, Tony Thomopoulos delivered the keynote address that Gentry had prepared.

"Hello, Beverlee?" Pierce said over the telephone. "I told you I'd call. I'm a man of my word."

A month after his breakfast meeting with Beverlee Dean, Pierce officially put her on the network's programming team.

"I'll call you a consultant," he said.

A network lawyer in New York drew up a one-year employment contract, renewable for a second, starting July 1, 1978. Dean would be paid $24,000 a year to give advice directly to Pierce. It was not a high wage by network standards, but she would share the privilege of reporting directly to Pierce on TV programming with only one other person at ABC, Tony Thomopoulos, who was still unaware of this agreement. Pierce's secretary in Los Angeles was to telephone ratings to Dean at her home in Encino, and scripts would be sent for her review. The network also provided her with a three-quarter-inch video cassette machine so that she could preview rough cuts of new pilots as soon as they arrived from suppliers.

"You just give me your opinion of them," Pierce told her.

Before the deal was sealed, however, he called and made one last stipulation.

"I would not like this to be known," Pierce said.

Dean reluctantly agreed to keep the secret.

7

Future Tense

In the 1930s, an FCC edict pro-
scribed the use of the public airwaves by "fortune tellers" and other
persons deemed to have a pernicious influence on the general
citizenry. Before the days of White House astrologers, voodoo
economics, and state-run lotteries, such things mattered to the
government.

In 1978, the edict was still on the books, but network television, and the Washington bureaucracies that regulated it, had
grown too remote and byzantine to remember. The origins of government had been obscured by its dependence on television. And
the roots of broadcasting had been lost in its ongoing relationship
with Hollywood.

Broadcasting for many years had served as the leading tool of
private industry for sculpting the American economy. Consider the
railroads and broadcasting. Each ushered in a different stage of the
nation's commercial development. In the nineteenth century, railroads carried farm and manufactured goods from town to city. In
the twentieth, radio and TV networks delivered the programming
and advertising that sold those goods to America's emergent con-
sumer class. Both industries were the "common carriers" of their

respective eras, and both owed their birthright to government grants. The railroads acquired right of way over public land. Radio and TV networks acquired rights to use the airwaves. Both were natural monopolies, requiring a sole proprietor or manager-by-proxy to make the most efficient use of the natur.l resource.

"It was something new to see a knot of adventurers possess themselves of an artery of commerce more important than ever was the Appian Way," the author Charles Francis Adams wrote of the Wall Street battle for control of the Erie Railroad after the Civil War. Like the robber barons of the railroads, Sarnoff, Paley, and Goldenson could use a broadcasting network to "make levies, not only upon it for their own emolument, but, through it, upon the whole business of the nation."

Monopoly paid a price, of course. "When private property is affected with a public interest it ceases to be *juris privati* only," the Supreme Court ruled in the celebrated case of *Munn* v. *Illinois*, which in 1876 set the precedent for regulating American big business. "When, therefore, one devotes his property to use in which the public has an interest, he . . . must submit to be controlled by the public for the common good."

The Interstate Commerce Commission, which was established in 1887, was designed to protect this "public interest" in the railroad, telephone, and telegraph industries. Washington regulated them as public utilities, fixing a tariff or schedule of rates, that the public could be charged. The ideal of common-carrier regulation (not always realized) was to treat private industry like the Post Office: No matter who was placing the call or mailing the letter, first-class postage and long-distance rates remained equal for all.

For broadcasting, however, the legislators took a different route. The Radio Act of 1927 had a clause in it that prohibited "obscene, indecent, or profane language"—from which, ultimately, the rule against "fortune tellers" was derived—but otherwise the government exacted only a loose promise from licensed broadcasters to operate as "public trustees." Instead of fixing a tariff, the legislators opened up the public airwaves to the free market of advertising supply-and-demand. Local stations could air whatever programming advertisers would pay the most money for. This created a kind of fuel-injection system for consumerism. Advertisers flocked to the network airwaves to display their wares, and listeners flocked to the stores to buy them. Starting with the Depression and accelerating during World War II, radio and TV advertising became a carburetor revving the nation's economic machine.

ABC, the weakest of the Big Three networks, was for many years a leading beneficiary of this laissez-faire broadcasting policy. The public interest rulings that Washington did make tended to go in its favor. The FCC's antitrust ruling against David Sarnoff's two-network colossus in 1943 gave birth to ABC as a network company. Its decision to grant the company five TV station licenses after World War II allowed ABC to leap from radio into TV. And the FCC's approval of the merger between ABC and United Paramount Theatres in 1953—a bold step at the time, given the Supreme Court's recent divorcement decree—enabled the company to survive in the network TV era.

Washington occasionally acted in inadvertent ways to help ABC. The Justice Department's refusal to sanction the ITT merger in the 1960s had saved the network from becoming a subsidiary of ITT and Harold Geneen. Even the Congressional ban on cigarette advertising on radio and TV, which all three networks fought bitterly at the time, worked to ABC's short-term advantage.

In 1970, before Congress took the Marlboro Man off the airwaves, tobacco advertising accounted for 10 percent of all network revenues. Removing that money from the Madison Avenue marketplace would affect the existing balance between the networks' supply of commercial air time and advertiser demand. Prices would drop. At ABC, Goldenson called ABC's top managers into his New York office and said, "Gentlemen, we have no choice. We're going to have to cut ten percent of our costs across the board."

At the same time that Congress imposed its ban, however, the FCC was winding up a television inquiry of its own. Network schedules ran from 7 to 11 each evening, but the FCC was concerned about the programming dominance of the Big Three. In 1970 it adopted the "prime time access rule," one of three interlocking measures designed to lessen the influence of ABC, NBC, and CBS, and forced them to give back one half-hour each night to their affiliates. The idea was to encourage locally created programming; instead, most local stations filled the 7:30–8 P.M. time period with syndicated programs like "Wheel of Fortune," "Entertainment Tonight," and "The New Hollywood Squares."

For ABC, the adoption of the prime time access rule was a short-term godsend. The Congressional ban cut revenues and advertising demand by 10 percent, the half-hour access rule cut program costs and commercial inventory by 17 percent. The Madison Avenue marketplace tightened. At all three networks the business effect of the two Washington rulings was to cancel each other out—and Goldenson's network benefited most of all. It shed poorly rated programs and put stronger shows in the new lead-in time period. Instead of competing for diminished dollars during a period of weak advertising demand, the third-place network gained ground on CBS and NBC.

Washington's indirect role in the Family Viewing Hour, which again scrambled prime-time schedules to ABC's advantage in 1975, proved to be the network's last assist from regulators for quite some time. By the 1970s, a public policy-making shift in Washington and new technologies of network distribution were beginning to turn broadcasting on its head. "Geosynchronous" satellites—orbiters circling the earth at the speed of the globe's rotation that, in effect, "stood still"—were reshaping the business for the first time in more than fifty years.

Ever since David Sarnoff signed the papers that gave birth to NBC, AT&T Long Lines had transported network signals from New York to local affiliates around the country. Leasing Long Lines was an expensive, full-time proposition. Between AT&T's monopoly and the limited number of VHF stations that were available to local outlets, it had been financially and technically impossible for more than three TV networks to exist. But twenty years after Sputnik, geosynchronous satellites shattered the old oligopoly, and new networks began challenging the Big Three.

In 1966, Goldenson had petitioned the FCC for permission to operate a domestic satellite system, with the stated aim of lowering the cost of distributing the network signal through a satellite alternative to AT&T. And in 1972, the FCC responded with its "open skies" decision, formally defining satellites as "common carriers" and making satellite technology available to all companies that could afford the tariff. The ruling barred AT&T from participating in satellite leasing for three years, and effectively broke the Long Lines monopoly on network TV distribution. In short order new, satellite-delivered networks sprang up in specialized programming niches alongside the Big Three. Home Box Office was the first of the new competitors. In 1975 the Time, Inc.-owned pay channel leased a satellite transponder and beamed a new network signal in a wide electronic "footprint" across the country. The transmission quality was postcard-perfect, like the satellite-delivered Olympic images that ABC had sent from Innsbruck and Grenoble. The difference was that HBO was transmitting live, continuous coverage of the "Thrilla in Manila," and that viewers were watching Joe Frazier and Muhammad Ali on cable, instead of broadcast network TV.

During the second half of the 1970s, as the satellite era slowly picked up steam, the reverberations from Silverman's programming were still echoing through the industry, and few people paid attention to newcomers like HBO. The action in broadcasting was taking place in America's heartland, in Andy Griffith's home state of North Carolina, not far from Mayberry, R.F.D.

"A vale of humility between two mountains of conceit," is how an antebellum historian described North Carolina. Unlike Virginia and South Carolina, its more aristocratic neighbors, North Carolina cleaved to small-town republican virtues, and refused to put on

111

airs. It was modest and plutocratic in spirit, boasting bankers and insurance executives, tobacco growers and furniture manufacturers, Southern Baptists and rednecks, all in egalitarian proportions.

Charlotte, the biggest city in the state, was located in the red clay hills of the Piedmont region. An early gold-mining settlement, it once supported a government mint. After the gold mines closed down, the downtown streets covered over the shafts and the original mint was rebuilt as the Mint Museum of Art. Charlotte, the largest Southeastern city between Washington and Atlanta, became a kind of mini-Dallas to local residents. Its two local VHF stations, meanwhile, turned into a new type of gold mine for local owners and two of the three networks in New York.

What with Greensboro, Winston-Salem, High Point, and, just over the South Carolina line, Greenville and Spartanburg, there were too many cities in the Piedmont region for each one to get three VHF stations when the FCC divvied up the spectrum after World War II. Charlotte got just two VHF stations, and so did Raleigh-Durham. In 1978 Charlotte was the largest American city with only two VHF stations—WBTV on Channel 3 and WSOC-TV on Channel 9, affiliated with CBS and NBC, respectively. They benefited from the buffered local marketplace, for until WCCB-TV, a UHF station on Channel 18, came on the air in the 1960s, they had the local airwaves to themselves. For ABC, Charlotte was the prime example of its distribution handicap—lack of affiliated outlets in small and medium-sized TV markets all over the country.

"Affiliates didn't think much about changing networks in those days," recalled Dick Beesemyer, the dapper, gravel-voiced friend of Elton Rule who was given the job of fixing ABC's affiliate problems in Charlotte and elsewhere across the country. "Once they signed up, they were married for life."

In Charlotte, WBTV was owned by Jefferson Pilot Broadcasting and had grown out of WBT-AM, one of the first radio stations in the Carolinas. CBS had owned WBT-AM outright in the 1930s, and Jim Babb, the president of Jefferson Pilot Broadcasting, had been a recent and highly active chairman of CBS's affiliate board of governors.

WSOC-TV had an equally strong network tie to NBC. Eddie Jones, a local life-insurance executive, had started its radio forerunner as an NBC affiliate during the Depression. A former NBC president named Niles Trammel had been a close family friend. Freeman Jones, the son of the local founder, still managed the TV station.

The bond between a network and its local, independently owned affiliates was so strong that NBC's standard practice at renewal time was to append a new clause to the existing contract and send it out for signature. The FCC required that all affiliate contracts be renewed every two years, so that the fiction of local station independence could be maintained. But the $150 million that each network collectively paid its affiliates (with the exact amount that went to each station geared to the size and competitive structure of local markets) was the only sticky glue in the arrangement. That, and the local ratings garnered by the network's programming, which local stations sold to local advertisers.

No sweeping changes had ever occurred in the Big Three affiliate lineups in the twenty-five years of modern network TV. CBS still had a superb national system, covering every nook and cranny in the country. The NBC lineup was equally powerful in all but the smallest rural communities. ABC was still the distribution laggard.

But by 1978, ABC's ratings were so strong and NBC had become so lazy that Dick Beesemyer could approach Freeman Jones at WSOC-TV (NBC) with an attractive offer to switch. One stroke of the pen added the Charlotte station to the growing ranks of ABC affiliates. Two target stations in Baton Rouge and San Diego had switched shortly before. TV stations in Atlanta, Knoxville, Gainesville, and Jacksonville quickly followed suit. Beesemyer marched across the South like Sherman.

"We raped and pillaged," Beesemyer fondly recalled.

In the North, key stations in Dayton, Indianapolis, and Minneapolis switched. Altogether, using competitive business tactics and Silverman's prime-time schedule as his calling card, Beesemyer induced twenty-two NBC stations in big cities and ten smaller-

113

market CBS affiliates to change their network allegiance to ABC. It was the most significant shift in the long-term balance of network power since Paley's talent raids on NBC after World War II.

When *TV Guide* caught up with Beesemyer, who traveled solo and hid out on the road while trying to persuade local TV station managers to switch, it titled the story "Operation Station-Stealing."

When Leonard Goldenson visited Charlotte later that year, Freeman Jones, the man responsible for the new association, hosted a gracious, Southern-style dinner party on the gold-mining property that he and his wife owned just outside town. Goldenson's visit contained a lot of memories for him. As the president of the Paramount theater division, he had once regularly traveled the Carolinas, checking up on local movie outlets there. In 1978 he had sold the Southern Theatres division, the last vestige of United Paramount Theatres. One of the dinner guests invited by Freeman Jones—at Goldenson's special request—was Sara Kincey, the widow of the local Paramount exhibitor in Charlotte.

Howard Cosell, who joined Goldenson in the Carolinas, had also known Charlotte from previous trips. He was a Brooklyn boy, but he had been born in Winston-Salem, just eighty miles up the road. Much to his chagrin he found himself back in the Bible Belt, where the world was still dry.

"Just take me to the neighborhood bar," Cosell told Jack Callahan, then Freeman Jones's lieutenant at WSOC-TV.

"Howard, we don't have bars down here."

"You don't?" exclaimed Cosell. "How do you live?"

Callahan took him down to the Charlotte City Club, where the private liquor lockers opened at a respectable afternoon hour. On the way they passed the Barringer Hotel, a relic of Charlotte hostelry circa 1950. Cosell had been there before. His father had died at the Barringer while on a business trip, and as a dutiful son, Cosell had come down from New York to claim the body.

Ted Turner, the newest network buccaneer, got his start near Charlotte too. Turner owned two UHF-TV stations, Channel 17 in Atlanta and Channel 36 in Charlotte. Neither was a network affiliate, and consequently neither was very profitable. In past years Turner had attempted in vain to convince Dick Beesemyer that his UHF station in Atlanta should be an ABC affiliate, but Atlanta was a three-VHF station market, and Beesemyer ignored him. In Charlotte, Turner had a better time.

Before ABC's affiliate switch in Charlotte, Turner's UHF station there was so strapped for funds that he went on the air in person and beseeched local TV viewers for donations. His fund-raising telethon followed a time-honored local tradition—Billy Graham, the granddaddy of TV evangelists, was a Charlotte native and had begun his ministry there; Jim and Tammy Faye Bakker's Praise The Lord Club had dug its roots down as well. Turner, however, was a commercial broadcaster not a charitable organization, and later had to give the money back.

Turner needed funds badly because, like HBO, he had leased transponder space on a new geosynchronous satellite. He turned his local UHF station in Atlanta into a national "superstation," was in desperate need of money for programming, and looked to Charlotte to get it.

In 1978, when WSOC-TV (NBC) switched its affiliation to ABC, Turner got his main chance. NBC was bumped off the VHF airwaves in Charlotte, and WCCB-TV, the UHF station that had formerly been ABC's local affiliate, went independent. The advertising marketplace in Charlotte was big enough by then to support such a full-time move. WCCB-TV began airing old movies and network reruns, and rented its facilities to Jim and Tammy Faye Bakker's PTL Club for religious fund-raising. The turn of events in Charlotte was good news for Turner's Channel 36, because NBC had no other outlet in town to turn to besides it. In a matter of days, the brash upstart from Atlanta had signed a new affiliate agreement with the oldest network company in America.

At the dinner in Rockefeller Center that was held to celebrate the new agreement, Turner decided to impress his New York partners.

115

"I'd like y'all to see a picture of my family," he said in a Georgia drawl, pulling a photograph from his wallet. Turner passed it around the table.

He reached into his wallet again. "And now I'd like y'all to see a picture of the little lady I see when I come to New York."

Ted Turner had more than saucy photographs up his sleeve. After introducing Home Box Office, Time, Inc. was slow to follow up on its success. He had a second idea for a satellite-delivered network business that was destined to make him the leader in the field. He needed $20 million to start it, but no bank would lend him the money. As soon as he snared the NBC affiliation in Charlotte, Turner approached Group W Broadcasting, a top local station group owner, and lured them into a purchase agreement for his Charlotte UHF outlet. Except for the new NBC contract, nothing had changed there. The station was still nearly bankrupt, and would not turn a profit for years.

But Group W agreed to pay Turner $20 million for it, and on the strength of the purchase agreement Turner borrowed the same amount of money from the banks. It went directly into his newest satellite-delivered venture. In June 1980, Ted Turner's Cable News Network went on the air.

In the first few years of their existence, the new networks like HBO, WTBS, and CNN nibbled away at the Big Three networks like mice on the big cheese. To most network officials they were a sideshow, a mere nuisance. But to Goldenson, who understood the relationship between Hollywood and broadcasting better than anyone in network TV, they represented a major long-term broadcasting disease.

Take an analogy from the oil industry: In a country with only three pipelines, the smart oilman owns a pipeline. In a country with twenty pipelines, he wants to own the oil.

Satellite technology had opened a Pandora's box of UHF-TV stations and local cable systems hooked into twenty or more national

TV networks. Not all of them would compete for national advertising. One of the attractions of Home Box Office and other "pay tier" cable networks to viewers was that they were commercial-free. But each new network would compete for programming and for the viewer's attention. And cumulatively they were altering the age-old balance between Hollywood and network TV.

Hollywood owned most of the "oil" in the entertainment industry, and it was now in a better position than at any time since 1948 and the breakup of its own studio-theater combines to squeeze the networks hard. There had been a sea change in antitrust regulation of the networks in Washington. During the FCC's adoption of the prime time access rule in 1970, the agency had defined the networks, for the purposes of limiting their power, for the very first time. Two corollary rules on program ownership restricted the networks' Hollywood deals. Ever since Goldenson's negotiations at Warner Brothers and Walt Disney, the networks had licensed the shows they aired on TV. Now Washington had decided they *had* to license what they aired.

Rule after rule was piled on, until the restrictions ran three deep. The "financial interest" rule kept the networks from owning any part of any prime-time show that they did not produce themselves; sports, news, and daytime shows were exempt, because they did not come from the studios. The "syndication" rule kept ABC, NBC, and CBS from distributing all TV shows, including programs produced in-house, to nonaffiliated TV stations after they aired on the network. And in 1978 and 1980, capping a decade-long antitrust fight, the Justice Department forced ABC, NBC, and CBS to sign consent decrees in which they forfeited the right, until 1990, to produce all but a tiny number of prime-time shows themselves.

Meanwhile, with the growing number of independent TV stations and cable networks, the marketplace for off-network and first-run syndicated programming was poised for an explosion. The Big Three networks were trapped. Washington's antitrust policy had closed off the easy avenues of business expansion just as its satellite rules had opened the door for new network competition. All the new rules of the game favored the production studios, and Hollywood was beginning to flex its long-dormant muscles.

As the curtain fell on the Silverman years, a shadow passed over network TV. Network television was about to undergo a metamorphosis. Like Gregor Samsa, the Kafka antihero who wakes up one morning to find himself transformed into a giant cockroach, the networks had grown oversized, odd, misshapen. At the turn of the new decade, Wall Street analysts and industry trade journals called them "dinosaurs."

8

A Gathering of Wolves

When Leonard Goldenson's affiliates gathered in Los Angeles in May 1979, few imagined that ABC might belong to a species that was doomed to extinction. "Mork & Mindy," the "Happy Days" spin-off starring a fresh new comedian named Robin Williams, was network TV's hottest new hit. Garry Marshall, its creator, was the TV industry's hottest comedy producer. "Taxi," another new comedy from Paramount, had won the Emmy for best comedy series, and also ranked in the Nielsen Top Ten. The network ratings juggernaut that Fred Silverman had put in motion was still gathering speed. During the 1978–79 season ABC had aired fourteen of the Top Twenty shows, eight of the Top Ten, and had a full programming house—all five of the top five shows. ABC's accountants, meanwhile, were logging record balance sheet numbers—$1.3 billion in network revenues and $186 million in pretax profits. It was the first time ever that a TV network had broken the billion-dollar revenue mark.

The network partied in Hollywood that May as though there were no tomorrow. Black tie was de rigueur for the main Century Plaza hotel banquet. Roast pheasant was on the menu. Donna

119

Summer regaled the guests with showbiz tunes. Robin Williams' live comedy act had them roaring with laughter in their seats.

But after all the out-of-town guests had packed and left, Leonard Goldenson stayed behind on the West Coast for an extra day. He had to attend a family funeral. Esther Goldenson, his ninety-three-year-old mother, had died in a Los Angeles nursing home.

Esther Goldenson had always been a wellspring of energy in her son's life and career. She had urged him to apply for admission to Harvard College, encouraged him to seek his fortune in New York as a young man, even taught him the rules of poker at an early age. His standing as a patriarch in Hollywood and among broadcasters derived largely from his mother's strong matriarchal qualities.

Retirement was on Goldenson's mind on the day he delivered his mother's eulogy. Speaking to a small group of family members and friends gathered in the chapel of a Jewish cemetery next to Paramount Pictures, Goldenson reflected on why she was being buried on the West Coast instead of in Scottdale, where he had grown up. He remembered the telephone call that his mother had made to him in New York a quarter-century before, informing him that his father had suffered a heart attack.

"I went to Scottdale and saw my father and told him, 'You're finished. You're going to California to live in a warm climate,' " Goldenson said.

"My mother said, 'You're the only one who can make him do it.'

"It broke my heart to see a man who had been in business for more than fifty years have to give it up. Because a man's work, fifty years, can all of a sudden be nothing."

Since his own heart attack in 1971, Goldenson had taken scrupulous physical care of himself. He drank alcohol rarely and did not smoke. But a half-century had passed since the start of his own career, and his mother's death made him pause. Goldenson's network was on top of the world, but he was glimpsing the void.

Goldenson might have packed up his bags and turned his company over to Elton Rule to run, but in the late 1970s he did just the opposite. As soon as his mother's funeral was over, he returned to New York, tapped a hidden reserve of energy, and forged ahead. He had already achieved most of his goals in life. There was only one goal in broadcasting left for him to conquer—being measured for the same industry pedestal as David Sarnoff and William Paley.

It was a curious fact of life on Broadcasting Row at the turn of the decade that Leonard Goldenson, the least-known network founder, was the only one of his patriarchal peers still alive and in full control of his company.

David Sarnoff had clung to power at RCA and NBC until a few years before his death in 1971; Sarnoff was convalescing in Lenox Hill Hospital from a mastoid operation when the RCA board, acting on the advice of doctors, voted away his chairman's title in 1969. Robert Sarnoff, his son, had taken over as RCA's chief executive until 1975; then he, too, was forced to step down. Without a firm hand to guide it, the company had diversified its operations and gone badly to seed during the 1970s. Fred Silverman's whirlwind style at NBC had accelerated the decay of its core businesses. RCA was struggling when Thornton Bradshaw, a caretaker chairman with a management style like George Schultz's, arrived in mid-1981 to nurse it back to health. One of Bradshaw's first decisions was to relieve the exhausted Silverman of his duties as NBC's chairman, and to hire Grant Tinker from the Mary Tyler Moore company in his place.

At CBS, William Paley was faring little better. "He told me they'd have to carry him out with his boots on," Sarnoff told an RCA colleague after his final lunch with the CBS chairman in the late 1960s. Paley was so determined to hold onto power that he turned the CBS presidency into a revolving door. After Frank Stanton, his longtime president and would-be successor, retired in 1971, Charles Ireland died after a few months on the job. And Arthur Taylor and John Backe, Ireland's successors, were forced out by Paley after four-year stints. Paley seemed to take a perverse pleasure in firing anyone who might one day replace him, and his board of directors began to worry about the company's long-term stability.

When Thomas Wyman, CBS's fourth president in eight years, arrived from the Green Giant Company in mid-1980, Paley grimly announced, "My successor is in place." Wyman hid his ambition behind a dour exterior, but he had few compunctions about dethroning Paley. Aided by actuarial logic and a compliant board, he was named chairman, president, and chief executive in 1983. Paley retired as "chairman emeritus" the same year. (He got an honorary new lease on life under Laurence Tisch, who dethroned Wyman in 1987.)

Goldenson, however, was far from finished. When ABC's board of directors—a group no less distinguished or independent than the boards of RCA and CBS—inquired about his retirement plans, Goldenson was said to have replied: "I have no intention of stepping down so long as I am in good physical condition and of sound mind." And he reportedly joked, when asked who would review his continuing sanity, "I will."

Goldenson, in short, had a rare opportunity. He could do for broadcasting in the eighties what Sarnoff had done in the twenties and Paley in the fifties: dictate the industry's future course. Goldenson had decided to start all over again—this time with enough "house money" to follow his gambler's instincts to the hilt.

All he needed was someone to help him place the chips on the table—someone like Elton Rule in 1968.

The network sported several new faces in 1979. Not new in the sense of newly arrived. They were new in the sense that few people outside the company had ever heard of them before.

One was Michael P. Mallardi, the chief financial officer. His nickname at ABC was "the Prince"—because of his Italian roots, and because of the copy of Machiavelli's masterpiece that he was reputed to keep at home for bedside reading.

The Prince, a sixteenth-century political treatise, discusses topics like "Types of Monarchy and How They Are Acquired," "Hereditary Monarchies," "Mixed Monarchies," and "On Those Who Have Become Princes by Crime." Machiavelli wrote the masterwork in exile, hoping it would restore him to favor with Medici princes in Florence. Published posthumously, it became a primer for statesmen worldwide, and foreshadowed, in the words of one commentator, "the centralized bureaucratic state."

As the network digested the success of the 1970s, the shadow of corporate bureaucracy lengthened over the company, and Mallardi thrived in the new ambience. He had an insider's ability to advance his own career without arousing more powerful executives' suspicion. And he had benefited from ABC's tendency to cast off outsiders like rejected organ transplants. The previous chief financial officer, a former Michigan State football star hired from another company, left within months of arriving; he couldn't fit in. Elton Rule, when asked by the corporate headhunter to rate Mallardi, the inside candidate, "on a scale of one to ten," answered, "About a five."

"Hire him," the headhunter replied. "He'll do better than an outsider who rates a nine or a ten."

A second top-level insider, wielding more power and influence than Mallardi, was Everett H. Erlick, the company's general counsel (not to be confused with Lew Erlicht, Pierce's programming protégé). Erlick had a small head and came from a rich Jewish family in Alabama, and had worked closely with Goldenson since 1961, longer than anyone else at ABC. Erlick had also been a network director longer than any other employee, and fancied himself as much more than the network's chief legal counsel and top Washington lobbyist. A graduate of Vanderbilt and Yale Law School, he had been moderately active in the civil rights movement and spent vacations going after bonefish in the Florida Keys. To many colleagues, Erlick seemed to think he was the most eminently qualified of Goldenson's possible successors.

Thanks in part to Erlick, a key figure was missing from the picture—I. Martin Pompadur. Pompadur, Rule's *muy simpatico*

123

network aide, had arrived in 1960 in a $7,500-a-year staff lawyer's job after hearing of an opening from an actress-girlfriend named Connie Hines. (She played Mrs. Wilbur Post on "Mister Ed," the show about a talking horse.) Pompadur was a leading member of the "new boys" network in its early days. Rule had named him the network's general manager in 1968, and over time Pompadur became Rule's alter ego for operations in every area of the company. With Rule's backing, he was elected to ABC's board of directors before Fred Pierce in 1974, and moved to an office on the thirty-ninth floor along with Goldenson, Rule, and Erlick. For several years, Pompadur ran all of the company's nonbroadcasting businesses, which still comprised a substantial portfolio. And each new promotion brought him closer to the job for which Rule seemed to be preparing him—his own, when he replaced Goldenson. Among his closest colleagues, there was no doubt that Rule coveted the chief executive's job.

Rule was sensitive to the founder's prerogatives (which was perhaps why he sought them for himself) and far too astute a corporate politician to disclose his aims directly. "Elton played Leonard like a Stradivarius," one associate recalled. It was not Rule's style to undercut his own corporate patron.

But Rule's ambitions had collided directly with Erlick's as early as 1968, when Rule arrived from California to run the network. He and Erlick had been drinking buddies before then. As long as Rule was in charge of KABC-TV in Los Angeles, Erlick could harbor strong contender's hopes in New York. In 1969, they had a serious falling out.

For years, Erlick's main responsibility as general counsel was the job for which Goldenson had originally invited him to join ABC—to watch over the network's business affairs. Hollywood contracts, studio negotiations, and program licensing were intricate and involved, and in 1961, when Erlick arrived, Ollie Treyz had made a mess of them. Goldenson had asked Erlick to clean up the mess, and Erlick had done so quickly. In 1962, about the time that Ollie Treyz left, Erlick was rewarded with a seat on the network board of directors.

But in 1969, after he assumed control of the network, Rule lobbied Goldenson for control of its business affairs and put an executive of his own in charge. His relationship with Erlick grew frosty thereafter.

In addition to directing the network's lobbying activities in Washington, Erlick's principal job after 1969 was to steer ABC clear of any criminal activities that might lead to the loss of its valuable TV station licenses. The FCC scrutinized the character of all broadcasters at license renewal time, and looked unfavorably on obscene broadcasts, unfair editorializing, and illegal business behavior—corporate kickbacks, bribery, and unfair advertising pricing all qualified. Licenses were almost never revoked. In twenty years of lax FCC review, only two stations, in Jackson, Mississippi and Boston, lost their right to broadcast—the first because of persistent racial bias, the second for impropriety in the original licensing.

Erlick took his watchdog role quite seriously, hiring the New York law firm of Hawkins, Delafield to pursue special internal investigations that were too sensitive for his own legal staff to handle. Through Hawkins, Delafield, Erlick had access to outside auditors and private investigators, too. These minesweeping powers were a source of great resentment and fear among many of Erlick's network colleagues. He spent millions of dollars each year on outside attorney's fees to hold everyone at ABC accountable, but he himself was accountable to virtually no one. When challenged, Erlick could always claim—like the CIA's national security claim—that station licenses worth hundreds of millions of dollars were potentially at risk. His outside auditors were regarded with awe by employees who worked in-house in the same area.

In 1976, not long after ABC filed an offering of public debentures with the Securities and Exchange Commission in Washington, Erlick's outside auditors detected a discrepancy in one of Pompadur's divisions. Pompadur and two other executives had purchased new Chryslers for personal use at a reduced rate from a company supplier. Erlick was duly informed of their executive misdemeanor.

In the past the network had never stated a general policy about conflicts-of-interest. Goldenson had reportedly commingled personal and company funds in tax-shelter movie theater deals in the 1960s; everyone then had looked the other way. Now ABC was rich, and had more to protect. And in the misdemeanor of Pompadur, Rule's closest colleague, Erlick had a vehicle for revenge. The other two executives were slapped on the wrist for their infractions (and subsequently promoted). Pompadur got different treatment. As Erlick pointed out to Goldenson, he was an ABC director, and the company was "in registration" at the SEC. Technically, the network had to disclose his indiscretion in a footnote to the SEC filing—or Pompadur had to step down from the board.

With a clean, lawyerly precision, Erlick had highlighted Pompadur's mistake in capital letters. The only way for Pompadur to avert having his prospects blemished permanently was to take matters into his own hands. Instead of simply resigning his board seat, he decided to leave ABC for good. A few months later, he was named president of Ziff-Davis, a publishing company, and began plotting its expansion into broadcasting.

Elton Rule was so upset at this turn of events that he ate oatmeal for a week to calm his stomach.

"It's your basic all-America executive suite saga," gossiped Page 6, the scandal page in the *New York Post,* in November 1978, "wherein hot young man propels ABC-TV to unparalleled heights and now lusts for the job of the somewhat less inspired (and older) man above him.

"Fred Pierce has reportedly made it clear that he wants ABC Inc. president Elton Rule's job. And all the middle and upper-level management types are busy choosing up sides."

For two-and-a-half-years after he left, Pompadur's office on the thirty-ninth floor of Hard Rock remained empty. In April 1979, when Goldenson and Rule named Pierce as ABC's new executive vice president, Pierce moved upstairs and filled the vacant space. It was a symbol of changing times.

Rule, the president and chief operating officer of ABC, was still Goldenson's closest professional confidant and the only person in the company—other than Sandy Merkel, Goldenson's personal secretary—who had uninterrupted access to his office. Rule had also instituted structures of institutional generosity that bound the company together in the lower echelons. When new employees were hired, he often sent back his copy of the memorandum announcing their arrival with a handwritten note, "Welcome to ABC, Elton Rule." His employee benefits program was an in-house system of corporate generosity that mirrored his individual personality. When one twenty-year network veteran resigned involuntarily after being caught out in a conflict-of-interest, Rule offered to pay for his three sons' college education out of his own pocket.

But ABC was changing so fast that even Rule, with his masterly political skills, could not keep up. Goldenson was holding steady and I. Martin Pompadur was no longer available to guard his flank. Rule was boxed in, caught in an intramural competition over who would be Goldenson's next heir apparent. An African tribal saying expressed his predicament best—"Power is like the skin of a leopard. Two people can't sit on a single spot."

As Rule and Pierce squared off, seemingly insignificant issues of authority defined the larger struggle. Who should run the public relations department, for instance? It had been Rule's since 1968, but after Pierce's promotion Pierce asked that it report to him. Rule granted the request, only to discover that his former top aides were being shunted aside and replaced by new staffers. Pierce now wanted to make himself more visible as a leading company spokesman. The compromise was to split the department in two. The majority of the staff worked directly for Pierce on network publicity. A splinter group still serviced Rule in corporate relations.

The divisions between the network and the corporate faction bored slowly through the company, fracturing old loyalties like an underground fault line. And as Goldenson's newly appointed executive vice president, Pierce had the better of the battle. He was now responsible not just for ABC Television, but also for "the development of programming for the new communications and entertainment forms."

In the summer of 1979, he faced a group of Wall Street analysts at a fortieth-floor dining room luncheon—the representatives of the insurance companies, pension and trust funds, and professional money managers who controlled more than 80 percent of the company's publicly traded stock. This was Wall Street's first "up close and personal" look at Pierce, who was widely hailed as the architect of the network's past and current success. The analysts had lots of questions about the future.

What were Pierce's plans, one analyst wanted to know, for relieving the pressure on network profit margins? A combination of flat advertising, rising costs, and inflation were eating into real revenue gains at all three networks. High interest rates, meanwhile, were leading many investors to take their money out of "equity instruments" like ABC stock, causing them to plummet in value, in favor of "fixed instruments" like money-market funds, which provided a safe financial yield.

Standing at the makeshift podium, Pierce paused perceptibly before answering. When they met with top company managers, Wall Street analysts usually acted like members of the press at Presidential news conferences, asking hard questions but expecting little in the way of firm answers. They homed in on body language and verbal nuances instead.

"Margins" was a new concept for Pierce. He wanted to talk about *ratings*, which in his view were the key to the network's business. ABC's ratings were just fine, he replied. While Pierce groped for an answer, his Wall Street audience squirreled away his glimmers of discomfort like a nut for winter.

Although he was unversed in elementary business concepts like "margins" and "return on equity," Pierce in 1979 was getting his fair share of good press coverage. The network had improved on its first-place ratings performance for the first season after Silverman's departure, and he seemed to be the reason. *TV Guide* had described Pierce as having "the best brain in television." Alan Hirschfield, the head of Columbia Pictures, had courted him to run a movie studio. *New York* magazine had called him "the smartest man" in broadcasting. Such words of praise led industry pundits to coin a new label for ABC. The network was no longer just "Leonard's candy store"; the shingle now said "Goldenson & Son."

Pierce enjoyed favored-son status, but his plaudits depended on the continuing success of Silverman's prime-time schedule—and it would not last forever. In Hollywood, in fact, a programming crack-up was already in the works.

The tension between Fred Silverman's programming team and the incoming Fred Pierce team of Tony Thomopoulos and Lew Erlicht surfaced at the beginning of the new programming cycle for the 1979–80 season. That was when ABC Entertainment first experienced the hole that had been opened by Steve Gentry's death.

In late May 1978, Brandon Stoddard, Marcy Carsey, Tom Werner, and a handful of other top staffers gathered at a country hotel in the mountains above San Diego for a "think tank" retreat. It was the spring after Silverman's departure, and for the first time since the twenty-fifth birthday party the programmers had no pressing tasks to distract them from reflecting on the events of the previous five months. Silverman's decision to leave for NBC had been an unhappy circumstance, but Gentry's death had left them spiritually battered.

"Nobody wanted to go, but it happened anyway," Gentry's West Coast assistant recalled of the season-end meeting. "It was on the calendar."

Instead of invigorating the staff, as other informal spring planning meetings hosted by Diller and Silverman had done, the retreat turned into a hospital ward of bodily ailments and emotional distress. Tony Thomopoulos had twisted his neck and wore a brace through the sessions. Marcy Carsey, the vice president for comedy development, had wrenched her back and had to lie prone. Even the countryside and hotel setting reinforced the overriding sense of malaise. The hotel was new and seemed to have been cut out of the mountainside; one staffer remembered thinking that it felt "like Charles Manson country." The group was served meals by waiters who were blond and so well groomed that another staffer was reminded of the Hitler youth.

As soon as the retreat was over, Pierce and Thomopoulos attempted to shore up morale by awarding most of the key entertainment programmers new long-term contracts. The sweetener in the deal was a "back-end" provision in which the network contractually promised to buy new pilots, made-for-TV movies, and series episodes that they might create as independent producers. A second provision foreclosed the possibility of their leaving ABC to work at another network. Pierce was being generous in a self-interested way. He wanted to lock in top-quality shows for the network in the future. He also wanted to make sure that his top programmers would not follow the Pied Piper to NBC.

"These moves are being made not only to make our operation more effective and efficient but to express our appreciation to an extraordinary team of creative program executives," Thomopoulos said, announcing the promotions.

The network had reached a Continental Divide. Later that summer, Pierce dispatched Lew Erlicht to the West Coast as the new general manager of ABC Entertainment, taking over the administrative duties that had belonged to Steve Gentry's old job. Tony Thomopoulos was still based in New York, but he joined in the migration too, and began spending most of his time in Hollywood. Fred Pierce had mastered the research and sales side of the network business. Now, as his cadre of insiders moved west, he took over the creative side for the very first time.

As the program development for the 1979–80 season progressed in Hollywood during the winter and spring of 1978–79, almost everyone involved in the process in Century City seemed a little bit out of sync. The current programs on the network's prime-time schedule were still extraordinarily successful, but no one on the programming staff seemed to have a clear idea about the future. Tony Thomopoulos, whose reputation as a "gent" was confirmed by everyone who came in contact with him, was nonetheless at sea when it came to providing a sense of urgency and direction to his staff. The network's Hollywood programmers, most of them in their late twenties and early thirties, were ambitious to succeed in the creative mold of Diller and Eisner and Gentry. To their chagrin, they discovered that Pierce had sent out a "suit" to watch over them.

"There was no *there* there," one programmer recalled of Thomopoulos.

"If you stuck your finger into him," said another, poking the air for emphasis, "it just kept right on going."

Thomopoulos at least was friendly. While he developed his skills as West Coast diplomat for Pierce by turning himself into a path of least resistance with whomever he met in Hollywood, Erlicht proved to be inexperienced and bristly to boot. Whenever Marcy Carsey and Tom Werner held meetings to discuss comedy ideas that were in development for the upcoming season, they made it a point not to invite Erlicht along. He had no authority as yet to make creative decisions, and he appeared to them like a Gentry-in-training, someone whom Pierce had destined for the top West Coast job but had deemed unready. Carsey and Werner naturally resented the idea that they should provide creative instruction to a would-be boss.

In place of the old white-office collegiality, a new "boutique" mentality crept through Century City. Individual programmers and groups of programmers worked in isolation, effectively ending the staff cross-fertilization that had been so important to the division's past success. Brandon Stoddard, the most accomplished programmer on the network staff, had always worked on a separate timetable in miniseries and made-for-TV movies, which were produced on a different calendar from prime-time series. Stoddard had a built-in excuse for remaining aloof in the Thomopoulos regime. But he ran drama development during the 1979–80 development season as well, and even so withdrew into his corner office at 2040 Avenue of the Stars, setting a distant tone for the rest of the staff.

The white office itself remained empty—a symbol of the political tug-of-war between Marcy Carsey and Lew Erlicht.

In the management vacuum and West Coast disarray, a new Hollywood figure emerged—the network's vice president for special projects, Gary Pudney.

Pudney, with a reputation for being a not-so-closet homosexual, had deep roots at ABC that went all the way back to an anthology "quality" television series called "Stage 67." Leonard Goldenson had put it on the air in the mid-1960s after being awarded the Distinguished Service Medal of the National Association of Broadcasters. "Stage 67" was short-lived, but it gave Pudney a running start in working in musical theater with marquee Hollywood stars. He had stayed on as head of network specials, left the company in 1973, and then resurfaced as the "executive in charge of talent" for ABC's Silver Anniversary jubilee in 1978. After assembling a cavalcade of Hollywood stars for the televised party, he rejoined the West Coast staff with Goldenson's blessing, reporting directly to Thomopoulos.

While the white office was vacant, Pudney moved in next door and turned the adjacent conference room, where Michael Eisner had once held staff meetings to discuss new scripts and pilots, into a private office. An adjoining bathroom came with the space; Pudney liked having a mirror nearby. And as the network's leading representative with on-air talent, he turned himself into a close confidant and aide-de-camp to Thomopoulos, treating him in the same deferential manner that he used with Hollywood stars.

Pudney and Thomopoulos were both small, elegant men who walked on the balls of their feet and for whom manners and physical appearance were of paramount importance. Pudney knew all the "right" ways to behave in Hollywood, and took Thomopoulos in hand as a novice, deciphering the social codes in advance. Vanity and professional need cemented the relationship.

"I'll have to spruce him up a bit," Pudney would say whenever Thomopoulos looked out of sorts. Later, he used the same words to describe his relationship with Pierce.

The rough-and-ready "No Shine," like Thomopoulos, was

putty in Pudney's hands. While the network coasted on the inherited programming strengths of the Silverman years, Pierce used part of the 1978–79 season to relax and let off steam, visiting the West Coast with more regularity than in past seasons.

Thomopoulos, meanwhile, was cultivating his reputation as a leading ladies' man. Although based in New York, he settled nearly full-time into Cottage 96, a hideaway cabaña at the Bel Air Hotel. Special telephone lines were installed in his rooms in the pink adobe Stone Canyon hotel, just fifteen minutes' drive out Sunset Boulevard from Century City, connecting them with Pierce's office and network headquarters in New York. During his first year as president of ABC Entertainment, Thomopoulos was often seen in the company of Marilu Henner, the leading actress in *Taxi*.

At the end of Thomopoulos' first development season, one of the jokes circulating in Hollywood was, "As long as he doesn't bump into the furniture in Silverman's office, ABC should stay in first place." But Pierce and Thomopoulos aggressively tried to make Silverman's schedule *theirs*, and moved returning shows around.

"We get input from about ten people," Thomopoulos told *American Film* magazine at the start of the 1979–80 season, "but then Fred and I go into a room together—we go *somewhere*—and we work it out."

When the fall season began, ABC's most highly touted new series, a New York law firm comedy called "The Associates," faltered within a few weeks of its premiere. "Mork & Mindy," which had been moved from Thursday to Sunday night, slipped badly in the ratings and eventually died. "Fantasy Island" and "Laverne and Shirley," which had also been moved to new nights and time slots, lost considerable ground. For the first time since 1974 and the "Year of the K," ABC failed to place one of its new shows in the Nielsen Top Twenty. And for the first time since 1975, the network finished second in the November sweeps.

As the network was heading for a virtual tie with CBS in the prime-time ratings at the end of the 1979–80 season, Leonard

Goldenson reached a major strategic crossroads. ABC had once been a fairly diversified entertainment company, with businesses that included movie theaters, records (Jim Croce and Steely Dan were ABC artists), and theme parks like Disneyland. These non-broadcasting profit centers, many of them money-losers, had all but evaporated since I. Martin Pompadur's departure. Except for a Silver Springs vacation park in Florida and a few small publishing companies, ABC was turning into what the Wall Street analyst community called a "pure" broadcasting play.

ABC Publishing was the exception to the rule. A California entrepreneur named Seth Baker had turned it into a division with more than $350 million in annual revenues. Baker had founded *Los Angeles* magazine, sold it to ABC in 1977, and joined the company with a mandate from Goldenson and Rule to build publishing into a brand-new business leg for the company.

Baker brought an empire-building mentality to his task, and for that reason alone was disliked by many network executives; even Eddie Byrd, the shoeshine man, called Baker "Slick" and "Snake." The *Los Angeles* magazine buyout had made Baker a wealthy man, unlike most of his colleagues, and his free-wheeling business style, which endeared him to Goldenson, threatened to upset the delicate balance of in-house power. On different weekend evenings, Elton Rule and Everett Erlick and their wives were invited to join the Goldensons at movie screenings at the founder's home in Mamaroneck. Shortly after he arrived, Baker was invited along too.

In November 1979, pursuing a strategy of growth-by-acquisition, Baker had targeted Macmillan for purchase—a major publishing company with strong but badly managed trade and educational lines, and blue-chip businesses like the Berlitz language and Katherine Gibbs secretarial schools. His own publishing division was on the verge of becoming a billion-dollar business unit within ABC. If the deal went through, ABC would become more corporate and less network, more Rule and less Pierce.

The ABC board of directors had formally approved the buyout, but before the agreement was officially signed, three top managers—Everett Erlick, Michael Mallardi, and Fred Pierce—joined forces in an impromptu alliance to nix the deal. Pierce, who was tardily informed of the negotiations, responded by preparing a memo outlining the anticipated cash needs at ABC Television for the coming season, including the $220 million that the network anticipated paying for broadcast rights to the 1984 Los Angeles Olympics, and $150 million that it planned to spend in order to upgrade its engineering facilities. There were also programming cost overruns in Hollywood to consider. Video Enterprises, the new technologies division which Pierce had just been given authority for earlier in the year, would need money too.

In a matter of days, the outlook for the Macmillan purchase changed from a deal that ABC could easily afford to one that could not be justified from a cost point of view. Rising interest rates, coupled with the fact that the money for the buyout would have to be borrowed, helped to doom the transaction. On the day that the deal papers were scheduled to be signed, Mallardi had a private lunch with Goldenson. When venturing outside movies and television, the chairman was highly susceptible to last-minute advice. And Mallardi, who acted cautiously, delivered strong opinions only when sure it was politically opportune to do so. As they walked downstairs, Goldenson asked, "So you really think this is a bad deal, Mike?"

"Leonard, it's worse than a bad deal. It's a terrible deal," Mallardi replied.

Upon reaching his office, Goldenson called Raymond Hagel, the Macmillan chairman, and read a statement that Everett Erlick had prepared. It was "not in the best interests of ABC to proceed," Goldenson said. When pressed for a further explanation, he repeated the same line. Erlick kept Goldenson to his prepared text, to avoid potential litigation over the sudden change of heart.

No one was more surprised than Seth Baker when he learned that his deal had been killed later that same afternoon. Instead of becoming a leading force in American publishing, his division became an orphaned enterprise within a company whose business interests still resided almost exclusively in broadcasting. Baker left the network a few years later and went back into business for himself.

Eight years later, Robert Maxwell, the British media baron, bought Macmillan for $2.7 billion, almost three times what ABC had agreed to pay.

At the turn of the decade Elton Rule's power to control or direct the course of events at ABC had been badly eroded. As long as Goldenson held onto power, he had little prospect of succeeding him. Fred Pierce was advancing on his lines of operational authority. Michael Mallardi's stealth and patience were like those of a crocodile close to shore, motionless and half-submerged in water. And Everett Erlick's legal stiletto seemed always to be drawn and ready.

And before Rule had adjusted his footing in this precarious network environment, he was thrown off-balance by another series of events in Hollywood. This time, the damage originated with his friend Aaron Spelling, the company's leading program supplier.

Spelling was a slightly built, white-haired creator of high-gloss "trash" programming, and a reigning genius in the entertainment industry. He had started his career in Hollywood as a bit actor in B-movies, moved on to jobs as a drama coach and director of Los Angeles theater, and worked as a staff producer at ABC. In 1968, through Rule's patronage at the network, he began producing shows for television, gradually becoming one of the most prolific and successful producers of programming in the history of the medium.

"The Mod Squad," Spelling's first series television hit, premiered on ABC in 1968. "The Rookies" followed in 1972, "S.W.A.T." and "Starsky and Hutch" in 1975, "Charlie's Angels" in 1976, "The Love Boat" in 1977, "Fantasy Island" and "Hart to Hart" in 1979, and "Dynasty" in 1980.

While compiling a brilliant record as a producer of TV shows, Spelling cultivated an image as a Hollywood loner. He was an oddball, a phobic personality. He would not fly in airplanes and was known to take to his bed in moments of stress, making the network's programming staffers pay him court as though visiting stricken royalty. His blond young wife had the improbable name "Candy." But Spelling was rich as Croesus, thanks to Elton Rule, his own creativity, and his long working relationship with ABC.

Most TV producers, unlike Spelling, worked for Hollywood studios and tried to sell new programming ideas to all three networks. If one network turned down the idea for a new show, the producer could shop it to the other two buyers in town. The most that a top-rank producer could hope for in his or her network dealings was a "first look" deal, in which a network paid a small premium in return for the right to be first in line for new projects.

Spelling, by contrast, produced his programs through an "exclusivity" arrangement with ABC. Under the terms of his deal, one network and only one could license his creative product. And in return for his willingness to forgo the right to shop his ideas to CBS and NBC, ABC had agreed to the most favorable terms granted to any programmer in the business. It promised to air at least one new Spelling-produced show on its prime-time schedule each season. Since open time slots were a scarce commodity, Spelling wound up having more clout in Hollywood than most studios. Other producers wanting access to ABC's prime-time airwaves entered into partnerships with him, most notably former programming executives Leonard Goldberg, Douglas Cramer, and Esther Shapiro. The terms of Spelling's deal enabled him to build a mini-studio of network suppliers who had learned their trade at ABC.

Since Spelling and his partners owned the copyright to every show that they produced, the additional revenues that came in from reruns of "Charlie's Angels" and other series from TV stations in the United States and from sales abroad were theirs to keep. His exclusive licensing arrangement was worth hundreds of millions of dollars to him personally. But Spelling's prime-time factory involved a labyrinth of cost accounting as well. And in 1980, this more shadowy side of his business surfaced in a Hollywood cause célèbre of cover-up and greed that almost toppled Elton Rule.

At the network, it was known as the Jennifer Martin affair, after the young West Coast business affairs attorney whose job it was to sign off on all network payments to Spelling-Goldberg. In the summer of 1979, Martin spotted what she thought was an inconsistent billing pattern. Spelling-Goldberg (the two producers then working in partnership) charged ABC for their personal services and program licensing through a Los Angeles business manager named J. William "Bill" Hayes. The billings normally involved payments for the ongoing costs of series production after the episodes were delivered. But under the heading of "exclusivity," Spelling-Goldberg had added a separate, unsubstantiated charge of $25,000 for several episodes of "Charlie's Angels." Spelling's contract with the network did not authorize additional payments for his exclusivity, so Martin did not sign the invoice. Instead, she queried her boss, a West Coast vice president named Ronald Sunderland, who instructed her to proceed.

"It is not a payment for Aaron Spelling's exclusivity, but for the entity of Spelling-Goldberg as long as 'Charlie's Angels' is on the air," Martin recalled Sunderland saying.

The answer was vague at best, so she again refused to sign. Sunderland lost his temper.

"Okay. You want to know what it's really for? They're fucking the Robert Wagners out of their money. We've been putting it into 'Starsky and Hutch' until now, but since 'Starsky' is off the air, the money's got to go somewhere. So we're calling it 'exclusivity.' "

In the accounting for Hollywood shows, profits were often split among multiple profit participants, and the actor Robert Wagner and his wife Natalie Wood were part-owners with Aaron Spelling and Leonard Goldberg of "Charlie's Angels," along with the writer-creators of the show. (Wagner starred in "Hart to Hart," another Spelling-Goldberg show.) Depending on how ABC's payments to Spelling-Goldberg were invoiced and authorized, the money transfer that Jennifer Martin was being asked to sign off on for "Charlie's Angels" could flow either to the show's producers for "exclusivity" or to the Wagners and the other profit participants as their financial share. In this instance, it would flow directly to Spelling and Goldberg.

Martin considered the network's handling of the transaction to be grand theft, and confided her misgivings in a set of confidential memos to her boss. To dissociate herself from what she saw as criminal activity, she then took the additional step of blind-copying her memos to the Los Angeles district attorney's office. The entertainment industry and the district attorney's office were highly sensitized to such allegations at the time. David Begelman, Columbia Pictures's studio head, had forged two checks in Cliff Robertson's name and committed other financial improprieties in a similar vein the previous year, and a special task force had been set up to investigate charges of widespread corruption in Hollywood.

Sunderland forwarded copies of the memos to his boss and to Fred Pierce in New York. Grand theft was just the sort of criminal charge that, if proved, could lead to the lifting of ABC's TV station licenses, so Pierce duly informed Erlick. The paper trail began to widen and grow. Jennifer Martin had opened up a can of worms.

ABC's top outside counsel for legal problems on the West Coast was Frank Rothman, a prominent Los Angeles and Hollywood attorney, and Erlick asked him to conduct an investigation instead. Rothman had the right credentials for the case: As David Begelman's lawyer, he had succeeded in getting an admitted forger off the hook virtually scot-free. Rothman looked into Martin's charges and returned with a report completely exonerating ABC. An oral agreement with Steve Gentry (now conveniently dead) was said to provide a basis for the "exclusivity" payments to Spelling-Goldberg, and the two "Charlie's Angels" producers were owed the additional money for cost overruns incurred at the network's behest.

But Rothman's written report, while discounting Jennifer Martin's claims, went on to raise questions about Elton Rule's relationship with Spelling.

Rule, who had been a friend of Spelling's since the days when he ran KABC-TV in Los Angeles, still served as his main contact at ABC. Even after relinquishing oversight of network programming to Pierce, he had remained responsible in an informal way for managing this sensitive relationship in Hollywood. Spelling's track record as a program supplier had begun on Rule's watch, and the extraordinary success of his shows continued to reflect well on Rule. The two men had overlapping business interests as well. In 1968, Rule had introduced Spelling to J. William Hayes, his own personal business manager, and through Hayes the two men were blind coinvestors in several southern California real estate deals. Rule's three children had also worked at various times in the 1970s for Spelling-Goldberg. Rothman's report itemized many of these facts and put Rule under a cloud. The district attorney's office now had two sets of allegations to investigate.

Since the network was in the clear, Jennifer Martin was, by implication, insubordinate, so after Erlick received Rothman's report he ordered that she be fired. Although there was no documentation substantiating the claim, her superiors on the West Coast concluded that her on-the-job performance even before the flagging of the Spelling-Goldberg invoice warranted her dismissal. Martin responded by filing a lawsuit against the network for wrongful discharge.

The Jennifer Martin affair simmered for almost a year before exploding in a front-page series of articles in the *New York Times*. They described an investigation by the Securities and Exchange Commission of the network's ties to Spelling and Goldberg under an obscure antibribery provision of the Foreign Corrupt Practices Act. Rule's friendship and apparent conflict-of-interest with Spelling featured prominently in the story. The *Times* implied that it was just one symptom of the broader conflict-of-interest in the network's Hollywood dealings that were under scrutiny in Washington.

The Los Angeles district attorney's office had dropped its inquiry in the meantime, but it reactivated the case. For several tense months, the network maintained an official "no comment" legal front. And when a colleague asked, "Why don't you do something to end the speculation?" Rule smiled wanly, shook his head, and pointed a finger down the hall at Erlick's office.

"I can't. He's handling this one," he replied.

While the investigations dragged on, and Rule twisted slowly in the wind, some network executives elected to go out-of-town on vacation in order to avoid taking calls from Goldenson, who was actively seeking information about the potential fallout. Other executives, sensing Rule's weakness, moved in for the kill. Roone Arledge put a crackerjack ABC News investigative team on the story, sent a camera crew to hound Ronald Sunderland at his West Coast office, and cloaked his own power play under the guise of "objective" news coverage. The network's evening news aired a four-and-a-half minute segment with helicopter footage of a warehouse and shopping center in Los Angeles in which Spelling, Rule, and other J. William Hayes clients were business partners.

No indictments were ever filed. The SEC and the Los Angeles district attorney's office finally dropped the case. When all the investigations were over, the head of the special task force on Hollywood corruption held a news conference praising Spelling and Goldberg as "completely cooperative" and "very respected members of the entertainment industry," and issued an eighty-one page report that stated: "There is insufficient evidence to prove beyond a reasonable doubt that Aaron Spelling, Leonard Goldberg (or the others) are criminally responsible for conspiracy, grand theft, or embezzlement."

The district attorney did suggest, however, that any disputes stemming from the case might best be settled in the civil courts— and several were. Jennifer Martin won a reported payment of $975,000 in her wrongful discharge suit, and after a careful audit of the producers' books Robert Wagner, Natalie Wood, and the writer-creators of "Charlie's Angels" also received substantial out-of-court settlements. After the proper payments were made, the matter gradually died away, and everyone involved emerged unscathed.

Everyone but Elton Rule. After the Jennifer Martin matter

was resolved, he spent the next summer in self-imposed exile in California, and never participated actively in network programming again. He was finished as a major player at ABC.

Rule had not changed, but the company around him had. By the end of 1980, the happy network family had turned into a den of snarling wolves. And while Rule stayed on the job, waiting in case Goldenson should decide to change his mind and step down as chairman, he refused to lead the pack.

Aaron Spelling, for his part, was aghast at having inadvertently done anything to harm his greatest network patron. When Spelling met Ivan Goff, a "Charlie's Angels" writer-creator who had won an out-of-court settlement, in a Hollywood restaurant, his eyes filled with crocodile tears. "My God, what have we done?" he whispered as an apology.

A few years later, Spelling was feeling better. At a dinner with Rule in Hollywood, he made a big to-do about wanting to help with Rule's farewell speech to the affiliates. The words had to reflect the deep affection and esteem in which Rule was held, he said, and he asked to speak with the writers about the contents.

A few days later, when asked precisely what he wanted to say, Spelling replied, "Tell them the network will always have continuity with its program suppliers."

9

Falling Out of the Saddle

Ln July 1979, Fred Pierce renewed Beverlee Dean's contract. The psychic from Encino had stopped giving late-night readings, but she got another $24,000 from ABC plus a 25 percent raise of $6,000. And in the second year of her contract, she fulfilled her long-standing dream—she became a producer for network TV.

One of the clauses in Dean's contract gave the network "first option" on her ideas for daytime and prime-time programming. One of her Hollywood producer-friends owned a made-for-TV movie property about the life of Mother Elizabeth Seton, the American nun who was canonized in 1975, and Dean pitched the idea to Pierce. Pierce sent her to Thomopoulos, who bought the project during the 1978–79 season, while the network was still in first place in the ratings.

For more than a year, scripts, ratings, and cassettes of new pilots were delivered by the network to Dean's home in Encino. She met with Pierce when he visited the West Coast, and often made programming and scheduling suggestions. Dean claimed credit for the decision not to cancel "Fantasy Island," and for moving "Hart to Hart" to Tuesday night. "I knew he listened to every-

143

thing I said," Dean recalled, but for Pierce the meetings were mostly a diversion or a joke. Her biggest battle, Dean said, was trying to persuade him to air a weekly five-minute segment called "Good News," focusing on uplifting, positive news items. He told her the local affiliates wouldn't buy it. No one ever asked why the man running America's most successful network would spend his time with a woman like Beverlee Dean. To almost everyone at ABC, the relationship remained a secret. But during their meetings, as she eagerly tried to humor and please him, Pierce and Dean forged a personal bond.

"You're the only one who can make him laugh," Pierce's Los Angeles secretary told Dean one day while giving her the weekly ratings over the telephone.

Gradually Dean began to sense that she was operating out of her depth. She got so nervous before one of her meetings with Pierce that she broke out in hives. And Thomopoulos, with whom she had to deal on the Mother Seton project, had disliked her from the start.

"Tony thought I was a jinx," Dean recalled. "He couldn't wait to get rid of me."

Two weeks before the Emmy Awards in 1979, Pierce took her out to lunch at the Century Plaza Hotel to meet Gary Pudney. Pudney, who had officially been put in charge of talent as well as special projects, was made her new network liaison.

"Because you're so good with talent, someone had to be your contact," Pierce told Dean.

Turning to Pudney, he added, "Gary, nobody knows this. This is a secret, and it must remain a secret. If she needs anything, you get it. If she calls about talent, listen to her."

"Fred, I can't believe this," Pudney marveled, as though a secret of Minerva had been vouchsafed. "Nothing in this town gets past me."

He took on the assignment by procuring a ticket for Dean to the Emmys, seating her at a table with Tim Flack, the network's head of casting, and Marcy Carsey, the head of prime-time series development. But not long after, people began calling her at home with queries. A *National Enquirer* reporter, phoning from Florida, woke her up early one morning to ask what she did for ABC. The secret had leaked.

Dean called Pierce in New York and told him she didn't trust Gary Pudney.

"Oh, dear, what have I gotten you into?" Pierce worried.

When Pudney began ignoring Dean's recommendations, she got frustrated and called Pierce again. By now it was May 1980, and her original two-year contract was about to expire.

"Beverlee, this is too dangerous," Pierce told her. "We've got to figure out something else. I'm a man of my word. Once Mother Seton airs, I'll be able to . . . " He let his voice trail off.

A Time for Miracles, the made-for-TV movie on the life of Mother Seton, was scheduled as a Christmas special in late 1980. It was Dean's last, best chance to prove her value to Pierce as a programmer. She promised him the movie would get a 40 share and be a big success. Instead, it got a 20 share and flopped. Pierce stopped taking her calls.

An out-of-work Dean broke her vow of silence the next spring, speaking out in the *Los Angeles Times*. In a front-page article called "The Psychic Who Came in from the Cold," reporter Deborah Caulfield exposed Dean's tale in chapter and verse, including a photostat of Pierce's handwritten scrawl: "I am three feet taller than Tiny Tim." The moral of the story, as the *Times* presented it, was that Pierce had put Beverlee Dean on the payroll to compensate for Silverman's defection. And the punchline? ABC had dropped out of first place in the ratings in the same month that Dean's contract expired.

Pierce called up Dean and told her off. "What the hell are you trying to do to me? I trusted you. How could you do this to me?"

"Why don't you ask Gary Pudney about it?" Dean replied defensively. Dead silence greeted her from the other end of the line.

"What do I do now?" she asked in a small voice.

"It's a little too late," Pierce said and hung up.

Later that same year, when ABC's ratings were down even farther, Pierce called again and asked her to remove her "hex" on the schedule. After that, they never spoke again.

In Leonard Goldenson's briefing book for the annual meeting of network shareholders that spring, one of the hypothetical questions posed was, "Why did ABC pay sizable fees to psychic Beverlee Dean to provide guidance in programming?" The network's official answer was "We hired Ms. Dean as a script reader, and during her tenure with us she also served as associate producer of the television movie *A Time for Miracles*, the story of Mother Seton. Ms. Dean had a two-year contract that expired and was not renewed."

Period, paragraph. Next question please.

No one bothered to ask. That, it seemed, was that.

Except for Mindy Naud. The star of "Operation Petticoat" had moved on in Hollywood since the cancellation of her first TV show, and in the spring of 1981 was auditioning for a new role on "Fantasy Island." Herve Villechaize was retiring, and the casting directors at Aaron Spelling Productions wanted to put a beautiful young actress in the part. Mindy Naud met their specifications, and they had all but promised her the job. All they had needed was network approval.

Naud's role in the Beverlee Dean affair was still a closely held secret. Dean had made a point of not revealing her name to the *Los Angeles Times*. Besides wanting the spotlight on herself, she also wanted to protect her friend. After the article was published, Pierce and Thomopoulos were the butt of entertainment industry jokes. Johnny Carson dressed up in Merlin the Magician clothes, and did a late-night sketch of an ABC programming meeting that featured voodoo dolls, tarot cards, and a witch doctor hovering over a bubbling cauldron. While the network played mum, issuing an official "no comment," Pierce and Thomopoulos had become a laughing stock, and any mention of Naud's name would only add to their embarrassment. She was being referred to in Hollywood

146

as "Deep Throat"—the Watergate term for a secret source.

Naud's role in the affair was secret, but Gary Pudney and Tony Thomopoulos still had final approval over network casting decisions. One day she had the "Fantasy Island" part, the next day she didn't. This sequence of events led the actress to believe she had been blackballed.

"All of a sudden, people were going around saying Mindy Naud was crazy," she remembered.

The high-spirited actress soon found herself unable to find work on any new TV show in Hollywood. Naud's once golden career turned distinctly ungolden. She finally left town and took an extended trip to Italy.

Hollywood in the early 1980s was in a ferment of box-office hits, profits from syndicated TV shows, and the prospect of additional revenue from satellite and cable distribution. The studios' self-assurance was a 180-degree turnaround from their hesitancy a decade earlier, and no studio epitomized the new mood more than Paramount. Barry Diller and Michael Eisner were in the process of transforming it into a Hollywood production powerhouse.

Diller and Eisner, still in their thirties, were too young to be considered movie industry titans, and as former network TV programmers aspiring to Hollywood leadership both had to overcome the taint of their second-class-industry origins. But Diller, the first TV executive ever to run a studio, endured the early hostility of the West Coast creative community, and with Eisner at his side, Paramount was pumping out hits. *Saturday Night Fever* and *Grease* had caught the disco wave in the late 1970s. *Raiders of the Lost Ark* and the *Star Trek* sequels were setting the 1980s trend in adventure movies. A string of comedy and drama hits—*Airplane, An Officer and a Gentleman, Trading Places, Flashdance*, and *Terms of Endearment*—were in the Paramount production pipeline. The studio was creatively and financially astute, usually produced low-budget pictures, and used money from outside limited partners to reduce the financial risk. It aggressively sought out

balance sheet tricks to offset occasional losses from big-budget failure. A safe-harbor leasing deal with a British bank generated sav-
ings of more than 20 percent on Warren Beatty's *Reds*.

Even more than successful movies, popular TV shows made
the studio profitable. The growing number of nonaffiliated TV stations and available time slots made reruns of "Happy Days" and
other hits more valuable than any single motion picture. The same
was true for other studios as well. ABC's long-term production deal
with Paramount was not yielding any new hits, but Diller and
Eisner, as studio executives, were able to reap the financial benefit
of their old program development in the continuing flow of syndication revenues. They also kept a watchful eye on the movie
distribution business. After an antitrust ruling prohibited a consortium of Hollywood studios from starting their own pay cable
movie channel in competition with Home Box Office, Diller licensed a package of Paramount movies to Showtime—a move that
helped Showtime become a competitive force and kept HBO from
gaining a monopoly in the field.

These and other business decisions added to Diller's mystique
as a shrewd, occasionally ruthless man. Although largely unchanged
from his days at the network, Diller was now under a Hollywood
spotlight, and whatever he could not control he tended to shy away
from. His top priority was not to make a splash; it was to remain
in favor with Charles Bluhdorn, the chairman of Gulf & Western,
Paramount's parent company. One visitor to the Bluhdorn vacation
home in the Dominican Republic, where Gulf & Western owned
vast sugar plantations, recalled Diller barefoot and quiet as a cat,
listening in on his boss's telephone conversations. As the second-
ranking studio executive, Eisner mined his creative ideas out of a
rich vein of boyish enthusiasm, but was becoming as renowned in
Hollywood for his never-say-die negotiating techniques with outsiders as for the loyalties that he developed with his staff.

These two Paramount executives were just the most prominent
ex-ABC executives making significant headway in Hollywood.
When a group of entertainment and business affairs staffers who
had worked at Goldenson's network were reunited at lunch one

day, more than forty showed up. In 1981, their numbers were strengthened by the disbanding of Silverman's old programming team. Barbara Gallagher, Bridget Potter, Pam Dixon, and Esther Shapiro had all left the network by the beginning of the 1980–81 season. Marcy Carsey, who had worked with Tony Thomopoulos as the head of prime-time series development since 1979, left at the end of that year. Tom Werner, Carsey's top colleague, followed a few months later.

The motivation for many of the departures were the back-end deals that Pierce and Thomopoulos had instituted several years before. A network programmer had little incentive to stay on the job when a network was contractually bound to put him or her into business as an independent producer. Several successful Hollywood producers, including Leonard Hill and Esther Shapiro, owed their starts to the network's largess.

But the strategy of priming the production pump through back-end deals was not paying off for ABC. In the fall of 1981, the network was ensconced in second place in the prime-time ratings. ABC still led in most key demographics, but its new fall lineup featured "safe" law-and-order dramas with titles like "Code Red," "Strike Force," and "Today's FBI." Six years had passed since Garry Marshall's breakout success with "Happy Days," and more than ten since Norman Lear's with "All in the Family." NBC was struggling to find a prime-time hit of any kind—its most popular show was "Real People," not "Hill Street Blues." And CBS had a schedule overloaded with "Dallas" spin-offs.

The innovative programming on network TV in the early 1980s was not in prime-time series, but in news, long-form miniseries and made-for-TV movie programming, and daytime. Since taking over ABC News in June 1977, Roone Arledge had turned the staid world of nonfiction TV on its head. The "star" system in network news was in full swing.

When Fred Pierce hired Barbara Walters from NBC with a contract worth $1 million a year in 1976, the pendulum of news coverage swung decisively toward entertainment personality–based journalism. Arledge inherited most of the on-air reporters and anchors who would make ABC News the best news division in TV. Frank Reynolds, Peter Jennings, Ted Koppel, and Sam Donaldson were already on the payroll when he arrived. But he created the programming franchises that turned them into stars. He adapted the production techniques of ABC Sports—split screens, satellite relays, "remotes" and computer graphics—and launched a three-anchor format on "World News Tonight" in 1978. "20/20," a new prime-time newsmagazine, also started that year. And the following year Arledge adeptly translated his special, late-night coverage of the Iranian hostage crisis into the "Nightline" format, which made a star of Ted Koppel and added a new half-hour of programming five nights a week for ABC News in the process.

As the only person at any network with *two* live TV divisions, Arledge was the virtual czar of live television. His extraordinary influence on the nation's airwaves became apparent when ABC Sports covered the Winter Olympics at Lake Placid, and turned the U.S. hockey team's gold medal and defeat of the Soviet Union into a patriotic lovefest. Only Arledge could capitalize on a confidence-eroding hostage crisis *and* give the country a morale boost from a sports event within the span of a few months.

In 1981 ABC News was preparing to move into a new, state-of-the-art Washington bureau. The network built it to accommodate the division's office needs for the next twenty years; within a year, the bureau was already full. Arledge put new shows into every available "fringe" time period on the network's schedule—"World News This Morning" in the early-morning hour before "Good Morning America," with Steve Bell and Kathleen Sullivan as anchors; David Brinkley on a new Sunday morning show, "This Week with David Brinkley"; even a new show that lasted for a few months in a late-late nighttime period after "Nightline." Each new program brought in new advertising revenues; and since ABC News, unlike other network divisions, was under no obligation to turn a profit, the revenue was pumped right back into ABC News. Arledge used it to raid the other two networks—especially CBS, which had the strongest bench of news talent in the business—of their best producers and correspondents. After Walter Cronkite retired, CBS gave Dan Rather a long-term contract worth more than $20 million simply in order to keep Arledge from hiring him away.

While laying the foundations of an improved news division, Arledge built an inviolable wall around himself. One year when the top network brass traveled from Miami to a board of governors meeting in Barbados in a rented propeller plane, he arrived in an ABC News–chartered jet, leaving as soon as his presentation was over. When the other executives flew back to Miami, fighting a strong wind, the ride was bumpy and cramped. One executive remembered thinking that if the propeller plane had crashed, every top network official would vanish at sea—except Arledge, who traveled alone.

In Hollywood, Brandon Stoddard exercised dual powers in entertainment production not unlike Arledge's in sports and news. Before the 1979–80 season, after watching Diller and Eisner run up a string of Paramount movie successes, Goldenson had put him in charge of a new unit called ABC Motion Pictures. While acting as the network's "bespoke" programmer in made-for-TV movies and miniseries, Stoddard was also overseeing the development of feature films like *The Flamingo Kid, Silkwood,* and *Prizzi's Honor.* During each May, February, and November sweeps period, a programming *oeuvre* from Stoddard goosed the prime-time ratings— Jane Seymour in "East of Eden," Peter O'Toole in "Masada." Stoddard adapted Albert Speer's *Inside the Third Reich* for television, and had "Thorn Birds," "The Winds of War," and "The Day After" on the drawing boards. Almost single-handedly, he had created a new form of network TV entertainment—"event programming." The ratings and quality of their programming gave Stoddard and Arledge a unique freedom from their higher-ups.

The money machine that supported all this activity was daytime television—the most lucrative part of the ABC schedule. Jackie Smith's afternoon soap operas produced one-fourth of the network's revenues; in 1981, they generated almost three-fourths of the profit. Smith was one of two women left in a senior-level

151

programming job, and the only holdover from Silverman's old programming team, and she had developed a soap opera theme called "Love in the Afternoon"—a euphemism for soft porn for housewives. "General Hospital," "All My Children," and "Ryan's Hope" were the network's top-rated afternoon shows, and they delivered more women in the 18–49 group to advertisers than the daytime shows of CBS and NBC combined. The wedding of Luke and Laura, the stars of "General Hospital," had college students across America cutting classes and crowding into campus lounges; it was the biggest event in network TV since "Who shot J.R.?" Hollywood stars like Elizabeth Taylor were lining up for cameo guest appearances on their favorite ABC daytime shows.

Because ABC, unlike CBS and NBC, owned most of its soap operas (the other two networks had started their daytime schedules in the 1950s, before the radio tradition of sponsor-controlled programming died out, and changed late in the game), it could convert its high daytime ratings directly into profit. Women viewers in the afternoon were allowing the network to float into the new decade on a reservoir of cash.

If Leonard Goldenson had been a Wall Street raider instead of an old-fashioned gambler, he would have "bought in" ABC shares in 1981, when interest rates were high and stock prices were depressed. Then he would have waited for the Wall Street tide to turn and sold his company to the highest available bidder. Instead of being merely wealthy, Goldenson would have become fabulously rich, like John Kluge of Metromedia, who made $3.5 billion while taking his public shareholders to the cleaners.

But Goldenson wanted to build, not manipulate, assets. He wanted to create new money. And Video Enterprises, the company's new-technologies division, was where he gambled with his network's house money.

Not a month passed during the 1981–82 season without Video Enterprises making a headline about its activity in the age of satellites and cable and the new technologies. ARTS, for the Alpha

Repertory Television Service, was an ABC joint venture with the Hearst Corporation to offer cultural programming via satellite and cable to viewers around the country. Daytime, another Hearst coventure, targeted women viewers with another special-interest cable network. Video Enterprises also joined forces with Group W Satellite Communications in two proposed twenty-four-hour cable news networks called Satellite NewsChannels, and acquired a minority stake in the sports network ESPN. And while all these new-technologies businesses were being announced, a top-secret project with the code-name "Project Gorilla" was moving ahead behind-the-scenes at ABC in hush-hush, top-level meetings.

Early entry, maximum entry, and minimum risk—that was the Video Enterprises plan, and it contrasted sharply with new developments at the other two networks. For ABC's five cable programming services, CBS and NBC were plodding along with just one apiece, both cultural networks like ARTS. While CBS Cable and RCA invested in the Entertainment Channel, ABC was spreading new-technologies tentacles widely into news, sports, and entertainment.

Goldenson's direct personal involvement in his company's deal making set it apart from the competition. When ARTS debuted but was not available on his local Manhattan cable channel, he requested cassettes of the first day's programming, took them home, and watched them on a VCR in Mamaroneck. The next day he telephoned the vice president in charge of programming with his comments and congratulations.

David Johnson, ABC's vice president for strategic planning, was in Goldenson's office in the fall of 1981 when the opportunity to buy into ESPN crossed the chairman's desk. Fred Pierce and Herb Granath, the likable, square-jawed executive in charge of Video Enterprises, interrupted a meeting to tell Goldenson that the Rasmussen family, which had founded ESPN, wanted to sell, and that Getty Oil, which was footing the bills, was looking for a new partner in the still unprofitable network.

Johnson listened skeptically to the informal presentation made by Granath and Pierce. He had a Harvard MBA, and his long-term strategy involved ABC buying a movie studio so as to integrate its business vertically and gain control over prime-time programming. Granath and Pierce had only the jotting on their yellow legal pads. But they argued that ESPN would give ABC a window on pay-per-view sports and help it bid for big sporting events.

"If we don't buy it, CBS will," they warned Goldenson.

Rule, who was also in the meeting, threw in his two cents: "If you're hanging your hat on pay-per-view, shouldn't you wait and see how it can come out of ESPN?"

Goldenson, turning to Rule, said, "Nope. First you place your bets. Then you look at your cards."

When the network lawyers set off to negotiate the details of the ESPN purchase, Goldenson instructed them, "Make sure you get an option to buy the whole thing."

Goldenson backed people and projects if they had the right feel, and the project in which he invested the most gambler's luck was "Project Gorilla," or TeleFirst. It was the only new venture *not* jointly undertaken with an outside partner. In the middle of the night, when the network did not broadcast a regular signal, ABC planned to transmit a scrambled signal to preset VCRs in subscriber homes. The VCR would then receive Hollywood movies, children's programming, and how-to instructional material, which could be replayed through a decoder at the viewer's convenience.

The elegant economy of TeleFirst and the auspicious omens that surrounded its development led ABC to stake a large portion of its long-term reputation on the project. The startup costs came to just $25 million, exactly what Goldenson had paid for ABC in 1953. Chicago, the test market, was where he had helped Paramount obtain its first TV station, in 1938. If TeleFirst worked, the network stood to reap a billion-dollar reward. It was a business idea that deployed an existing network resource, required no significant capital investment, and allowed the network potentially to corner the pay cable movie markets of HBO and Showtime and the home video rental market without the loss of so much as a single time period.

To overcome the technical obstacle of scrambling and decoding the TeleFirst signal, ABC turned to the Sony Corporation, which through its chairman, Akio Morita, had been involved as a potential joint venture partner from the start of the project. When Morita learned that TeleFirst, as a for-pay transmission over licensed American airwaves, would require an FCC waiver, he backed off, not wanting to hand the politicians in Washington a new issue in the trade arena between Japan and the United States. But Sony agreed to design and manufacture the decoders, and its participation gave the project an exciting international angle. If TeleFirst worked in America, the network planners reasoned, it would work abroad too, and ABC could export it under license to Sony in the Middle East, Japan, and Europe.

The TeleFirst idea flourished at ABC like a favored grandson, the namesake to carry Goldenson's company into the next generation. It was the only Video Enterprise project housed at Hard Rock. Good luck seemed to come along with the package. When Arthur Cohen, the Madison Avenue executive whose marketing skills made him a natural as TeleFirst's new president, was waiting for a lunch date in the downstairs lobby a few days after his arrival, he looked down and found five $20 bills lying there on the floor, waiting to be picked up and put in his pocket.

Cohen, meeting Goldenson at lunch the next day, told him, "Leonard, this is my kind of company."

In the summer of 1981, Goldenson signed a new four-year contract as ABC's chairman and chief executive officer. "Leonard's going to hold on to the candy store for another four years," a network insider was quoted as saying.

Besides wanting to leave his mark on broadcasting history, Goldenson had compelling business reasons for holding on to his network power. High interest rates and cable television's long-term promise had combined to send network stocks plummeting on Wall Street. As ABC's stock bottomed out, market opportunists began investing in the company. Laurence Tisch, a neighbor of

155

Goldenson's in Westchester County and fellow member of the Temple Emmanu-el in Manhattan, was the most notable. He and his brother, Robert Preston Tisch, had built the Loew's Corporation into a multibillion dollar conglomerate, mostly by buying stocks on the cheap. Laurence Tisch had a good idea that the network was worth more money than its stock: In 1965 he had acted as Harold Geneen's go-between in Goldenson's almost-merger with ITT. In early 1981, Tisch invested his own family's money in the network's stock, and did not stop until he owned just under 5 percent. Then he waited for Goldenson to respond.

Tisch and Goldenson were acquaintances, but Goldenson did not view Tisch's investment as friendly. Business was business. After Goldenson politely requested that he not allow his block of shares to attract other, unfriendly speculators, Tisch sold his network stock. Goldenson was still firmly in charge.

The political jockeying inside the network intensified behind the scenes that summer when the all-purpose consulting firm of Booz, Allen, and Hamilton delivered a report on long-term company strategy to Goldenson, Rule, and the company's board of directors. Compiled at a cost of $1 million, many of the findings contradicted the idea that the network was performing well financially, and indirectly called into question Pierce's management capabilities. The network was superbly run as a revenue machine, the consultants reported, but its percentage of ratings-to-profit was poor.

"If you don't watch out, you're going to be another division of General Electric in a couple of years," one consultant warned in the meeting of top network managers.

The Booz, Allen report had been commissioned to give Goldenson a new road map for the next decade, but except for a general dictum about cutting costs, the company followed few of its recommendations. Goldenson's decision to stay on for another four years rippled down in the form of new four-year contracts for Rule and Pierce. Cosmetic promotions were handed out in long-term strategy and personnel (which was renamed "human resources"). The only change of real note, an attempt to link compensation with performance, was the company's adoption of a new stock-option plan for its senior executives. Eighty top managers were given annual awards of restricted "share units" that were scheduled to vest—that is, become tradable shares—at the end of four years. If network profits had risen in the meantime, the board of directors reasoned, its stock price would have risen too, and thus the executives would receive their just reward. If not, not.

The new emphasis on corporate responsibility also called for Pierce to relinquish the presidency of ABC Television and to concentrate, as executive vice president, on the company's new technologies ventures. Pierce tried to appoint Tony Thomopoulos in his stead, but Goldenson and Rule both vetoed the move. Thomopoulos was still "too untested," they said. Indeed, when the network had slipped into second place in the prime-time ratings, the *New York Daily News* speculated that Thomopoulos might lose his job altogether. "ABC Ratings Skid Puts Tony in Tight Spot," the headline said.

The round of promotions accompanying Goldenson's announcement that summer ended with Pierce's orchestration of a top-level game of musical chairs. He shifted ABC Entertainment's base of operations from New York to Hollywood, and Thomopoulos officially moved to the West Coast full-time, adding new responsibilities in the area of on-air promotion and business affairs to his existing portfolio. Lew Erlicht moved into the white office job of comedy and drama development. Pierce's loyalists consolidated their control over the heart of ABC's business.

With the company's future now resting squarely on his shoulders, Pierce turned ever more granitelike with professional resolve. His daily calendar was filled with business meetings, strategy sessions, and long-term planning—a rapid-fire whirl of activity as exhilarating as that of any of his industry peers. While Pierce inhaled deeply of this heady atmosphere in New York, Thomopoulos seemed to relax into an increasingly sybaritic West Coast lifestyle of his own. In the spring of 1981, when ABC televised a miniseries based on John Steinbeck's *East of Eden*, he was seen squiring the actress Jane Seymour, who played a villainous wife in the TV show, around town. It was hardly abnormal for network chief program-mers to escort their stars to Hollywood parties, but Thomopoulos's interest appeared to go beyond the purely professional. He was seen socially in the company of ever more beautiful leading ladies as he progressed in his Hollywood career. Pierce seemed to enjoy his colleague's activities vicariously from a distance.

After Thomopoulos' promotion was announced, the two men spent the month of August 1981 on a yacht with their wives, sailing off the coast of Greece.

Except for "Dynasty," which was slowly climbing the charts, ABC had not had a new Top Ten hit since "Taxi" and "Mork & Mindy," but the second season of 1981–82 seemed to turn the schedule around. "Joanie Loves Chachi" and "T. J. Hooker," two new series, premiered in March and did well. "Joanie Loves Chachi" was a "Happy Days" spin-off whose comedy tempo and characters revisited Garry Marshall's ten-year-old pilot. "T. J. Hooker" was an Aaron Spelling confection starring William Shatner of "Star Trek," Adrian Zmed of "Dance Fever," and Heather Lock-lear of "Dynasty."

Although ABC's new series were feeding on the past, the viewing public had not yet caught on. Tuesday night, in the half-hour time period after "Happy Days," "Joanie Loves Chachi" tied for third in the year-end ratings. Leading off on Saturdays at 8 P.M. "T. J. Hooker" shored up the faltering "Love Boat" and "Fantasy Island." With one successful entry from the fall—"The Fall Guy," starring Lee Majors of "The Six Million Dollar Man"—the new spring entries brought the network neck-and-neck with CBS in the prime-time ratings, and helped it win the second season.

The second season was an auspicious moment for Tony Thomopoulos. Because he had moved to the West Coast full-time and taken hands-on control of the prime-time schedule just the fall before, he could take full credit for the turnaround. And when the second-season win was placed alongside the new-technologies ac-tivity at Video Enterprises and added to the highly rated programming of Roone Arledge, Brandon Stoddard, and Jackie Smith, Pierce could take full credit for leading the entire company to its best-ever business plateau.

With all the vital signs strong, *Forbes* prepared a story on the network that spring, putting a big picture of Leonard Goldenson in a broadcast studio on the cover. His arms crossed over the controls, the old founder still looked vigorous. The caption read, "ABC's Leonard Goldenson: A Shrewd Strategy for Staying on Top," and the magazine gushed about his company's multifaceted achievements. "Staying Tuned for Tomorrow" was the story title. A second photograph featured Goldenson, Rule, and Pierce at the same studio controls, with portraits of the network's other top executives in the TV monitors. "ABC's Longest-Running Series," the second caption read.

Forbes had it pegged—ABC's senior management had scarcely changed in more than a decade. But for the first time since 1972, when Rule had been appointed the company's president, Pierce was standing next to him and Goldenson in an official company photograph. Goldenson spelled out the meaning of the visual choreography in a last-minute insertion to his speech to network affiliates in May 1982, putting Pierce in line to succeed Rule.

The long-term impact of the announcement was not clear until after the affiliate board of governors met in December in Acapulco. Emilio Azcarraga, the head of Televisa, Mexico's biggest network, threw a private party with fireworks exploding over Acapulco Bay. Pierce was in high spirits and flaunted his newfound power before the network's top executives and its affiliate guests. In confidential conversations with Goldenson, Rule had reluctantly agreed to become the network's vice chairman.

Only a few insiders knew that spring that Rule had reluctantly agreed to make way for Pierce by becoming ABC's new vice chairman. The move was a titular ratification of his ebbing power and of Pierce's new status as Goldenson's official heir apparent. One insider who did know was Thomas Murphy, the head of Capital Cities Communications, ABC's largest affiliate group, who invited Pierce to speak at his annual gathering of TV station managers in

Phoenix. It was the first chance for Capital Cities to meet privately with the executives who filled their local airwaves with programming.

Pierce was feeling bullish about the future and spoke expansively to Murphy. "If they ever change the seven-seven-seven rule," he said, referring to the FCC rule limiting network ownership to seven local TV stations, "we ought to get our companies together."

It was the first mention that Capital Cities and ABC might merge. Pierce, of course, assumed that the network would be doing the buying and Capital Cities the selling.

In May 1983, Elton Rule stood at the podium of the Century Plaza ballroom and delivered his concession speech. The affiliates listened closely as he spoke in a measured and dignified tone.

"In the twenty-five years I've been attending these affiliate meetings, I've worn a number of different hats," Rule began, and listed the various titles he had held during his long career. "Next year at this time you'll see me wearing a different hat. I will be Elton Rule, private citizen."

Rule did not expound on his reasons for leaving. All he would say publicly was, "This hasn't been an easy decision for me to make. When you've given as much of your life to an organization as I have, and when you've enjoyed it as much as I have, it's difficult to walk away. But it seems to me this is the *right* time to leave." He had told Pierce and Goldenson privately, "You can't have three men running a company." So instead of staying on and jollying the network through the rest of the decade, the odd man out had decided to resign.

Even as Rule announced his departure, the affiliates had to be reassured. The outgoing executive was called on to convey the upbeat message. "Legacy," "caring," "grace," and "sunshine"—the words other speakers employed to bid him farewell—were mixed with "management team still in place" in Rule's speech-making that day.

But his stately veneer broke down near the end of his prepared remarks. Rule's voice wavered as he described what he was leaving behind, and his eyes shone with tears. When he had finished, the affiliates rose as a group to their feet, and gave him a standing ovation.

Goldenson, with moist eyes too, followed Rule at the speaker's podium.

"Several years ago Elton informed me there would come a time when he would want to move on," Goldenson began. "That time is here, and this is his own decision. I'm going to miss him."

He looked straight at Rule.

"Elton, I have an extraordinary, special feeling about you."

The two men embraced on stage, Rule stepped off and kissed his wife, and then Pierce took him by the elbow and led him back up again.

"It's going to be difficult for me," Pierce began spontaneously. With no text to guide him, he paused and dabbed his wet eyes with a handkerchief. Rule leaned forward to the microphone.

"It's easy for me," he joked.

"We've worked together fifteen years," Pierce continued. "He's been a teacher, a terrific boss, a wonderful associate . . . "

Pierce stopped, again at a loss for words.

"Don't let it get you, Fred," Rule said. The difficult moment was over, and he now wore a broad grin.

"And above all, he's been a terrific tennis partner," Pierce went on. "Somehow I was always the guy running back for the lobs."

"It's going to remain that way," Rule interrupted gleefully.

"That was the first time I knew I was going to have to do the work," Pierce said, still speaking of the past, "and Elton was going to do the leading."

A loud guffaw erupted in the back of the ballroom at the implied criticism in the remark, and Pierce involuntarily joined in the laughter, releasing nervous tension.

161

10

Hollywood Fleece

At the beginning of the 1982–83 season Fred Pierce was on top of the world. In the twenty-seven years that had passed since he had first arrived at the network as a chubby ex-accountant in network research, he appeared to have changed in all the right ways. Pierce was lean and strong in his middle age. When he walked through the revolving doors at 1330 Avenue of the Americas in the morning, the *New York Times* and *Wall Street Journal* tucked under his arm, the skin drawn tight against his jaw, and his fingernails lacquered and polished, he looked every inch the part of a modern corporate president.

After ten years of running ABC Television, Pierce was accustomed to the trappings of power. He oversaw contracts totaling billions of dollars. His annual take-home salary was nearly $1 million, not counting year-end bonuses and stock options (which Pierce promptly sold). It was a long way from Bensonhurst to the Colorado Rockies, where he owned a condominium. Pierce taught himself to ski with the same rugged resolve that had brought him to the top at ABC. He wasn't quite there yet, but he was within reach of the brass ring. With Goldenson almost eighty years old, the actuarial clock was ticking away.

Pierce's new appointment made barely a ripple in the company rank and file. His signature replaced Rule's on employee ID cards, and that was it. Everyone turned in their old cards, sat for a new picture, and waited for it to be laminated in plastic. It was like getting a driver's license renewed. For employees, there was nothing much to improve. Matching stock, full medical coverage with provisions for maternity leave, and a company-sponsored dental plan were all part of the benefits package that Elton Rule had instituted. Camera operators, broadcast engineers, news and sports producers, and other union personnel even had a clause in their contracts guaranteeing first-class air fare when they traveled on company business.

Members of the new-boys network benefited the most from Pierce's rise. When the appointment was announced in early 1983, Thomopoulos and Gary Pudney put on a fete. Pudney arranged the party details. Thomopoulos flew from Hollywood especially for the event. As the waiters at the 21 Club poured Cristal champagne into tall, thin-stemmed glasses, the small crowd milled around the Puncheon Room, confident in the knowledge that "their" man had won. Joan Wechsler, Pierce's secretary-cum-confidante for nearly twenty years, moved joyfully through the room. To one guest she looked like a Jewish bride dancing a hora.

Like Rule before him, Pierce put his own personal stamp on the company. He promoted Everett Erlick, the network's general counsel, and Michael Mallardi, its chief financial officer, to executive vice presidencies—moves that left them in the same posts with a cosmetic title change. He named Mark Cohen to the executive committee of the company management, a first leg up toward a seat on the board of directors. When Brandon Stoddard refused the presidency of ABC Entertainment, Pierce promoted Lew Erlicht to the job instead. Tony Thomopoulos, he installed atop a brand-new division—the ABC Broadcast Group, which comprised all operations in radio and television. Thomopoulos once again began reporting directly to Pierce.

When the music had ended and the chairs were filled, the

new regime looked exactly like the old one, except for new titles and higher salaries. But the network had changed from being an organization that prized audacity and youthful creativity to one where authority was bottled up for fear of failure. The new-boys' network had become a sycophantic old-boys' club.

By the simplest network measure—the prime-time ratings—the bottom began to fall out from under Pierce at the start of the 1982–83 season. "Joanie Loves Chachi," the "Happy Days" spin-off, which had scored well at 8:30 on Tuesday night, was moved to Thursday, a night where the network had experienced ratings difficulties since the problems with "Mork & Mindy" three years earlier. Only the modest success of "The Greatest American Hero," an hour-long comedy from producer Stephen J. Cannell, had kept ABC in the running on Thursday.

Pierce and Thomopoulos shifted "Joanie Loves Chachi" and "Too Close for Comfort," an established Tuesday night series, in the expectations that they would anchor a new Thursday lineup. Against CBS's "Magnum, P.I." and "Simon & Simon," both shows promptly died. Decay was slowly spreading through the entire prime-time schedule.

Thomopoulos, who along with Lew Erlicht was the executive most responsible for the programming decline, displayed a curious insouciance toward the prime-time series genre. Series "are not the essence of this business," he told *American Film* magazine in 1979. "They make it happen, but they're not the essence." Thomopoulos' interest as a programmer had always run toward feature films.

Unfortunately for ABC, prime-time series were the essential ingredient of any successful network schedule—and in late 1982, the network was floundering in this regard. It had not aired a new, sure-fire concept in situation comedy since "Happy Days," and the "Happy Days"/"Laverne and Shirley" brand of comedy was on its last legs, as the failure of "Joanie Loves Chachi" had demonstrated.

ABC had a new show called "Ripley's Believe It or Not" on Sunday at 7 P.M. It was up against the perennial favorite "60 Minutes" and had little chance of a real success. ABC chose the heaviest viewing night of the week to cut its losses by scheduling low budget shows like "Ripley" and "Those Amazing Animals" in the lead-off time period.

For public consumption, Thomopoulos tried to make light of the network's faltering series lineup. One Tuesday when the weekly Nielsens had just come out, showing an even more dismal performance than expected, he stepped into a crowded Century City elevator and joked about the new Sunday night show: "There are more people in this elevator than there are watching 'Ripley's Believe It or Not.'"

It drew a light laugh, but when Peter Boyer, then a TV reporter for the *Los Angeles Times*, overheard the remark and used it in a story about ABC's declining ratings, the joke suddenly didn't seem so funny to Thomopoulos. Thomopoulos called up Boyer.

"You cocksucking asshole liar!" he screamed at him over the telephone.

By the beginning of the 1982–83 season, Thomopoulos was beginning to feel cornered. He had been riding Pierce's coattails for almost a decade, doing what little he could to maintain the programming legacy that Silverman had left behind. He had tried to work with Marcy Carsey and Tom Werner, whom he had appointed as virtual coheads of new series development between 1979 and 1981. But as Pierce's yes man, Thomopoulos' power to fashion a competitive schedule was inherently limited. When entertainment staffers from the East Coast visited his office in Hollywood, Thomopoulos would ask them to leave the room whenever Pierce telephoned. Pierce issued his instructions; the subordinates were then ushered back in, and according to one of them, "Tony looked like he'd been hit over the head with a pile of bricks."

Pierce took his programming comfort where he could find it— in Esther Shapiro's "Dynasty," and in the continuing success of Brandon Stoddard's made-for-TV movies and miniseries. Backed by the network's most intensive on-air promotion campaign ever,

Herman Wouk's "The Winds of War" aired that February. "The Thorn Birds," Colleen McCullough's steamy melodrama of the Australian outback, was broadcast in March, and it scored the highest ratings of any TV miniseries since "Roots." But except for Stoddard's output, ABC was coasting on high-gloss Aaron Spelling melodramas and tired, recycled comedies.

During the program development cycle for 1981–82, Pierce had redefined the audience orientation of ABC's prime-time programming. The baby boomers were growing into their middle years, and research data in New York indicated that Madison Avenue advertisers were more likely to buy air time on TV shows that appealed to older viewers. So Pierce tilted the network's target demographic upward. Instead of developing new series for teenagers, like "The Brady Bunch" and "Happy Days," the staff in Hollywood was told to come up with new recipes to attract an average thirty-year-old viewer.

Pierce had hoped to widen the network's existing edge in audience demographics with this programming shift. What he discovered instead was that switching prime-time formulas in New York was easier than finding new creative ideas—and producers to execute them—in Hollywood. "The Fall Guy," a new series starring Lee Majors, was the only ABC show to fit Pierce's specifications in the 1981–82 season, and it attracted an audience typically associated with CBS shows—older, rural viewers. ABC had lost its handle on younger city dwellers. In allowing research to dictate programming development, Pierce had played into CBS's strength and provided an opening for third-place NBC.

One new pilot in development at ABC in the fall of 1982 was "Hotel," a high-gloss melodrama from Aaron Spelling based on Arthur Hailey's popular novel. Another was "Concrete Beat," a police show along "Hill Street Blues" lines; it was produced by Glenn Gordon Caron, who later created "Moonlighting," but when the two pilots came up for review, "Concrete Beat" lost out to "Hotel." There was only one time slot open on the schedule: 10 P.M. on Wednesday night, right after "Dynasty." "Hotel" followed "Dynasty" naturally, and during the 1983–84 season it would turn into ABC's first Top Ten hit, except for "Dynasty" itself, since 1979. But the decision to go for "Hotel" turned as much on the network's contractual need to fulfill its on-air commitment to Spelling as on creative considerations. In spurning Caron, a new talent, ABC had lapsed back to the tried and true. However strong its Wednesday night programming combination of "Dynasty" and "Hotel" might be, it was essentially an imitation of CBS's "Dallas"/ "Falcon Crest" pairing on Friday. The network was playing catch-up with the competition.

With the development pipeline clogged, the odds that a young producer in Hollywood could get a pilot on ABC were so slim that emerging talent stopped pitching their best ideas at Century City. Even big-name, proven suppliers were having creative troubles at the network.

Every new season there was a highly touted and highly promoted program from ABC that seemed destined to become a hit. In the second season of 1980–81 it was "Tenspeed and Brown Shoe," an hour-long show from producer Stephen J. Cannell. The next spring it was "American Dream," a "realistic" hour-long drama about a working-class family produced by Barney Rosenzweig. The next fall it was "Best of the West," a half-hour farce from Paramount. All of them were adroitly conceived, well-cast, and launched with fanfare. All of them scored high ratings at first—and then rolled belly-up. The "Mork & Mindy" syndrome, in which hit shows suddenly flopped, seemed to have spread through the schedule like a disease.

The typical response of Pierce and Thomopoulos when a show did not pan out was to juggle the time slot, put it "on hiatus," and then cancel it outright. Besides offending Hollywood producers, such quick cancellations tended to accelerate the ongoing talent drain. A show's cancellation usually involved a promise by the network to pick up a fresh pilot from the studio that owned the rejected property. Then, instead of choosing freely among a wide variety of producers, the programming staff at Century City had to fulfill contractual obligations imposed by scheduling decisions made in New York.

In late 1981 when Lew Erlicht was promoted into the white office, ABC Entertainment had fifty-one script and pilot commitments to "burn off." Some dated as far back as the multipilot deal that Pierce and Thomopoulos had made with Paramount, during the 1978 "Happy Days" renewal. Others were more recent, but the overwhelming backlog did not bode well for the development of fresh new programming.

Stephen J. Cannell, one of Hollywood's leading independent producers, got an especially bitter taste of ABC's mishandling of its creative commitments. As a writer-producer at Universal Television, Cannell had forged one of the best records in Hollywood. He regularly took series ideas from concept to script, to pilot, to full series. He had helped put "Baretta" on ABC's schedule during the second half of the 1974–75 season, and produced "The Rockford Files," an hour-long private eye show that starred James Garner; it was an audience favorite on NBC in the late 1970s.

In 1979, when Cannell went into business for himself, Thomopoulos signed him up at ABC. The first-look, three-pilot deal gave Cannell start-up money for his new company. The network bought an option on his first three shows, and agreed to pay penalty points if it did not buy the pilots and air them as series. A first-look deal was the next best thing to an on-air guarantee, like Aaron Spelling's. Thomopoulos hoped that Cannell would develop into a network supplier along Spelling lines.

Cannell's first series for ABC was "Tenspeed and Brown Shoe," featuring an "odd couple" team of private eyes. Jeff Goldblum played the white stockbroker, Ben Vereen the black ex-con artist, and the show premiered midway through the 1979–80 season in the Sunday-night time slot just vacated by "Mork & Mindy." Thomopoulos billed "Tenspeed" as the cornerstone of ABC's second-season effort, and backed it with an extensive on-air promotion campaign. It broke big, got a large audience sampling, and then fell precipitously. Pierce and Thomopoulos moved it to a new night and time period; the show sank further. They moved it again, and it dropped out of sight.

"The Greatest American Hero," Cannell's second series, fared better. This mild Superman spoof premiered in the second season of 1980–81, and lasted for a full season on Thursday at 9 P.M. "Hero" was not a big hit, but it attracted teenagers and scored consistent ratings.

In April 1982, when ABC introduced its fall season lineup for 1982–83 to Madison Avenue, Lew Erlicht stood on stage in the Ziegfeld Theater on 54th Street in New York. The network was still flush with Thomopoulos' second-season win, and advertisers were curious to find out whether it had been a flash in the pan. Nothing would tell them more quickly than what Erlicht announced for Friday night in the time period against "Dallas."

At the time, CBS still held the Number One spot in the prime-time ratings. Except for "Little House on the Prairie," NBC had not had a Nielsen Top Ten hit since 1977. But NBC had hired Grant Tinker, the respected Hollywood producer, to replace Fred Silverman, and Tinker had kept Brandon Tartikoff as president of NBC Entertainment. While airing "quality" programming, NBC had fallen badly in the ratings during Tinker's first year and a half on the job. It was now in even worse shape than Silverman had left it. At Century City Tartikoff was remembered as the guy in current comedy who couldn't get a development job, and NBC, the third-place network, was the butt of jokes.

Erlicht introduced the new ABC lineup night-by-night, time period by time period. Friday night was the last one projected on the big Ziegfeld screen. And "The Greatest American Hero," Cannell's Superman spoof, was scheduled against "Dallas." While the audience gasped, Erlicht gave mumbo-jumbo assurances about "two-television homes," implying that "Hero" would be watched by kids while adults watched "Dallas." In fact ABC was ducking CBS, reverting to counter-programming, and had consigned Cannell's show to cancellation. No self-respecting teenager would be caught dead at home on a Friday night. To rub salt in the wound, Pierce and Thomopoulos had scheduled Cannell's third series, a throwaway called "The Quest," at 10 P.M. on Friday, where it would have to face "Falcon Crest." Both series were headed for extinction.

The logic to this cavalier treatment dated back two years, when "Tenspeed" was taking its nose-dive in the ratings. After producing a brilliant pilot, Cannell had experienced disastrous budget over-runs, and called Thomopoulos.

"Look, I'm in real trouble here," Cannell said. "I'm going to have to pull back the production value on the show, or you guys are going to have to come up with more money."

If Hollywood studios like Paramount went over budget, they usually ate the short-term losses and made up the difference with the next successful series. But Cannell, who was just starting out as an independent producer, faced bankruptcy.

"We won't let you go under," Thomopoulos replied. "We won't wash you clean, but we won't let you go under."

After ABC had bailed out Cannell on "Tenspeed," and Thomopoulos had swallowed his pride at having the show fall flat, Thomopoulos and Pierce thought they owned the producer and could do whatever they pleased with the series that remained in his original contract. But circumstances interfered.

Although he was now working on budget in 1982–83, Cannell once again faced bankruptcy. The networks were insisting that Hollywood producers deficit-finance new series—that is, produce them at a loss, making up the difference later through syndication sales (in which the networks were forbidden by the FCC to share). Cannell had a $100,000 deficit on each episode of his remaining series, yet neither seemed likely to survive long enough to go into syndication.

Cannell did, however, have one old pilot commitment left from his days at Universal, and when "Hero" and "The Quest" died on ABC, he fell back on it. Brandon Tartikoff was toying with a new second-season idea: He wanted to develop a hybrid of "The Dirty Dozen" and "Mission: Impossible," using the action-adventure genre to appeal to kids. Sensing that Cannell was in trouble, Tartikoff called him up and proposed that he produce the new series for NBC at Universal.

"The A Team," Cannell's new series, premiered on NBC right after that network's broadcast of the Super Bowl in January 1983.

It was the real McCoy—a breakout hit, a Top Ten show that found its own audience without any help from existing shows. "The A Team" yanked NBC out of its lethargy, and Tartikoff, making matters worse for ABC, ingeniously scheduled it against "Happy Days," at 8 P.M. on Tuesday night. In short, Cannell, whom ABC had put into business as an independent producer, had ended up delivering his first hit series to a competing network.

To rub it in, Mr. T, "The A Team" 's star, appeared in a special on-air promotion during the Super Bowl. Brandishing a Mohawk-style haircut, Mr. T jabbed a black finger at the TV screen, rattled the gold bracelets around his linebacker-sized forearm, and said in a gruff, mean voice: "Fonzie, your happy days are over."

Teenagers all across America heard the line and laughed.

"It was like 'Happy Days' was hit with a bullet," Lew Erlicht recalled ruefully.

"I'm going to bring in Hollywood," Leonard Goldenson had vowed in 1953—and for almost three decades Hollywood and network TV had observed an uneasy truce. In 1983 they abandoned all pretense of belonging to the same industry and waged a war over prime-time profits in Washington, D.C.

No new situation comedy had swept the American TV audience off its feet for years, but Hollywood was about to perpetrate a hilariously entertaining joke. The premise had to do with the government agency that regulated broadcasting and the "D" word, or deregulation.

The deregulation tide had started under Jimmy Carter with the natural gas, airline, and financial services industries on the principle that fixed prices and commissions were less efficient than free-market competition. By the time Ronald Reagan was elected, Washington had already dismantled many of its old rules and procedures. Except for network TV, the broadcasting and telecommunications industries had been largely deregulated. AT&T was in the midst of an antitrust proceeding that would lead to the court-ordered breakup of its massive corporation. Satellite technology had prompted the FCC to repeal many of the rules that had hindered the growth of the cable industry in the past. Charles Ferris, the outgoing FCC chairman, had started to relax the procedures for renewing government licenses at local radio and TV stations.

When Mark Fowler, Reagan's FCC chairman, arrived in town, network TV was the only industry sector not yet touched by the deregulatory fervor—and Fowler had big plans for it. A lanky ex-radio broadcaster from Florida and staunch proponent of "getting government off the backs of business," Fowler followed two basic principles. He believed that the only valid purpose of regulation was to facilitate the workings of a free marketplace. He also believed that the First Amendment did not allow him to interfere with the rights of broadcasters.

"I am not your shepherd, and you are not my flock," Fowler said shortly after taking office in 1981. "The public interest is what interests the public."

Fowler looked through the Federal Register for several months, searching for rules to discard while building the majority among his fellow commissioners that he would need to implement his agenda. Then he stepped smack into the most sensitive area of Hollywood-network relations—the 1970 financial-interest and syndication rules.

Whenever a new TV show entered development, a number of touchy issues had to be resolved. How much would the series cost per episode? What would the license fee be? How could the interests of both parties—the network and the studio producer—be accommodated if it was canceled?

Until a few years before Mark Fowler, such questions had been answered through an elaborate set of network customs and Hollywood rituals. The networks mainly paid the bills, and the actors and producers bowed and scraped. There was no question about where the ultimate power in television entertainment lay. The TV networks, the buyer and distributor, held the industry purse strings.

Washington's rules kept the networks from actually *owning* the TV programs that Hollywood produced, so the $1 million on average that ABC, NBC, and CBS paid for an hour-long series was just a license fee. It allowed a network to air the program twice, in one original and one repeat broadcast. The studio usually owned all the rerun returns.

Just as Mark Fowler took office, the old programming customs and rituals started to break down. Independent TV stations and cable networks developed as new sources of off-network revenue. ABC, NBC, and CBS resorted to deficit financing and forced producers to supply series for which the license fee did not cover all the costs of production. Producers, in turn, were more open in their resentment toward network intrusions in their creative decision-making.

If Fowler was successful in lifting the program-ownership rules, the networks would use their vast distribution leverage to negotiate a financial interest in the programs they aired. ABC, NBC, and CBS would eventually take over the studios or form new ones. They would be freer to monopolize the entertainment business than anyone had been since the breakup of the movie-theater chains after World War II.

That was why Hollywood decided to fight.

One old Hollywood hand in Washington took a special interest in Fowler's deregulatory plans for network TV—Ronald Reagan. In the late 1940s, when his career as an actor began to fade, Reagan's career as a politician was just beginning. He was president of the Screen Actor's Guild (SAG) before and during the red-baiting McCarthy years. As an FBI informant, Reagan added fresh names to the Hollywood blacklists at a time when more than 2,000 of his fellow actors, producers, and writers were losing their livelihoods in the studio slowdowns that resulted from the 1948 divorcement decree. In 1952, using these out-of-work actors as his justification, he helped orchestrate a SAG waiver that put his movie agent, Lew Wasserman, the head of MCA, into the TV programming business.

Wasserman, a former theater usher from Cleveland with al-leged mob ties, wanted to get a jump on the competition by adding a TV production arm to MCA's talent-agency business while the movie studios were still boycotting the medium. In the final year of Reagan's SAG presidency, he asked the guild for a waiver of an old rule prohibiting talent agencies from producing movies. The principle, which also related to the production of TV shows (and, in the financial-interest and syndication rules, to the Big Three networks entering the syndication market), held that it was unfair to the competition to be both a buyer and a seller of the same product. A talent agency that produced prime-time shows would favor its own client list; a network that owned "Happy Days" would give it a prime scheduling slot and sell it to independent stations ahead of a Hollywood-owned series.

No minutes of the crucial SAG meeting were kept, but Reagan steered Wasserman's request through to unanimous approval—a blanket waiver of the rule in MCA's behalf. Nancy Davis, the actress who would shortly become Reagan's second wife, was one of the Guild members who voted to approve Wasserman's petition. When other Hollywood talent agencies later asked for similar ex-emptions, they received only limited waivers, which allowed them to produce for TV on a show-by-show basis. MCA alone regularly buttered its bread on both sides, so to speak. It produced TV series *and* represented actors and prospered through the 1950s—and Reagan was a leading beneficiary of its success. In 1954, when he was washed up as an actor and needed cash to pay back taxes so badly that he had worked as a "greeter" at society parties, Wasserman hired him as the host and program supervisor of "Gen-eral Electric Theater," a show that MCA produced for CBS. The salary was $125,000 per year. Among his new duties, Reagan toured the country as General Electric's spokesman—the role that even-tually became the launching pad for his career as a politician.

Reagan still wasn't disenchanted enough with liberal politics to serve as a convincing spokesman for conservative interests, but his actions on behalf of MCA led to a humiliating Washington experience that provided ample motivation. By 1960 MCA's profits from its TV shows far surpassed its earnings as a talent agency, and Wasserman engineered a takeover of Decca Records, which owned Universal Pictures, one of Hollywood's biggest studios. The antitrust aspects of the buyout led Robert F. Kennedy, then the Attorney General, to conduct a lengthy criminal investigation of the company (perhaps inspired by Wasserman's alleged mob ties as much as by the suspicious SAG waiver); Reagan was questioned at length by Justice Department investigators.

"I spent a long, unhappy afternoon being interrogated by a federal lawyer who'd seen too many 'Perry Masons,' " Reagan recalled in his autobiography, *Where's the Rest of Me?*

Kennedy ultimately dropped the criminal investigation without filing charges and allowed MCA to buy Decca-Universal—after forcing Wasserman to sign a consent decree relinquishing his talent-agency business. Reagan was forced to resign from his job on "General Electric Theater." The termination was the final straw in Reagan's rupture with mainstream 1960s politics; by 1964 he was an ardent spokesmen for the kind of government noninterference that Mark Fowler, his FCC chairman, was espousing twenty years later. Wasserman fared better immediately—with Universal under his wing, he became a worthy successor to Adolph Zukor and Nick Schenck as the new dean of Hollywood. In 1966 he selected Jack Valenti, the terrier-sized special assistant and confidant of Lyndon Baines Johnson, as the new head of the Motion Pictures Association of America, to ensure that Hollywood got the best treatment possible in Washington.

Hollywood, the Big Three networks, and other interested parties argued their cases, for or against, "on the merits" before Mark Fowler and his fellow commissioners. These discussions continued for almost a year before the agency issued its first tentative ruling. The three "neutral" Reagan Administration participants—the Federal Trade Commission, the Justice Department, and the Commerce Department—all sided with the networks during public hearings. Unless extraordinary pressures were brought to bear,

Hollywood would have to bid against its own former customers, the networks, for the ownership of America's TV programs.

Then Tim Wirth, the Colorado congressman who chaired the House Telecommunications Subcommittee and was an avid Hollywood supporter, traveled to the West Coast. Meeting with movie-industry representatives—Barry Diller and Michael Eisner were among them, lobbying hard to defeat the measure—he exhorted them to use the most powerful weapons at their disposal.

"Get me *real people*," Wirth implored. And so the stars came to town.

The Fonz visited Washington during cherry-blossom season, when Capitol Hill was packed with tourists who gawked and stared at the Hollywood star ("You're right, it's me," he greeted them cheerfully). As Wirth had expected, his presence made the Hollywood case more real to people who, when they returned home, changed back from tourists into voters.

While "Happy Days" was faltering in the ratings, the actor Henry Winkler had fallen back on the long-term development deal he had signed with ABC in 1978, and was now an aspiring producer as well as one of America's best-known sitcom stars. The last thing Winkler wanted to lose, now that he owned a stake in his programs, was the special negotiating leverage and subsidies that the financial interest and syndication rules gave him in his dealings with ABC. In the office of Congressman Bates of California, he described the positive influence that his "Happy Days" role had exercised on an entire generation of young TV viewers.

"Hey, anyone can own a library card," was one line Winkler remembered particularly. The "Happy Days" writers had wanted to show that tough guys like the Fonz could read books too. But the network censors often abused their buyers' prerogatives, Winkler said, by trying to delete socially redeeming dialogue in scripts.

Bates interrupted the lobbying session to take a telephone call from his daughter. After talking briefly to her, he handed the receiver to Winkler. "You're talking to the wrong person," he said.

Winkler took the receiver. "Hello, whatever your name is," he said gruffly, gliding smoothly into the role of the Fonz. "What are you doing? I hope you're doing your homework. You're not? You're playing with a girlfriend? When are you going to do your homework?"

It worked like a charm. As the lobbying session ended, the Washington professional who was accompanying Winkler turned to Bates: "Now will you co-sponsor our bill, Congressman?"

The bill, proposed by Henry Waxman, the Congressman from Hollywood, mandated a five-year moratorium on any change in the FCC rules.

Bates smiled. "Not yet," he replied. "But you're on the right track."

A few weeks later, Alan Alda of "M*A*S*H" came to town. Like Winkler, he was both an actor and a producer, and well-versed in the art of subtle persuasion. After making the lobbying rounds with the FCC commissioners in the morning, he stopped to get something to eat at the corner fruit stand outside the agency.

"How much is it?" Alda asked the vendor after selecting some fruit. The vendor, looking up, opened his eyes wide in disbelief.

"Hawkeye! Hawkeye! Jesus, God! It's Hawkeye!" he gasped. "Take 'em, take 'em!"

The politicians were no different from the man in the street. When Alda arrived on Capitol Hill for his first afternoon appointment, there were camera crews from the Congressman's local TV station setting up equipment. Cosponsoring the Hollywood bill was a small price to pay for the privilege of appearing with Hawkeye Pierce on the evening news in Pittsburgh. The actor's lobbying session was the politician's photo opportunity.

A few weeks later Hollywood rolled out its biggest gun—J. R. Ewing. He came to visit Congressman Jim Wright of Texas, who happened to be his old high school boxing coach in Weatherford, Texas, where J. R., a.k.a. Larry Hagman, had grown up with his mother, Mary Martin. The former boy mayor of Weatherford had invited the star of "Dallas" to speak at the bipartisan luncheon of the Texas delegation that took place in Washington every Wednesday while Congress was in session.

J. R. was wearing a pale-gray suit, black alligator-skin cowboy boots, and a ten-gallon hat. He carried a black alligator-skin-covered walking stick. Little white oil derricks were woven into his thin black tie. He went right to the point. "Why give more power to the cartel?" J. R. asked.

The Congressmen all laughed. The men from Texas knew what Hagman meant. They had the Seven Sisters of the oil industry to compare with the Big Three of network TV.

As the summer of 1983 progressed, finding a way to stop Mark Fowler's deregulatory initiative became a top priority of the Reagan White House. Fowler had put Reagan in a difficult position. Any White House intervention in Hollywood's behalf would lead to glaring publicity about the favor Reagan had performed for Wasserman in 1952. The past incident was so unethical that bringing it to light would embarrass the President.

Early in the fall the White House staff summoned Fowler to brief Reagan on FCC activities. The meeting was not on the President's public calendar. Fowler arrived with an aide and was ushered into the Oval Office, where the entire senior staff of Reagan's first term—Edwin Meese, James Baker, Michael Deaver, Richard Darman, Craig Fuller, and David Gergen—greeted him. Knowing that Caspar Weinberger had deployed visual aids in his presentation for the Pentagon military buildup, Fowler brought out charts and graphs to help the President grasp the essentials of the FCC rules change. Instead of MX missiles, tanks, and soldiers, however, Fowler's charts displayed the syndication revenues of "M*A*S*H," the most profitable TV sitcom that Hollywood had ever produced. The point he wanted to make was that the networks were being excluded from sharing in the off-network profits.

"CBS charts," Richard Darman remarked dryly.

"Yes, but they're right," Fowler replied.

Reagan, who in this case didn't need the benefit of charts, hardly spoke at all during the hour-long meeting. He let a deeper message sink in. "Change your mind while it's still possible," he seemed to be saying to Fowler. "Larger forces than you are at play here."

Hollywood's Competition in Television Act, which would deny

Fowler "the authority to take any action before July 1, 1988, to repeal, amend or otherwise modify" the financial interest and syndication rules, was in subcommittee as the summer ended, but Jack Valenti still counted on Congressional disaffection with the networks to push it through. To say that there was no love lost between most of Washington's elected officials and the networks was a royal understatement.

The politicians and the networks both tended to appeal to the lowest common denominator in the viewer and the voter. Both had grown bloated at the trough of the "public interest." And both shared the dirty secrets of lovers who detest yet depend on each other. Incumbent politicians depended on the "fairness" of election-year coverage as much as they did on campaign advertising. And network broadcasters depended on Washington's licensing largess for the pursuit of their immensely profitable business. The guilty consciences of both parties, who depended on each other for their existence but were loath to admit it, had turned the networks' Washington dealings nasty and brutish. Hollywood, by contrast, practiced a pure form of corruption—edifying most when it instructed least. It could be hypocritical and free of cant at the same time.

On a variety of issues ranging from perceived liberal news bias, to the network's use of exit polls and willful disregard of the needs of children's programming, many Washington politicians wanted to teach ABC, NBC, and CBS a lesson—and Jack Valenti, Hollywood's top lobbyist, handed them an excuse. With help from compliant legislators, he attached the substance of the Competition in Television Act as a rider to the supplemental appropriations bill that Congress *had* to pass that fall to keep the government functioning. Senator Ted Stevens (R., Alaska), who chaired the Republican-led Senate Appropriations Committee, was Hollywood's leading sponsor. Stevens was the special guest at a political fundraising party hosted by Lew Wasserman in Los Angeles. In October, when the supplemental appropriations bill came up for a vote, a vote *for* the bill would be counted as a vote to deny Fowler the money he needed to change the FCC rules.

Leonard Goldenson in 1980 Ben Weaver, Camera 5

David Sarnoff, wireless operator. Sarnoff (left) with Guglielmo Marconi
Culver Pictures

William Paley as a young man
Culver Pictures

Adolph Zukor Culver Pictures

Elton Rule Elton H. Rule

Roone Arledge Ken Regan, Camera 5

Fred Silverman Peter C. Borsari

*Barry Diller with Barbara
Walters* Peter C. Borsari

*Michael Eisner with Cindy Williams (left)
and Penny Marshall* Peter C. Borsari

Howard Cosell Ben Weaver, Camera 5

*Aaron Spelling with Linda Evans
(left) and Joan Collins*
AP/Wide World

Mindy Naud Melinda Naud

Beverlee Dean with Lorne Greene
AP/Wide World

Tony Thomopoulos and Cristina Ferrare
Peter C. Borsari

Fred Pierce Peter C. Borsari

Tom Murphy (left) *with Laurence Tisch* AP/Wide World

Senator Bob Packwood (R., Oregon), who chaired the Commerce Committee, had parliamentary jurisdiction over FCC matters, and was a network ally. A few hours before the Senate was scheduled to vote, Packwood attempted to delete the rider. Behind closed doors, Stevens refused to yield. The issue spilled onto the Senate floor, where Packwood rose to his feet and appealed to the Senate chairman. The upper chamber's parliamentary rules provided for the deletion of nongermane riders on appropriations bills, so the chairman ordered the rider removed.

All one hundred Senators were waiting to vote on the appropriations measure and had to choose sides in an up-and-down accounting of Capitol Hill sentiment about network TV. "How do I fuck the networks on this one?" one of their distinguished number, who had not previously been instructed on the issue, was overheard asking his neighbor.

When all the Yeas and Nays were tallied, fifty-seven Senators had voted against their own parliamentary rules to thwart Fowler's deregulatory initiative. The issue was still not closed, but the majority gave the White House the opening it needed to administer the coup de grace.

On November 1, less than twenty-four hours before Barry Goldwater's Senate Communications Subcommittee was scheduled to take up the matter in public hearings, the White House summoned David Markey and William Baxter, its Commerce and Justice Department representatives, to a late-night meeting. In previous testimony, both had spoken in favor of the network position. They were now instructed to change their views. A letter from Edwin Meese, special counsel to the President, communicated Reagan's official new policy on the FCC matter to Senator Pete Wilson (R.) of California.

"After careful consideration of this matter," Senator Wilson read gleefully into the record the next morning in Barry Goldwater's public hearings, "the President has decided to support a two-year legislatively mandated moratorium in the syndication and financial interest rule."

"What facts have occurred in the last two weeks to change the

Department of Commerce's position on this issue?" Bob Packwood asked David Markey.

"Well, no facts except that our boss, who is the President, has decided that there is a change," Markey replied.

"Mr. Baxter, is your position the same as Mr. Markey's now?" Wendell Ford (D., Kentucky) asked the Justice Department representative.

"Well, I would certainly not have agreed that the President changed his mind," Baxter replied.

"What is the extreme thing that gets the White House?" Ernest Hollings (D., South Carolina) fulminated. "They have got Grenada and Lebanon, and all of a sudden they find now that the President has studied this. I hope he is not studying it. He has got too many more important things to find out about than movie producers and network producers."

Barry Goldwater, the grand old Republican of the Senate, also found Reagan's intervention troublesome. "I have had only one conversation with the President, and that was at eleven last night," Goldwater volunteered. "I told him that I thought he was doing something he shouldn't."

Anyone seeking the source of the sleaze factor, illegal lobbying, and conflict-of-interest scandals in Ronald Reagan's second term should look no further than this exercise of Presidential leadership. In the battle over the financial-interest and syndication rules in 1983, Reagan followed his own example, the one he had set in his 1952 dealings with his former agent, Lew Wasserman. This time, his protectionism extended beyond helping out a friend for personal gain. It had saved the entire movie and TV production community from a deregulating network incursion.

While Everett Erlick, ABC's top lobbyist, sat fuming in the hearing room, Reagan neatly pulled out the rug from under Mark Fowler and the Big Three networks' hope of regulatory relief. The Capitol Hill solution to stalemate was to take the FCC matter off the rule-making calendar and to declare it a topic for "industry negotiations." While the studios retained their special-interest protection, the networks remained shut out of the program-ownership marketplace. Hollywood had kept the network wolf from darkening its door.

ABC, CBS, and NBC were now more vulnerable than ever. With new competition from independent TV stations and satellite-delivered cable networks, their traditional role as industry middlemen was rapidly melting away. And as the controversy over the program-ownership rules wound down, Mark Fowler quietly slipped a fresh item on the FCC's rule-making calendar. After failing to change the government's rules on program ownership, he wanted to try his hand at network distribution. One of the oldest rules on the books prohibited ABC, NBC, CBS, and other big-station groups from owning more than seven local TV stations. American broadcasting had taken shape around the 7-7-7 restriction. When it changed, the networks and the entire industry would go "into play" on Wall Street.

11

The Rot Sets In

At the start of the 1983–84 season ABC was skimming along at high speed without traction, like a car on ice—an accident waiting to happen. Its regulatory underpinnings were about to be removed in Washington. Its creative relationships in Hollywood were in serious disrepair. And Fred Pierce and most of the executives who worked for him were oblivious to the unfolding drama.

ABC's rerun of the miniseries "Masada" that summer gave a premonition of the chasm that was about to open underneath his feet. The miniseries told the story of an army of Roman legions advancing against a proud, stubborn band of Zealots. The Zealots, retreating into the desert, take refuge in a natural fortress of high wilderness rock, while the Roman commander, played by Peter O'Toole in a performance even more camp than his 1962 film portrayal of Lawrence of Arabia, lays siege in the hot plain. Reduced to starvation, the Zealots take their religious pride to the grave, preferring mass suicide to submission.

The "Masada" premiere in the spring of 1981 had been a big audience success, but the repeat broadcast, in the middle of a scorching summer heat wave, nose-dived to an 8.9 and dragged

ABC's full-week ratings to the lowest nonpolitical convention score ever.

Only six months into 1983, Pierce's grace period as president had abruptly ended. (It didn't help that Richard Pearson, his aspiring actor-son, had a bit part in "Masada.") His quick fix for the failure was to insert James Bond movie repeats into the summer schedule. But with the failure of "Masada," the perception had seeped into the company that Pierce himself was damaged goods. The miniseries reflected all too well the fortress mentality in his own personality. When bad news arrived, Pierce "bunkered down," pounded his fist on the table, and jutted his jaw forward. His closest associates had all learned to insulate him from new information that might make him uncomfortable.

"That's an interesting idea, but now's not the time to talk to Fred about it," said Mark Cohen, Pierce's top financial man, when a fresh proposal for off-balance-sheet TV-movie financing reached his desk in the midst of the "Masada" crisis.

It was even rumored that Leonard Goldenson had called Pierce into his office during the summer and given him a little talk about network leadership. The secretaries on the thirty-ninth floor had complained that he was walking right by them every morning without saying hello. A few bold strokes, some top-level firings— anything to shake the network out of its lethargy—would have helped Fred Pierce. But it was not to be.

There was a lot going on at ABC as the new season got underway. ABC was scheduled to air the Winter Olympics from Sarajevo and the Summer Olympics from Los Angeles during the upcoming year. A new presidential campaign was under way. At ABC News and Sports, Roone Arledge would be showcasing his skill at producing live television events, and Pierce was backing him up to the tune of $93 million and $220 million apiece for the broadcast rights alone to Sarajevo and Los Angeles. Together Pierce and Arledge had also committed the network to paying $450 million and $575 million for new long-term NFL and major-league-baseball contracts.

That November the network broadcast "The Day After," Brandon Stoddard's made-for-TV movie about nuclear warfare, whose rave reviews and high ratings momentarily erased the bad taste from "Masada." Under attack by right-wing pressure groups, ABC almost censored the show—until Stoddard flew to New York and threatened to resign if "his" program was altered. The network bowed to the pressure by arranging a "Nightline"-like roundtable after the broadcast, with luminaries like George Schultz and Henry Kissinger pontificating about the alleged impossibility of the show's scenario in real life, and ABC put "Amerika," a new miniseries, into development as a fictional Fairness Doctrine rebuttal.

At Video Enterprises, the bloom was off the rose. Until November 1982, Pierce and Herb Granath were still in an expansive mode. The division was on the verge of adding a joint venture with 20th Century-Fox, Columbia Pictures, and Showtime to its impressive list of new business activities. ABC, alone among the Big Three networks, seemed to be pushing into all key areas of new-technologies programming—in news, sports, and entertainment.

In the superheated environment in the cable industry in late 1982, the various deal makers were hopping in and out of joint ventures like promiscuous starlets into so many beds. Only Pierce believed in monogamy. Less than twenty-four hours before the luncheon meeting where he was supposed to buy a 50 percent stake in Showtime with Columbia and Twentieth Century-Fox, Columbia backed out. It was putting the final touches on a mutually exclusive deal just a few blocks away in midtown Manhattan. A few days later Columbia, HBO, and CBS announced that they were forming Tri-Star Pictures, a new movie studio.

During 1983, as the cable boomlet temporarily fizzled, Video Enterprises was forced to pull back from its earlier, ambitious plans. There were simply too many new cable networks and not enough advertisers and subscribers. CBS Cable went belly-up. So did RCA's Entertainment Channel. And one by one, the ABC ventures ran into difficulty, took on new partners, or expired. ARTS merged with the defunct remains of the Entertainment Channel. Daytime merged with Cable Health Network. "RSVP," the highly touted joint venture in pay-per-view sports with Getty Oil and ESPN, lost upward of $5 million when a boxing tournament organized by Don King turned into a mediocre closed-circuit affair.

But it was Satellite NewsChannel, the joint venture with Group W Satellite Communications, that took the heaviest hit. Initially projected as two twenty-four-hour news networks, Satellite NewsChannel never got past the start-up phase. It had to compete with Ted Turner's Cable News Network, and Turner pulled out all the stops to save his fledgling franchise. When Satellite NewsChannel tried to buy its way onto local cable systems, Turner matched its offer. He almost bankrupted himself in the process, but Satellite NewsChannel lost more than $80 million, and near the end of 1983, instead of staying the course and buying out Turner, ABC and Group W folded their operation and sold their subscribers to him for $25 million. Turner now had the run of the cable TV news field.

A few months after ABC and Group W blinked, the economics of cable networking began to turn around. As redundant networks fell by the wayside, local cable operators began paying carriage fees to the networks that remained—a few pennies per subscriber, but enough to make a palpable difference on Turner's bottom line. CNN, the shoestring operation that Turner had started when Group W bought his nearly bankrupt UHF-TV station in Charlotte, would soon be worth more than $1 billion. By pulling back from Satellite NewsChannel, ABC had lost a potential monopoly in cable TV news.

"I don't think the management of that company is very good," Turner gloated, after he bought Satellite NewsChannel's subscribers from ABC. "CBS and RCA took their losses [in cable] and got out quickly. ABC keeps hanging around, like the U.S. in Vietnam."

Video Enterprises still had TeleFirst in the wings, its late-night direct feed into subscribers' VCRs. In early 1984 it began a trial run in Chicago with an expensive marketing and advertising campaign. The Hollywood studios, most of which had refused to supply it with product, held their collective breath, waiting to see if the service would catch on. They did not want a new network owned by middlemen to control the home distribution of movies. During the first week, consumers flocked to the phones and placed orders.

"We know it's going to be a success, we just don't know how big yet," Arthur Cohen, TeleFirst's president, ventured nervously.

But within a matter of weeks, the bottom fell out of the venture. Many would-be subscribers canceled their orders after having the new service installed. ABC finally decided the project would remain still-born and shut down TeleFirst completely at a loss of $25 million, just three months after it began operations.

By now Video Enterprises had lost more than $110 million while failing to turn a profit, and Goldenson was losing patience. When the Wall Street battle between Pennzoil and Texaco for control of Getty Oil broke out in the spring of 1984, one of the fallouts was that Getty Oil's majority stake in ESPN was put on the auction block.

"Make sure you get an option to buy the whole thing," Goldenson had instructed the ABC lawyers several years before, so that now he had a right of first refusal on the cable sports network. Instead of relying on his gambler's intuition, Goldenson this time instructed Michael Mallardi to investigate all the details of the $220 million purchase. And Mallardi took advantage of the assignment to capitalize on the growing confidence gap between Goldenson and Pierce. When the ABC chairman telephoned him a few months later, shortly before the deal was scheduled to close and asked for an honest opinion, Mallardi replied, "I don't know, Leonard, we don't turn cash-positive on this deal for five or six years."

Five minutes later when Pierce called and asked the same question, Mallardi played on Pierce's enthusiasm.

"It looks terrific, Fred," he told Pierce.

With Rule out of the picture, Goldenson could not get straight talk from anyone but Pierce—and he was trusting Pierce's business judgment less and less. ABC finally agreed to buy ESPN, but

189

Goldenson hedged his bets and sold off 20 percent of it to Nabisco, where Don Ohlmeyer and John Martin, Arledge's former aides at ABC Sports, worked.

The news was bad, and getting worse. Eddie Byrd, the network's shoeshine man, died in December 1983, taking with him all the colorful nicknames he had given its top executives. That same month a new face arrived. Cristina Ferrare showed up at one of the network's Plaza Hotel parties wearing a black sequin dress and looking every inch the former *Vogue* model. Her picture would soon burst onto the front pages of newspaper tabloids and tabloid TV shows as the wife of John DeLorean, the General Motors ex-superstar who had been put on trial in Los Angeles for cocaine trafficking. Gary Pudney escorted Ferrare to the Plaza Hotel party, and Tony Thomopoulos soon began dating her.

While Thomopoulos and Ferrare partied, a creative fiasco was brewing at ABC Entertainment. Among the new shows pitched during the development cycle was one from Marcy Carsey and Tom Werner, the two former programmers from ABC. Carsey and Werner had gone into business together since they left Century City. Carsey, who liked to work with well-known stars, had produced "Oh Madeline," a sitcom with Madeline Kahn through her back-end deal with ABC; the show had been canceled in 1982 after thirteen episodes.

This time she had a high-concept idea for a new family comedy. The proposal lacked a script, but it had a famous star. The deal included an on-air commitment for thirteen episodes, $100,000 per week in salary for the star, and production in New York, where shooting costs were high.

Carsey, according to one participant, "pitched her heart out" during the Century City meeting that Lew Erlicht held to listen to her proposal. What Erlicht did not know was that she had already pitched the same project to Brandon Tartikoff at NBC, who had given it a cool reception. The show's star, though well-known, had a checkered career on network TV. His two previous comedy and variety shows had both failed. Except for appearing in Jell-O commercials, his principal employment at the time was as a standup comedian at Harrah's casino in Las Vegas.

Lew Erlicht weighed all the factors and then did something quite unusual. In Hollywood, new-pitch meetings with favored suppliers typically ended with a round of flattering remarks, with the worst possible response being "Let us think this one over" or "We'll be back to you in a few days." It was important to stay on good terms with any creative executive capable of producing a new series hit. But Erlicht liked to appear decisive, had no manners to speak of, and after their old white-office feud, was inured to Carsey's sales pitch. He rejected the idea unilaterally after one session, firmly and without the normal courtesies.

Marcy Carsey and Tom Werner took the project back to NBC, where Brandon Tartikoff gave them the go-ahead to produce a presentation tape. Tartikoff wanted to get the "feel" of the show without paying for a full pilot. When the twenty-minute reel clicked, NBC ordered up the series for the following fall.

Instead of Carsey and Werner's comedy, ABC was betting on a new hour-long drama, also a family show, about an Air Force test pilot, his wife and children. It was set in the Kennedy era, followed the lines of *The Right Stuff*, and was produced by Jon Avnet and Steve Tisch, two up-and-coming names in Hollywood. The show represented a step away from big-name suppliers like Aaron Spelling. Fred Pierce was moved to tears and took a rough cut home to show his wife. Leonard Goldenson was also impressed; after the screening he told an ABC staffer, "That's the best pilot I have ever seen."

Pierce decided to make "Call to Glory," as ABC's new show was eventually titled, the centerpiece of the network's 1984 fall campaign, backing it with an on-air promotional blitz during the Los Angeles Olympics. He could not help but remember the ratings blast-off that ABC had experienced in 1976 after its Olympic broadcasts from Montreal. There still seemed to be time for the network to correct its problems in prime time.

Despite the promotion, "Call to Glory" would be consigned

to oblivion in the fall, while Carsey and Werner's production, "The Cosby Show," would make the Huxtable family the biggest new attraction in network TV since Archie Bunker and the Fonz.

As the business soured and the network careened out of control, the minor personalities took their place in the spotlight.

Three executives at ABC shared power in public relations. Ellis Moore, a courtly graduate of Washington and Lee, was Elton Rule's old press aide. Patti Matson, a White House veteran who had worked for Julie Nixon Eisenhower and Betty Ford, was Fred Pierce's chief flack. And Jim Abernathy, the vice president in charge of Wall Street relations, played all the power angles.

When Rule and Pierce split the network public relations function into three separate zones in 1979, these three executives, each with his or her own turf to protect and ambitions to fulfill, started a vicious competition.

The roots of their mutual antagonism went deep. Ellis Moore, the senior statesman of the group, had once offered Abernathy a job at NBC when Abernathy was a young man not yet graduated from college, and the turn-down still affected their relationship twenty years later, when Abernathy was the boss and Moore the recalcitrant subordinate. But their antipathy was mild compared to the relationship between Abernathy and Patti Matson. In the 1970s, before squaring off in the office, they had dated briefly.

"They went to Plato's Retreat together," recalled one colleague, referring to the orgy-discotheque. "After that no one knew whether they disliked each other for personal or professional reasons."

Matson, a Nebraska farmgirl who wore Sally Jessy Raphael glasses, had learned the arts of corporate warfare in the Nixon White House. She oohed and aahed over episodes of "Laverne and Shirley" in Pierce's presence and ingratiated herself by sheer sycophancy. Abernathy was equally driven, but used a different style. He doubled up his early morning breakfast meetings at the Dorset Hotel, holding court with Wall Street analysts at a white linen-covered table while eating pink grapefruit and drinking black coffee. The maître d' shuttled the guests in one after another. Abernathy liked to lunch at La Côte Basque, an exclusive French restaurant, or the 21 Club. He scheduled trips to the West Coast to arrive on Wednesday, in order to be able to show up at the Polo Lounge with the weekly edition of *Variety*—which was printed in New York—under his arm before it reached Hollywood news-stands. He also cultivated his reputation as a ladies' man. At one meeting of Wall Street analysts, held as a special event during a West Coast affiliates' meeting, Abernathy peered out at the au-dience before taking the stage. A number of women were waiting for his presentation.

"I can't go out there," he joked. "I've slept with half a dozen women in the front row."

After the meeting, in which he greatly impressed Tony Thomopoulos, Abernathy was led to expect a big promotion. Thomopoulos had recommended him to Pierce, and Rule, before retiring, had increased his salary and put him in a direct reporting line to the corporate presidency. Abernathy was so sure of his chances that he turned down a high-level job at Columbia Pictures. Patti Matson's continued closeness to Fred Pierce, however, impeded his progress. Try as he might, Abernathy could never make Pierce trust him. Eddie Byrd had spotted the difference. Pierce's nickname was "No Shine"; Abernathy, who always liked to have his shoes polished, was called Shine.

In 1983 Abernathy began to work a new angle for promotion. Leonard Goldenson would turn eighty in 1985, and was still one of the best-kept secrets in the broadcasting industry. Abernathy aimed to help the network founder attain a crowning public rec-ognition. He wanted Harvard University, Goldenson's alma mater, to confer an honorary degree on the old man.

Harvard University had grown enormously in the sixty years since Goldenson had attended, and in 1988 was in the middle of a $400 million capital fund-raising campaign. Its solicitation of major gifts from rich alumni, however, did not extend to the direct sale of honorary degrees. Like other Ivy League schools, Harvard granted a dozen such awards each year, and these only at the discretion of its president, Derek Bok, who acted on nominations from the institution's faculties and Harvard Corporation members.

Abernathy tried an indirect route. The John F. Kennedy School of Government, with a new and rapidly expanding Harvard faculty, had plans to start a Center on the Press, Politics, and Public Policy. A Frank Stanton Chair on the First Amendment, named for the former president of CBS, who had always been network TV's spokesman on First Amendment issues, was its cornerstone. The only problem was that William Paley, his old boss, had endowed the professorship stingily. A Harvard chair cost at least $1 million. At Paley's direction, CBS had donated just $500,000.

The Abernathy plan involved ABC allocating $125,000 from its budget for corporate contributions to the Stanton professorship. Goldenson would then raise a similar amount from twenty well-heeled business acquaintances and friends, put the Center for the Press, Politics, and Public Policy on the map, and become a leading TV industry spokesman. All this, indirectly, was supposed to convince the Kennedy School of Government that it should exercise influence with Derek Bok and induce Harvard to grant Goldenson an honorary degree.

That was the plan. The skeptics, Ellis Moore among them, believed that Goldenson's long-standing philanthropic interest in United Cerebral Palsy and another underendowed professorship at the University of Missouri School of Journalism would interfere with the fund-raising effort for Harvard.

But the $125,000 contribution was made, and in 1983, at Goldenson's initiative, Harvard agreed to cosponsor a symposium in Washington on the decline of American voter participation. To help with the planning, Abernathy hired a woman from the League of Women Voters named Cecily Coleman.

An attractive blond in her late twenties with Democratic political leanings, Coleman was given an office at the ABC News bureau at 1717 DeSales Street in Washington, with marching orders to mount a first-class event. The Harvard symposium was to be a carte-blanche affair, no spending limits. Coleman also received an implicit promise from Abernathy that, if all went well, a full-time network job would probably await her.

The situation had all the elements of a daytime soap opera—compulsive male executive in early forties meets fresh female hire with idealistic leanings, and introduces her to a vipers' nest masquerading as a network public relations department. As the symposium planning proceeded, Abernathy began to evince more than a professional interest in his new Washington protégée. He made special trips to D.C., took Coleman to dinner, and inquired about her professional plans. Anticipating that Ellis Moore would soon retire, he told Coleman the job could be hers. But when he invited her to his hotel room one night after dinner, the reason for his "professional" interest became crystal clear; he was coming on to her sexually. Coleman did not reciprocate his sexual interest, but she did not back away either.

After the sexual high jinks of the jackpot years, on-the-job promiscuity at ABC had become deeply embedded in the fabric of the network organization. For every "Great Stone Face," "Bald Eagle," and "Tony the T," there was an equally telling female image—"Nurse Ratchet," "The Iron Butterfly," and "Black Widow."

In no other respect was ABC more truly a family company. The in-house sexual ritual pervaded every nook and cranny at the network. In Hollywood, shortly after separating from his wife and before taking up with Cristina Ferrare, Tony Thomopoulos was engaged to Candace Farrell, ABC Entertainment's head of on-air promotion. Lew Erlicht appeared to be carrying on a liaison with Christy Welker, a vice president for made-for-TV movies and miniseries. Michael Mallardi spent time out of the office with Anita Hecht, a handsome woman in charge of New York personnel. Mark Roth in the owned-stations division had long displayed an interest in Julie Hoover; she had left a vice presidency in broadcast standards and practices for a vice presidency in stations with his help. At ABC News and Sports, Roone Arledge was renowned for double dipping; his sexual intrigues straddled two divisions.

The implicit rules that guided sexual conduct at the network stated that any woman was fair game unless she said "No!" After a successful conquest, the men who held power were generally expected to protect the women who obliged them in bed.

Abernathy differed from this norm only in the degree of charm that he brought to the task of seduction. Instead of being overbearing, he played on Coleman's intellectual interests and emotions.

At the time, she was dating another man, who wanted to marry her. While she kept Abernathy at arm's length on a personal level, he held her in professional thrall. Her resistance heightened his ardor. Abernathy began making wild proposals: According to Coleman, he said he wanted to run away with her to Connecticut.

In September 1983, just before the symposium was to begin, the date for her wedding was set, and she ordered invitations from the printer. With the two deadlines, professional and personal, converging all at once, Coleman panicked. Which was more important, marriage or career?

Career, Abernathy told her.

Instead, Coleman mailed the invitations.

When the Harvard–ABC Symposium on American Voter Participation opened in late September, ranking Senate majority leader Howard Baker delivered the official welcome. A distinguished group of Congressmen, journalists, campaign consultants, pollsters, voter education experts, scholars, and the national chairmen of the Democratic and Republican parties all participated. Gerald Ford and Jimmy Carter made special ex-Presidential appearances. ABC chartered a Gulfstream jet to fly Derek Bok, Harvard's president, from a fund-raising dinner in Los Angeles to Washington. While Fred Pierce and a score of other bewildered ABC executives looked on from a roped-off gallery, the network videotaped the symposium proceedings in preparation for a half-hour ABC News special, which would be broadcast in a "fringe," Sunday-afternoon time period before the Iowa caucuses and New Hampshire primary. Cecily Coleman disbursed more than $500,000 of the network's money on the two-day affair.

A few months after the symposium, Harvard campaign chairman Roger Stone and a powerful delegation of university officials visited Goldenson in New York to ask for a contribution. They knew, and Goldenson did too, how important the Harvard connection had been to establishing him in his career. The university had come to cash in. Goldenson told them he planned to give a quarter of his estate to charity when he died and that one third of that would go to Harvard in equal allocations to the Medical school, the College, and the Kennedy School of Government. With an estate estimated to contain $40 million in ABC stock and $40 million in other assets at the time (the networks portion would soon increase dramatically in value), Goldenson was planning altogether to give his alma mater more than $6 million.

As the symposium ended, Cecily Coleman was still looking for a job. ABC News in Washington was looking for a new director of public relations and interviewed her, but since the job reported ultimately to Patti Matson, who regarded Coleman as a potential spy in her own camp, she never got it.

Abernathy, still acting as her mentor, arranged a job for Coleman as the executive director of the Advisory Committee on Voter Participation, a letterhead organization of Leonard Goldenson, Jimmy Carter, Gerald Ford, and Derek Bok, to "follow up" on the symposium's recommendations instead. The job paid four times what she had earned at the League of Women Voters, but for the first time it put her in a direct reporting relationship with Abernathy, whose ardor was fading. When she invited him to her wedding, he accepted but did not attend. Abernathy had already turned his attentions to another blond-haired, blue-eyed woman—a symposium participant—who proved more compliant than Coleman.

Through the fall and winter, as Abernathy's own plans for promotion stalled, he began to vent his professional frustration on Coleman. She may have been played out as a romantic fantasy, but she was still around as a sexual object. Trapped in a professional no-man's-land, she shuttled regularly between her new home in Washington and Abernathy's increasing demands in New York. Coleman grew nervous. Her health began to deteriorate.

In March 1984, when Coleman learned that Abernathy was

planning to fire her, she became desperate. Like a good corporate soldier, she took her case to a personnel officer in ABC News' Washington bureau and played it by the book: She asked for help. The personnel officer, another woman, told her that it was network policy to handle such complaints confidentially, listened to the story, and promised to look into it.

But when the personnel officer called up the network attorney in New York, a male, to ask for guidance, he demanded to know Coleman's identity. Within hours, word of her complaint had reached not only Abernathy, but also Everett Erlick, the top legal officer of the corporation. The network walls went up fast and tight, and she was left standing outside.

Cecily Coleman was in big trouble.

In the spring of 1984, the sexual tempest that was brewing at ABC caught up with Mark Fowler's plans for deregulating TV station ownership.

"The Commission, acting on its own motion, here proposes to modify that aspect of its multiple ownership rules commonly known as the 'seven station rule,' " the FCC announced—and on Wall Street the news item from Washington flashed like a stock message on a Quotron machine. The rule that Fowler wanted to change was a cornerstone of American broadcasting. Since the 1940s, only the limits imposed by the 7-7-7 rule had kept ABC, NBC, and CBS, and big station groups like Westinghouse, Capital Cities, and Storer, from expanding the number of TV stations they owned.

Now the smart money on Wall Street and the best brains in broadcasting were anticipating a merger and takeover opportunity. Investment banking firms like First Boston and Morgan, Stanley beefed up their media analyst staffs and mergers and acquisitions groups in preparation for the industry buyout spree. Everett Erlick, ABC's Washington lobbyist, briefed Goldenson on the new developments at the FCC. Mark Fowler was expected to announce the change in the 7-7-7 rule in August, just before the Los Angeles

Olympics, and the preliminary indications were that he wanted to repeal the ownership limits altogether, allowing the networks to buy up local affiliates all across the country.

In May, as ABC's affiliates gathered for their annual meeting in Los Angeles, Goldenson began collecting information from various members of his corporate staff about possible merger and takeover scenarios. Among those he asked for data was his top Wall Street officer. Goldenson's request for a merger in which ABC would acquire Capital Cities, its largest affiliate group, reached Abernathy's desk not long after Cecily Coleman's sexual harassment complaint.

Abernathy was in a curious bind. He liked to think of himself as an intimate player in the world of high-stakes finance, but his $140,000 annual salary was not large by Wall Street standards. He hobnobbed with business tycoons and could contemplate buying a $2 million Long Island estate, yet his lavish life-style was largely made possible by his generous corporate expense account. He counted the months before his restricted stock options turned liquid. And now, complicating his life further, he was being targeted for what he viewed as character assassination by a vengeful female subordinate.

When Cecily Coleman learned that the network had broken its promise of confidentiality, she had two options. She could say, "My complaint is not true, I didn't mean it." Or she could fight.

She chose to fight, and while the network was reaching into its deep pockets and hiring the New York law firm of Epstein, Becker, Borsody, and Greene to defend Abernathy and itself, she retained an attorney "on spec," without retainer, to represent what she viewed as her injured interests. Coleman's complaint had not yet reached the lawsuit stage, but the two sides were squaring off. ABC's attorneys had decided that Coleman was a virus to be isolated and contained. They instructed Abernathy to have no further contact with her and deployed what one attorney called "scorched earth" tactics to force her into submission.

Coleman, fighting fire with fire, put a lawyer named Mark

Lane on her side of the case. Lane was an attorney with a reputation. "What moves me most directly to action," his entry in *Who's Who* read, "is the fact that I hate bullies. What concerns me the most in contemporary America is the influence of the police and spy organizations with the national news media. Together these are bullies to contemplate and oppose."

Best known for his book *Rush to Judgment*, which disputed the Warren Commission report on the Kennedy assassination, Lane was a notorious anti-Establishment conspiracy theorist. A bright, competent trial lawyer, he was also a gifted publicity hound. Lane had worked on the Wounded Knee Indian trials in St. Paul, Minnesota, in the 1970s and was on the scene in Jonestown, the religious community in the wilds of Guyana, at the time of the Jonestown Massacre. Lane reportedly hid in the bushes while the cyanide-laced Kool-Aid was being served. By 1984, when he jumped on the Cecily Coleman case as a new vehicle for his crusade against the national news media, Lane's career had come full circle. He had built his reputation playing an establishment pariah. In the process, he had succeeded in antagonizing most of his anti-Establishment peers.

Even Mark Lane did not realize how much events at ABC corroborated Coleman's complaint. At the ABC News bureau in Washington, where many bright, well-qualified women had been hired since 1981, the sexual tensions were just below the boiling point. The quick stardom of Kathleen Sullivan galled other, more experienced on-air female correspondents. Sullivan received flowers from Roone Arledge at work and traveled to Paris with him after a special on-air assignment at the Sarajevo Olympics. To newswomen with ambitions of their own but no sugar daddy to look after their careers, it was humiliating to watch Kathleen Sullivan jump ahead in the celebrity queue. Their protected female colleagues, who got promoted, dismissed such feelings as "professional jealousy." But when producer Susan Morrison and correspondent Rita Flynn organized a potluck dinner to trade war stories, more than forty-five women showed up.

The next day White House correspondent Sam Donaldson, a relatively forward-thinking newsman, joked over the bureau's public-address system, "I heard there was a women's liberation meeting last night. I want to know who the perpetrator is."

Donaldson called up Susan Morrison, a former "60 Minutes" producer who had been needlepointing at her desk at ABC and told her, "You're ruining your career."

Dorrance Smith, an Arledge protégé in weekend news, who was known for selecting his girlfriends from the bureau staff, called Rita Flynn and invited her to lunch. "Don't bring your lawyer," Smith warned.

The Washington bureau chief's apology for the limited amount of on-air time that most of the women correspondents received was, "Women's voices are not as authoritative as men's."

A group of incensed newswomen retained the lawyer who had won the Washington State "comparable worth" class action lawsuit before the Supreme Court, in order to put pressure on ABC News. Meanwhile, Mark Lane raced ahead with Cecily Coleman's complaint in strictly confrontational fashion. Lane pressed a set of non-negotiable demands in his client's behalf, which the network perfunctorily refused. The network lawyers had conducted an investigation of their own. When they asked Abernathy, "Did you do it?" he said, "No."

For Abernathy the sexual harassment issue was not whether his infatuation had affected Coleman's job status, but whether or not she had been attracted to him. "I looked up 'sexual harassment' in the dictionary," he said. "The dictionary defined it as 'unwanted sexual advances.'"

Since she had never explicitly said, "No," in other words, he was innocent. Male vanity was the perfect defense.

In May 1984, after a month of legal maneuvering between Mark Lane and the network's attorneys, Coleman, in her capacity as executive director of the Advisory Committee on Voter Education, traveled to Las Vegas for an industry convention, taking her husband with her. The trip had been on her calendar for months, but the network didn't view it that way. Before she returned to Washington, she received a telegram informing her that she had been "terminated" for having taken an unauthorized business trip. The files were removed from her office. She was physically barred from the news bureau. Inside, the rumors were already circulating that she had been fired for misappropriating company funds.

Within days, Mark Lane had filed a $1 million lawsuit against ABC in federal court in Washington. The charges included sexual harassment, retaliation, and defamation, and the total damages sought would grow to $15 million.

Jim Abernathy, the principal defendant, was in Palm Springs attending the annual gathering of ABC Entertainment staffers when the lawsuit was filed. The end-of-season think-tank retreat that the programmer held to brainstorm about the upcoming development cycle had swollen under Tony Thomopoulos into a corporate event where guests from Hollywood and New York bathed in Jacuzzis and listened to professors and educators of worldwide renown. In May 1984, the topic was "The Brain and Beyond," a seminar focused on artificial intelligence and parapsychology.

As soon as he heard, Abernathy hurried back to New York.

Civil litigation is like a romance that ends badly. Both parties fabricate their own version of reality, convince themselves of its truth, and attack the opposing version as a self-interested fiction.

The network's public posture during the discovery phase of the Cecily Coleman lawsuit was to dismiss it as being "without merit." The reason Coleman had filed her charges was her "ultimate frustration at not being able to gain permanent employment," the network's attorneys said. While accusing her of providing false and misleading information on her résumé when she was originally hired, ABC froze her company-backed American Express credit card, leaving an unpaid balance of thousands of dollars. Confronted with a corporation willing to deploy all of its legal and financial resources to force her to drop her suit, Coleman fought fire with fire. She orchestrated fund-raising meetings at the National Organization of Women, taped telephone conversations with at least one former colleague without his knowledge, and prepared to duke it out with the networks in court.

Abernathy, on the other hand, faced a different set of problems. When discussing the case in private, most network executives simply shook their heads sadly or laughed out loud. What was funny to them was that Abernathy had to cover up for an alleged misdeed that, in their view, was a minor misdemeanor. After all, the affair had not even been consummated. All this, and Abernathy was still sweating. When he met with a New York speech consultant before his pretrial deposition, one colleague called the visits Perjury 101.

Through the summer the pretrial discovery period continued. The Coleman lawsuit would not end until the summer of 1985. But in August 1984 the network's in-house soap opera gave way in interest to the wider industry story. Mark Fowler unveiled his proposal to deregulate TV station ownership on August 3, with the change scheduled to take effect in thirty days. Wall Street was waiting for its own version of the LA Games to commence—it wanted to make money buying and selling any company, including the networks that owned TV stations.

The top network officials, meanwhile, were flocking to the West Coast to watch the Los Angeles Olympics. John DeLorean's trial for cocaine trafficking was still underway in Los Angeles, but Tony Thomopoulos arranged for Cristina Ferrare, DeLorean's wife, to sit near him in the Los Angeles Coliseum, and the two exchanged discreet "hi" signs. Promotional spots for "Call to Glory," ABC's prime-time series for the fall, inundated the airwaves during the Olympic competition.

Only Leonard Goldenson did not join fully in the party. On one of the days he spent in Los Angeles, Goldenson played a quiet game of golf at the Bel Air Country Club with Elton Rule and two highly influential members of the board of directors, Jack Hausman and Ray Adams. After lunch at the men's grill, the foursome played eighteen holes. Goldenson, sensing problems ahead, was quietly seeking outside advice.

The first sign of real trouble came in the August 13 issue of *Forbes,* the same magazine which had praised the network so lavishly just two years before. The article it now published had a decidedly different tone. "Lost Bearings," the title read. "ABC is doing well, but not as well as it should be doing, which is precisely why it may be takeover bait." The photograph of Fred Pierce carried a caption asking, "Simply not good enough?"

The *Forbes* analysis of the network's problems was as precise and detailed as an internal memo. It started the bad publicity. A few days later, in the August 20 issue of *New York* magazine, the "Intelligencer" column included an account of the network's most recent board meeting and said that the directors were in "open revolt" against Pierce. Frank Cary, the former IBM chairman who ran ABC's compensation committee, was said to have interrupted a European vacation in order to quash an overly generous restricted stock option newly proposed by Pierce.

The *Forbes* article made Pierce look incompetent. *New York* made him out to be greedy as well. Both pieces were grist for the Wall Street mill. From all appearances, someone at ABC was snitching to the press.

Meanwhile Richard MacDonald, the media analyst at First Boston, was reviewing the network's business in order to make a published sales recommendation to his clients. It was customary Wall Street practice for analysts to discuss their reports with company contacts, so MacDonald showed a prerelease copy of his report to Jim Abernathy, ABC's executive in charge of Wall Street relations. Abernathy usually treated MacDonald with mild disdain, but when the two met for a Dorset Hotel breakfast in early August, the reception was warm.

"Jim, what do you think of this?" MacDonald asked, handing Abernathy a draft of the report across the table. MacDonald's "buy" recommendation, which would be published with First Boston's imprimatur, began, "We believe the stock price of ABC does not reflect the value of the broadcast and publishing groups, the real estate, or the potential of ESPN. . . . Any major price appreciation, however, must await evidence of a dramatic longer-term operating

improvement or a move by an outsider in the relatively near term.
. . . We would be inclined to accumulate on weakness. . . . Something has to happen."

MacDonald was basically inviting investors to buy ABC stock,
on the premise that the network would be taken over. For a Wall
Street analyst, the recommendation could not have been more
inflammatory. Abernathy, who ought to have professed shock, instead looked up quickly and replied, "I love the opening lines."

Elissa von Tayn, Jim Abernathy's bustling, well-groomed secretary, had some information that she thought Fred Pierce ought
to hear. She had overheard her boss in the middle of a telephone
conversation that sounded suspicious to her.

Listening to executive conversations was an office ritual for
secretaries on the twenty-seventh floor of Hard Rock. All of them
had drop lines connecting their telephones to their bosses', and
Von Tayn, with Abernathy's encouragement, had been listening to
almost all his calls since she was hired the year before. Doing so
enabled her to keep "up to speed" with his hectic schedule; it was
both her privilege and her duty to stay informed.

The observation post had made Von Tayn an unwitting first-
hand witness to the various events that had led to Cecily Coleman's
sexual-harassment lawsuit. As part of his damage-control effort,
Abernathy had suggested to Von Tayn in no uncertain terms that
he would view any unfriendly court testimony from her in a very
unfavorable light. The relationship between boss and secretary had
become strained.

In mid-August, while Von Tayn was listening in on a conversation between Abernathy and a Boston stock-portfolio manager
named Bob Beck, she heard what she thought was truly shocking
information. Beck, acting for State Street Research and Management in Boston, had purchased ABC shares totaling more than 5
percent of the entire company. His firm controlled the largest block
of stock on the market. Von Tayn was unversed in high finance,
but she thought that Abernathy and Beck were discussing the

details of how much the company would be worth if the network was broken up and resold in parts.

After Abernathy hung up, Von Tayn sat and stewed. Finally, she confided her sense of alarm to another secretary, and was encouraged to speak to a network higher-up. In short order Von Tayn found herself describing Abernathy's conversation in detail to Fred Pierce in a private meeting at the Dorset Hotel.

Once before, Pierce had glimpsed the network's future. Beverlee Dean had warned him of Fred Silverman's betrayal. Now, in Dean's role, Von Tayn was telling him that Abernathy was the Benedict Arnold, trying, in concert with ABC's largest outside shareholder, to sell the company.

Pierce consulted with Everett Erlick, ABC's general counsel, who helped him lay the plans for Abernathy's dismissal. Between the negative publicity and a concurrent upsurge of trading in the network's stock, there was no time to obtain objective confirmation of Von Tayn's report. Wall Street was usually quiet in late summer, but since early August the network's stock had risen 10 points. On August 21, 475,300 shares changed hands, and on August 22 another 400,000 shares, far above the usual trading ranges of 60,000 shares per day.

After the Olympics had ended, Jim Abernathy was summoned back to New York from a family vacation on Nantucket. He arrived in the city on a hot, muggy morning. Pierce and Erlick kept him waiting for more than an hour, giving him time to visit the head of personnel and inquire about his restricted stock options. At 11 A.M. Abernathy went into a meeting with Pierce and Erlick. After two hours he emerged, red-faced and angry. Accompanied to his own office by a security guard, he was allowed a few minutes to collect his personal belongings and was then escorted to the lobby and out the front door.

The locks on Abernathy's office were changed. His files were sealed. The network took every precaution in its power to guard against theft and to nip in the bud what it had evidently deemed Abernathy's pending takeover plot. The one-line memorandum that went out from Pierce to all network department heads tersely conveyed the news: "This is to inform you that James L. Abernathy, Vice President, Corporate Affairs, and an officer of the corporation, has resigned to pursue other business interests."

Whether or not Abernathy was involved in a takeover conspiracy, the network could not have handled his firing more badly. ABC had signaled its weakness and set the Wall Street rumor mill churning just as Mark Fowler's proposed change in the TV station ownership rule was moving full speed ahead in Washington. The timing of the events had inadvertently put the network into play on Wall Street.

12

March to the Sea

There had never been a network takeover in the history of American broadcasting, or even a friendly merger since Leonard Goldenson's merger of United Paramount Theatres and ABC. But in the fall of 1984, the entrepreneurial artists on Wall Street and communications deregulators in Washington began beating their drums in unison, and the industry scrambled toward a takeover crescendo that no network leader could ignore.

When the Wall Street brokers and traders returned to their offices after Labor Day, they pounced on ABC. That Wednesday 662,000 shares crossed the Big Board, and the price of the network's stock jumped 6 points. On Thursday 1,112,000 shares changed hands, and stock closed up another 2⅛ points. More than 6 percent of the company had just been bought and sold as the *Wall Street Journal* remarked in its regular "Heard on the Street" column on Friday:

"Rumors of a takeover of American Broadcasting got high ratings on Wall Street yesterday. . . . "

"Talk of an ABC takeover or leveraged buyout has been circulating briskly for several weeks, and the latest rumored partner

209

was Capital Cities Communications. Both companies strongly denied the rumor. Nonetheless, many analysts believe that ABC's days of independence are numbered. . . . Few consider the company well-managed."

Richard MacDonald's "buy" recommendation on ABC stock, which First Boston had published in late-August, was cited as having "helped fuel takeover talk." MacDonald took advantage of the *Journal* news item to pay a visit to Fred Smith, a senior partner in mergers and acquisitions at his firm, and alerted him to the trading activity. MacDonald and Smith together went to see Bruce Wasserstein, the leading takeover artist on Wall Street, who with Joseph Perella, another First Boston partner, had engineered Texaco's $12 billion bid for Getty Oil earlier in the year.

Wasserstein placed a telephone call to Leonard Goldenson, who was vacationing in England. Leaving a message at the Dorchester Hotel in London, Wasserstein told the network founder, in effect, "Your company is under attack. You need to hire us."

When he returned to New York a few days later, Goldenson called Wasserstein back and put First Boston on retainer to advise the network in takeover defenses. Skadden, Arps—the law firm which had helped ABC during Laurence Tisch's earlier foray—was still on the payroll. By mid-September, the network seemed doubly fortified against any hostile bid.

Ironically, just as ABC was getting a case of the Wall Street jitters, the network was experiencing record revenues and profits. Pierce's $220 million investment in the Los Angeles Olympics had pushed revenues over $2 billion for the first time in network history. So after the summer holidays, Goldenson made one further move. A year before Pierce's contract was scheduled to expire, he renewed it for another five years, through 1989.

"This action by the board and myself is a clear indication of our support for Fred Pierce and the job he has done," Goldenson said on September 21. "We are coming off the best quarter in the company's history. . . . Our prospects for the future are bright indeed."

In spite of the board's optimism, ABC's prime-time schedule was finally caving in. When "Call to Glory," the hot ticket on the new fall schedule, premiered in the fall of 1984, it repeated the all-too-familiar pattern of network series in the past—instant success followed by instant failure. "Call to Glory"'s first episode scored high ratings, thanks to an Olympics lead-in and extensive on-air promotion. But the numbers trailed off drastically in the second episode, and by the third "Call to Glory" hovered near the ratings basement. Pierce and Thomopoulos moved the show to a new night, where its ratings dropped even further. Then they put it on hiatus. Then they canceled it altogether.

The circumstances of failure were different from the failure of other new shows in previous years. In the fall of 1984, the network had spent money on covering the Olympics and on the 1984 Presidential election which before had always been earmarked for "special event" programming. This year, for the first time since "Roots," Brandon Stoddard had no big made-for-TV movie or miniseries project in the development pipeline. ABC's comedy and drama series had to carry the programming burden alone. The outcome was the start of a ratings debacle—a prime-time performance during the regular season along the lines of the midsummer repeat of "Masada." Because while "Call to Glory" wilted on ABC, "The Cosby Show" premiered on NBC, building audience strength with each passing week and revitalizing the entire NBC schedule. "The Cosby Show" turned into a "locomotive" comedy, like "All in the Family" and "Happy Days" and pulled audience shares for "Family Ties," and "Cheers," two other NBC Thursday-night comedies, from the 20s to the 40s. The ratings of ABC's competition had doubled overnight.

A few weeks into the new season, although CBS still held first place, NBC surged past ABC in the Nielsen numbers. In a single month, the programming wheel had turned, and ABC was back in third place.

It had all happened with a cyclical Hollywood justice. "Creative" people—Diller, Eisner, Silverman, Steve Gentry, and even Brandon Tartikoff, Marcy Carsey, and Tom Werner—were the network's stock-in-trade. But now Diller and Eisner were rising movie moguls, Gentry was dead, Tartikoff had inherited Silverman's "golden gut" at NBC, and Carsey and Werner had produced "The Cosby Show"—not for Fred Pierce and ABC, but for NBC. The irony was that Pierce's back-end deals and Hollywood cronyism had precipitated an outflow of creativity that he was powerless to stop.

Pierce was left behind in the Hollywood shuffle. Most of Paramount's TV production had already shifted over to NBC before Diller and Eisner left to run separate studios. Grant Tinker and Brandon Tartikoff had hired Les Charles, Glen Charles, and James Burrows, the inheritors of Silverman's old writing team at Paramount, to create "Cheers" for NBC after Pierce canceled "Taxi" in 1982. And in place of Garry Marshall, the creator of "Happy Days," Gary David Goldberg, the producer of NBC's "Family Ties," was the bright new light of TV comedy at Paramount.

As ABC's programming disaster flowered in the fall of 1984, Fred Pierce began putting out feelers in Hollywood for a new chief programmer. Leonard Goldenson, on the other hand, bought a plane ticket to the West Coast. He wanted to conduct his own investigation of the network's performance there.

Through the fall, while ABC's ratings plummeted, the fact that the network was in play on Wall Street had still not registered on most company executives. No takeover suitors declared themselves after Labor Day, and the speculative trading flurry died away. ABC's business seemed to resume its normal course.

But the smart money on Wall Street, in fact, was just lying in wait. Wall Street was playing a chess game, and before it could capitalize on ABC's weakness, Washington had to make its move.

Since Mark Fowler's humiliation on the programming-ownership issue, the FCC's relationship with Capitol Hill had gone from bad to worse. On August 9, less than a week after making his proposal on the 7-7-7 rule, Fowler temporarily put the breaks on his deregulation of TV station ownership. His plan called for broadcasters to own as many as twelve local TV stations, regardless of market size, and included a "sunset" provision, which would abandon all limitation on the number of stations a network could own by 1990; the networks would then be allowed to own TV stations in *every* American market. The FCC seemed to be sending out invitations to the networks to buy their own affiliates.

The plan Fowler proposed in August, not surprisingly, did not last long on Capitol Hill. The legislators, prompted by Hollywood lobbyists, attached new legislative riders denying the FCC the right to spend tax dollars to change the TV station ownership rules. During October the price of ABC stock fell steadily on Wall Street. More than 800,000 shares were sold on consecutive days in November, and by early December the network had dropped 20 points from its post-Labor Day high. As the *Wall Street Journal* commented in another "Street" column, "ABC's Stock Slide May Have Some Investors Wishing They'd Never Heard Takeover Talk."

The takeover machinations reached a new stage in mid-November. In Washington, that was the time when the House and Senate Appropriations Committees met to cut budget deals. Since the government needed to pay its bills, Fowler had an opportunity to break the regulatory log jam. He paid a late-night visit to the Capitol Hill offices of Tim Wirth, the Colorado congressman who ran the House Telecommunications Subcommittee, and who was not one of Fowler's fans.

"Look, we've got a problem here," Fowler began. "I haven't listened before, but now I want to work it out."

"Good, so do I," Wirth replied.

After Wirth and Fowler came to a meeting of minds, an amended station-ownership proposal was adopted by the FCC in a closed session on December 19. As of April 1, 1985, any company could own up to twelve local stations, provided their combined audience did not reach more than 25 percent of the total American audience. Fowler's sunset provision was dropped.

Word of the new FCC proposal was not scheduled to be publicly released until February 1, but a leak catalyzed events in New York long before then. Capital Cities chairman Thomas Murphy called Leonard Goldenson shortly before Christmas and asked for a meeting. Since he ran the network's largest group of station affiliates, Murphy had often run into Goldenson at official ABC gatherings. As social acquaintances, they also played golf together occasionally at their respective Westchester County country clubs. But this meeting, in Goldenson's office, marked a new beginning.

"Leonard, I'd like to make you a proposition," Murphy started the conversation. "Please don't throw me out of the window when you hear it."

The two men were thirty-nine floors up, so what he had to say had to be important.

"What would you think about merging our two companies?"

Capital Cities, unlike ABC, was not a household name. Neither was David before he slew Goliath.

The company had been born in 1954 when a Harvard Business School graduate named Frank Smith, the broadcaster Lowell Thomas, and twenty-one other investors purchased a nearly bankrupt UHF station in Albany, New York.

Lowell Thomas, well-known for describing the Saharan exploits of Lawrence of Arabia or dining habits of New Guinea aborigines with equal aplomb, was by far the most distinguished member of the Capital Cities group. "Good evening, everyone," Thomas once began his 6:45 P.M. radio news program, and for many years, before Edward R. Murrow's "This . . . is London," it was probably the most recognized on-air signature in America.

Thomas met Frank Smith during the production of a wartime radio show called "Victory Is Our Business," and later hired him as a personal business manager after the war. The other Capital Cities founders, mostly well-heeled New York and Long Island businessmen, tended to be Republican in politics, Catholic in re-

214

ligion, and Irish in ethnic background. William Casey, later the head of the CIA, was one of them.

"Good broadcasting is good business" was Frank Smith's company motto, and responsibility for all operating decisions was delegated to him. Smith's first move was to hire Thomas Murphy, another Harvard Business School graduate and the son of a New York State Supreme Court judge, to run the Albany station.

As a UHF outlet, the Albany station lost a lot of money at the start, and Murphy, just twenty-nine years old at the time, was baptized as a broadcaster in the school of hard knocks. The station was located in a former Catholic convent, a mile and a half down a dirt road. Its studio was a converted chapel. When he gave the station a much-needed paint job, Murphy decided to save money and painted only the two sides that could be seen from the dirt road.

"What I learned," Murphy said later, describing his apprenticeship, "was how few people you really needed to keep things running."

The Albany station was upgraded to a VHF frequency in 1958, and Frank Smith by then had bought a second VHF station in Raleigh-Durham. Raleigh-Durham and Albany were both state capitals, so the company was christened "Capital Cities." Smith then began to buy other stations, adding TV outlets in Buffalo, Providence, and Charleston-Huntington (West Virginia), and nine radio stations besides. He looked for valuable, yet undermanaged, assets—for instance, stations that won 30 percent of the local audience but only 25 percent of local advertising. Then he sent in Capital Cities managers to improve sales and cut costs. With the increased profits, Smith then went out and bought more stations. Tom Murphy moved to New York in 1960 to oversee the growing station operations, and joined Smith in Villard House, a cluster of elegant nineteenth-century townhouses across Madison Avenue from St. Patrick's Cathedral, where Capital Cities was headquartered. Murphy's Albany successor was Daniel Burke, a younger brother of his roommate at Harvard School.

In 1964, when Capital Cities issued public shares, Frank Smith celebrated by inviting all the company's friends to a chartered day-long ocean-liner cruise. It was billed as "The Cruise to Nowhere." The guests played golf together at the Sleepy Hollow Country Club in Westchester County beforehand, and Smith, traveling around the course in a golf cart, stopped on a hilltop to take in his creation. The secret of Capital Cities, he told his golfing partner, was that its executives felt free to say what they thought, even if it meant disagreeing with one another.

"They can say exactly what's on their minds," his playing partner said, "because you've given them all enough money to say 'fuck you' and leave if their views aren't heard."

Smith laughed so hard that he nearly fell out of the golf cart.

In 1965 Capital Cities was a small, prosperous broadcasting company that owned five VHF stations—then the maximum number allowed by the FCC. It might have slowed down, passed profits along to shareholders, and stopped growing, but Smith's ethic of growth-by-acquisition was firmly rooted. In 1965, when Smith died, Tom Murphy kept right on buying, branching out into new territory in 1968 with the purchase of Fairchild Publishing, a large company which owned *Women's Wear Daily* and other prestigious titles. In 1970 Murphy followed up this transaction with the $100 million purchase of Triangle Broadcasting—the country's largest-ever TV station deal.

The Triangle deal involved three major-market TV stations in Philadelphia, Hartford-New Haven, and Fresno, and was sticky because Capital Cities was trying to buy and sell stations at a time when the FCC was enforcing its station-ownership policies quite strictly. WPVI-TV in Philadelphia, the nation's fourth-largest market after New York, Los Angeles, and Chicago and one of ABC's oldest affiliates, was the plum in the deal. Once in the 1950s, Walter Annenberg had considered selling it, until Leonard Goldenson advised him, "Hold on to it. That station will be worth a lot of money before too long."

Murphy finessed the necessary regulatory approval for the purchase from the FCC, and the increased revenue from Triangle stations helped turn Capital Cities into a major force in American broadcasting. As ABC's largest single affiliate group, Capital Cities got all the benefits of Fred Silverman's programming without paying any of the costs. Murphy and Burke never paid a dividend to their public shareholders. Instead, they reinvested their profits from TV earnings in newspapers and other media properties—the *Kansas City Star, Fort Worth Star-Telegram, Institutional Investor* magazine, and local cable systems.

By the early 1980s Capital Cities was still very tightly run, but it was a broad-based, billion-dollar company. Its reputation among broadcasters was that of an impeccably managed, public-spirited enterprise. In the newspaper world, where profit margins were lower and Murphy's and Burke's acquisitions more recent, it was seen as a union-busting cost cutter. But the company was the darling of Wall Street. In all their expansion, Murphy and Burke had never reported a "down" quarter. Capital Cities' stock had a better than 20–1 price-earnings ratio. Murphy's nickname among his colleagues was "the Pope," and he went on shipboard retreats with media and financial gurus like Katharine Graham of the *Washington Post*, Laurence Tisch of Loew's, and Warren Buffett of Berkshire Hathaway.

A change in the TV station ownership rules was the prerequisite for further Capital Cities expansion in broadcasting, and in December 1984 the Capital Cities chairman had his ear close to the Washington ground. Shortly after his difficulty in getting the Triangle Broadcasting deal approved by the FCC, Murphy had helped make Jim Quello, a former Capital Cities station manager, one of the FCC commissioners. Thus when Mark Fowler made his twelve-cities compromise with Capitol Hill, Murphy seemed to know all about it long before it was announced publicly.

Then he went to Goldenson and proposed that Capital Cities and ABC merge.

In his ABC office, Goldenson listened cordially to Murphy's offer, and said that he would think about it. Then he informed his

217

inside directors—Fred Pierce, Everett Erlick, and Michael Mallardi—about the visit. The news traveled quickly around the building. Patti Matson, Pierce's top public-relations aide, had taken over most of the deposed Jim Abernathy's responsibilities. When a network art director asked her in late December about next year's annual report, Matson gave a surprisingly gloomy reply:

"If there *is* a next year."

Jim Abernathy was only the first of a growing list of network casualties. At Christmas, instead of throwing parties, ABC was making an executive body count. John Lazarus, who ran ABC Sports sales, had been responsible for selling more than $450 million worth of commercials in 1984. More than anyone else at the network, Lazarus knew how to party. He would hire a bus, arrange to meet his guests at the Plaza Hotel, and transport them around the city, stopping at a different restaurant for every course: cocktails, dinner, and dessert, all in Ken Kesey style.

Just before the 1984 Summer Games, Lazarus had made the mistake of cosigning (on ABC's behalf) a $1 million note for a personal friend who happened to be an ABC catering supplier. The supplier went bankrupt, his creditors clamored for payment, and the network was left with Lazarus' signature and a lawsuit that alleged drug use at ABC as one of the motivations for Lazarus' unauthorized guarantee. After he resigned, the charges were settled out of court for an undisclosed sum.

The following spring, Peter Cusack, the head of personnel, would run into similar troubles, and by Christmas the rumors were already running rampant through Hard Rock. FBI agents and private investigators were said to be checking the in-house couriers and overnight pouch service between New York and Hollywood for drugs. The coffee carts that brought coffee and Danish around each morning were said to be dispensing Bolivian marching powder in little plastic sachets that the coffee boys neatly hid between two stacked coffee cups. From the mailroom to the highest levels of the company, no ABC executive was free from suspicion.

The edict came down at Christmas time that there would be no company-sponsored parties; employees could buy their own cake, punch, and cookies, and celebrate, if they did it quietly. Goldenson had a movie studio head's tolerance for offbeat and creative behavior, but it had to help the company's bottom line. With ABC's ratings going down the toilet and buyout proposals on the table, Goldenson was in no mood to tolerate further executive hanky-panky.

On January 20, the network broadcast Super Bowl XIX from Palo Alto, its first ever, the Miami Dolphins against the San Francisco 49ers. The $450 million multiyear contract that Fred Pierce and Roone Arledge had signed with the NFL had put ABC Sports into the Super Bowl rotation along with CBS and NBC, and ABC could boast that it had sold the industry's first million-dollar commercial minute. That was what Apple Computer and the other Super Bowl sponsors paid for sixty seconds of air time.

The million-dollar minute represented the culmination of fifty-odd years of growth in network broadcasting. Advertisers in 1931 had paid $3,000 for *thirty minutes* of network air time. In 1984, an unusual combination of election-year political advertising and Olympic spending boosted demand to an unprecedentedly inflated level. But in 1985, between new cable networks, syndicated programming, ABC's ratings shortfall, and lower demand, the outlook for the future was dim indeed. Michael Mallardi's staff had lowered its profit projections in the network's five-year plan.

The lower numbers shocked Fred Pierce. His experience as a broadcaster had led him to expect continually expanding revenues. During a review of the projections, Pierce told Mallardi's staff to come up with a higher number, and when a thirty-year-old MBA asked him how it would be met, he glowered, jutted out his jaw, and snapped back, "Because the creative people—*none of whom is in this room*—are going to make it happen!"

The Super Bowl gave Pierce an opportunity to make his own fervent pitch to Wall Street in his first meeting with analysts since the ill-fated encounter in mid-1979. ABC put on the dog with an all-expenses-paid trip to San Francisco, a private pregame banquet,

219

and tickets on the fifty-yard line. As Pierce sat with the analysts in the first-class section of the flight to the West Coast, he discussed the year ahead. "I *guarantee* we'll earn seven dollars and fifty cents a share," he promised.

What the Wall Street analysts knew, and he did not, was that Wall Street was already marching to attack. After the New Year, the news of Fowler's twelve-cities compromise leaked widely, and trading in ABC's stock picked up. More than 200,000 shares were changing hands every day, instead of the normal 60,000.

Shortly before the Super Bowl, John Sculley, a San Francisco money manager for Robert Bass, made a big purchase of ABC stock. Bass, one of the four Bass brothers of Fort Worth, Texas, was among America's most sophisticated investors. The Bass family fortune had been diversified out of oil and real estate and was growing rapidly in media. Robert and his brothers owned 25 percent of Walt Disney (it was through their influence that Michael Eisner had moved from Paramount to Disney as Disney's new chairman in the fall of 1984), and now had bought heavily into ABC. While the 49ers were beating the Dolphins, Sculley and Robert Bass called Leonard Goldenson's office and asked him for a meeting.

Goldenson, who was not yet entirely bereft of regulatory shields, used an ingenious tactic to ward off Bass and Sculley. Washington's program-ownership rules did not easily permit one owner to control a movie studio *and* a TV network, so Robert Bass's investment in ABC had the potential to jeopardize the four brothers' combined stake in Walt Disney. Sid Bass, Robert's older brother, was duly informed. Sid called Robert, who called John Sculley. On January 28, when the Robert Bass position in the stock was liquidated, more than 1.2 million ABC shares were traded on Wall Street.

Goldenson had beaten back one would-be corporate raider, but another quickly sprang up. After Gen. William Westmoreland's libel suit was settled in December—in CBS's favor—Jesse Helms, the Republican Senator from North Carolina, wandered into the budding Wall Street takeover arena.

Since no network had ever been taken over by an unfriendly bidder, there was no way that Helms could know how uncannily accurate his timing was. But Helms had honed his political skills in the 1960s as the on-air editorialist for WRAL-TV, the local ABC affiliate in Raleigh, and he was quick to attack when an opponent's flank was exposed. In mid-January, after Westmoreland had failed to vindicate himself in court, Helms's North Carolina-based political action committee set up Fairness in Media, an organization with the avowed aim of removing Dan Rather from the anchor's chair at CBS. Fairness in Media filed papers with the SEC announcing its intention to wage a proxy fight against CBS, and Helms signed a letter to his political constituents all across the country urging them to buy CBS shares.

The publicity that surrounded Helms's political fund-raising ploy put CBS into play on Wall Street and helped to camouflage the serious negotiations that were already underway at ABC. On February 7, less than a week after the FCC publicly announced its December 19 station-ownership plan, Tom Murphy called up Goldenson again.

"Leonard, the FCC has indicated it will change the seven-seven-seven rule," Murphy started off. "What do you think about my merger idea?"

He said he wanted to talk about a cash buyout, mentioning $90 per share. ABC's stock closed that day at 66¾; it was a 35 percent premium over the publicly traded value of the company.

Goldenson again informed Erlick, Pierce, and Mallardi of his conversation with Murphy, and this time the news did *not* travel. After the Jesse Helms announcement, every network stock on Wall Street had turned volatile. The day before Murphy's second call, ABC's stock rose 3 points on 723,000 traded shares. The day after, 879,000 more shares changed hands, and the price jumped again.

Only Everett Erlick, who had been at Goldenson's side through the failed ITT merger and the hostile moves of billionaire

Howard Hughes in the late 1960s, had traveled this road before. As the network's chief counsel Erlick was well positioned to interpret the long-term significance of Fowler's decision making in Washington. The first sign that Goldenson had decided to pursue Murphy's offer came on February 14 when Erlick called on a law firm in Washington to render an antitrust opinion about a possible merger with Capital Cities.

On Monday, February 18, Goldenson called Bruce Wasserstein and invited him and a small group of First Boston advisers to lunch later in the week. He called Tom Murphy the next day to inform him that he was interested in talking about a deal.

When he arrived at ABC the following Friday, Bruce Wasserstein knew nothing of Goldenson's conversations with Murphy and his pending plans. Wasserstein and the other First Bostoners were still on retainer as defensive advisers. Outlining a number of possible defensive strategies, Wasserstein told Goldenson that he could take ABC private in a leveraged buyout and become a controlling shareholder, or "buy in" shares and recapitalize, or buy another company and take on debt—Storer Communications, a large TV station and cable group owner, was one of the targets mentioned.

The one option that the First Boston advisers did not mention—and the one they most wanted to pursue—was that of selling ABC outright.

Goldenson listened politely through lunch and then invited them to his private office downstairs. Closing the doors, he recounted the substance of his two discussions with Murphy and said he wanted to sell the company to him—provided the price was right. First Boston's job was to find out exactly how much money ABC was worth, but Goldenson was quite direct in his instructions. Of all possible suitors, he had picked Murphy. He wanted to see the deal go through.

"This is the right home for this company," Goldenson said.

For three weeks, working in utmost secrecy, Goldenson proved that his old skills as a deal maker were still intact. Paralysis gripped his company. The senior-level staffers, who still believed they were running things, asked themselves, "Should we bring the old man in on this?" He was about to surprise them all.

A few days after asking Wasserstein to provide him with a high valuation, Goldenson met again with Tom Murphy. He told Murphy that he was interested, but that the price of $90 per share was too low. Murphy, on his return to Villard House, immediately telephoned Warren Buffett in Omaha, Nebraska.

If the Bass brothers were sophisticated investors, Warren Buffett ranked in the genius category. He had started in business in 1956 running a small mutual fund which in 1969 paid back $300,000 for every $10,000 invested by its partners. After liquidating the mutual fund, Buffett kept as his share a small New England textile firm called Berkshire Hathaway, and used it as his own semiprivate investment vehicle. During the 1973–74 bear market, he bought shares in advertising and in Capital Cities, and a sizable chunk of the Washington Post Company. He later bought the *Buffalo Evening News*, and by early 1985, still heavily but not exclusively invested in media stocks, had turned himself into a multibillionaire.

Buffett ran his one-man investment operation out of Omaha, his home town, but he flew to New York when Murphy called and at Villard House learned the full scope of the transaction that Murphy was contemplating. Capital Cities would have to borrow billions to buy ABC, and would have difficulty getting bank consent without a fresh injection of capital. Murphy invited Buffett to participate in this capacity as an equity investor. Although Goldenson had rejected his offer of $90 per share, Murphy said, he thought ABC would probably sell for "a little more than $100."

"Get a lockup," Buffett replied enthusiastically. Buffett feared that other, competing bids would emerge as soon as news of the negotiations was revealed. Buffett and Murphy jointly agreed that the next offer to Goldenson would be $3 billion, or a little more than $103 per share.

On the first of March, a Friday, Murphy got some news that almost nixed the brewing deal altogether. Goldenson believed that $103 per share was an unsatisfactory price and, in Buffett's words,

223

he "wanted a stock deal rather than a cash deal." "At this point," Buffett confided later in his notes, "[I] had the feeling that things were dead."

Wall Street deals of all sizes hinge on subtle distinctions and financing nuances like the one that threatened Murphy's plans for ABC. He wanted to pay cash for the network, to inherit control of the company outright with no strings attached. If he issued new Capital Cities shares and paid for ABC with them instead, the deal would be more of a true merger. The network's shareholders would participate in the future growth of the combined company, and the equity of his own shareholders would be substantially diluted. Moreover Goldenson, while not the controlling owner, would remain the new company's largest shareholder, because Warren Buffett would drop out of the deal.

Goldenson and Murphy took the weekend off to think the situation over. When the Capital Cities chairman called Goldenson back on Monday, he told him that he could be flexible on price but not on the principle of paying in cash. Goldenson, always willing to listen to a higher offer, agreed to meet with Murphy again.

On Tuesday, March 5, Murphy started off the intense negotiations with a bid of $115 per share for the company. Goldenson asked for $120. At this stratospheric level, each dollar-per-share was worth more than $29 million in buyout money. Murphy, preferring to split the difference his way, suggested a compromise of $117 per share—$500 million over his $3 billion offer, and nearly $1 billion over his $90-per-share bid. Goldenson, of course, wanted to split the difference the other way.

"Eighteen is my wife's favorite number," he countered. "Can you make it $118?"

The number 18 was engraved on Goldenson's tie pins and embossed on his luggage. The network's main telephone number was 887-7777, but his office line was 887-7018. To him—though he did not reveal it at the time—it meant *chai*, the Hebrew word for "life," for which Jews have great reverence. (The Hebrews, like the ancient Greeks, had no numerals and used letters as equivalents. The numerical equivalents of the letters in *chai*, 8 and 10, add up to 18.) Goldenson was selling his life's work, and when Murphy finally agreed to his price, this numerical symbol became part of the deal.

The following evening, the two men dined together at the Harvard Club, where it is a house rule not to discuss business on the premises.

13

On the Beach

On Sunday, March 17, a spring fever swept through the city. The sidewalks around St. Patrick's Cathedral were littered with debris from the St. Patrick's Day Parade. A sea of Celtic green had surged up Fifth Avenue on the day before the Sabbath, leaving its tidal marks on the cathedral's front steps, where Cardinal O'Connor had bestowed his annual blessing. Wooden police barricades, blue with white lettering, warning, "Police Line—Do Not Cross," lay stacked on the pavement.

The bargaining was over. The deal was done. It was a glamour deal in a glamour industry—at the time, the richest nonoil company transaction in United States business annals. And the fact that it was happening at all was something of a miracle. More than once Warren Buffett, who was investing $525 million in the deal, repeated his fear that it was "totally dead." Between March 6, when Goldenson and Murphy settled on $118 per share, and March 16, when the full-dress negotiations had ended, Goldenson had jacked up the price at every turn, asking Murphy to sweeten the pot with warrants and to guarantee ABC's employee-benefits package for a minimum of three years. Goldenson had the leverage of knowing that he could walk away from the discussions at any point and find another willing buyer. He forced Murphy to yield on almost every detail.

On Sunday evening, while Tom Murphy met over a meal with his Capital Cities directors in their old Gilded Age mansion head-quarters, the fact that buyout discussions had occurred at all was still a closely held secret. On Broadcasting Row, just two blocks west of where Murphy's dinner was taking place, ABC, NBC, and CBS were lined up like ducks, waiting to be toppled.

That weekend Goldenson issued a clarion call of his own. Wherever they happened to be, whatever they happened to be doing, the network's top executives left it to attend. Roone Arledge, on assignment with Ted Koppel in South Africa, took a jet to London and the Concorde to New York. Lew Erlicht, the president of ABC Entertainment, was struggling with the upcoming season in Hollywood, but he flew from LAX into Kennedy Airport. The network VIPs assembled like disciples at the Last Supper in the Plaza Hotel suite, and in the room where Barbara Walters conducted her celebrity interviews heard the news for the first time: Leonard Goldenson was selling the company out from under them.

While tossing and turning in bed that night, the ABC executives did not count sheep. It was time for them to begin counting restricted stock options.

The next day dawned simply enough. In the 66th Street studio where "Good Morning America" was broadcast, Joan Lunden and David Hartman interviewed musician Rod Stewart, former "Mork & Mindy" star Pam Dawber, Notre Dame basketball coach Digger Phelps, and the father of Terry Anderson, the AP reporter who had recently been taken hostage in Beirut. Goldenson's directors were already passing through the lobby of network headquarters by the time Steve Bell had finished reading the "Good Morning America" news. Alan Greenspan, not yet the chairman of the Federal Reserve, Frank Cary, the former chairman of IBM, and Leon Hess, the chairman of the Amerada Hess Oil Company and the

New York Jets were part of the parade of somber gray suits that filed into the express elevator, getting out on the fortieth floor.

When the New York Stock Exchange opened for business at 9:30, a bulletin went out over the Dow Jones wire. Trading in Capital Cities and ABC shares was temporarily suspended "pending an important announcement." This first public inkling of the news raced through ABC like a brushfire. Employees hurriedly spread the news, in low, urgent tones:

"Did you hear what's happening?"

"The stock hasn't opened."

"The game's up."

"We're being taken over."

Behind the closed doors of the board room, the directors sat down around the massive polished-walnut table. Bruce Wasserstein outlined the financial aspects of the deal. First Boston was charging ABC a $6 million fee for a written opinion that the transaction was "fair," so Wasserstein had plenty of charts, graphs, and illustrations proving the point. His advice to Goldenson during the negotiations had helped raise the sale price by hundreds of millions of dollars.

For Goldenson, it was a master stroke. He had preempted hostile moves against his company, enriched his shareholders, and solved his management-succession problems. He was selling out, true enough. He was selling out but in controlled fashion, before the rest of television caught on. Once again, he was setting the new industry standard.

While the directors were meeting in New York that morning, Elton Rule was driving to Los Angeles. Rule was among the handful of people Goldenson had consulted about his plans before acting, and he still held all the ABC stock that he had accumulated before leaving the company. The buyout would net him more than $14 million.

Jack Hausman, Goldenson's director of longest standing, interrupted a golf vacation in Palm Springs to attend the meeting by long-distance telephone. In 1950, Hausman, Goldenson, and their wives had cofounded United Cerebral Palsy, the nation's second-largest medical charity, so he was well apprised of Goldenson's intentions. When the meeting was two hours old, Hausman wanted to get out on the golf course, and he broke in.

"It's a good mix," Hausman said. "It's a good price. And most important, it's with the right people. I okay it. Now I'm going to play golf."

The board members in New York, with the outside directors voting first, gave their unanimous approval. In a few minutes, the first phase of the deal was officially done.

The boardroom doors opened. The deal makers, flushed with a nearly sexual excitement, milled about in the yellow-carpeted fortieth-floor reception area. At Villard House, the Capital Cities board of directors had voted its assent just moments before. Both sets of participants sensed that they were now part of broadcasting history. For the first time since 1953, a network was changing hands. For the first time since 1943, someone besides Goldenson was doing the buying. For the first time since 1928, all three networks were about to belong to new owners.

Tom Murphy and a contingent of Capital Cities directors and executives trekked across Fifth Avenue, walked into Hard Rock, and took the elevator to the fortieth floor to pay homage to Goldenson and claim their prize.

In the conference room one floor down, the network's senior managers had gathered to learn the results of the board meeting. Having started to digest the news the night before, most were ravenous for new information.

"Ah, Michael Moriarty, how are you?" Mark Mandala, the new president of ABC Television, joked as Michael P. Mallardi entered the room. As an inside director, Mallardi was a prime source of hard information, and with men named Murphy and Burke running things, it was never too early to affect an Irish lilt.

Pierce who had been sitting at Goldenson's side during the previous fortnight, stoically watching the company slip from his fingers, had the sorry task of addressing the troops. It was too late for him to change his spots.

230

"I've relied heavily on you guys over the years," Pierce began, his eyes glistening with tears. "In the next few months I'll be counting on you more than ever."

"Fred, to a great extent we're depending on where you stand with new management," Roone Arledge quickly said. "Where do you stand?"

"Well, I'll be vice chairman."

"Who will you be reporting to?"

"I'll be reporting to Dan Burke."

Arledge let it go at that.

The official press release about the merger spelled out the new hierarchy:

> Leonard Goldenson will serve as chairman of the executive committee of the new company, and Thomas S. Murphy will be chairman of the board and chief executive officer. Frederick S. Pierce will be vice chairman of the board . . . Daniel B. Burke will be president and chief operating officer.

When the afternoon feed of "Entertainment Tonight" was beamed by satellite across America, ABC News landed the signal and played it over the network's in-house closed-circuit system. "Entertainment Tonight" gave rank-and-file employees their first real news about the merger.

"Hello everyone, I'm Robb Weller."

"And I'm Mary Hart."

"CBS was the network some people thought might change ownership," Mary Hart said brightly in Los Angeles, "but ABC has beaten them to the contract table in a very hush-hush deal."

Dick Shoemaker, the show's New York correspondent, gave details.

"The merger of ABC and Capital Cities Communications came as a tremendous surprise to almost everyone in the broadcasting industry. The total deal is said to be worth three and a half billion dollars, with Capital Cities bringing in a totally new management team to run the giant company."

231

When everyone reassembled for a press conference at 5 P.M., even Everett Erlick, the company's ornery general counsel, was smiling.

"As discussions proceeded," Murphy and Goldenson said publicly, "we found that Capital Cities and ABC complemented each other particularly well in assets and common experience. We are convinced that the combination will be in the public interest."

The press in attendance danced around Roone Arledge, seeking pithy one-liners. Arledge obliged them later in *USA Today*. "It's a good marriage that uses the wife's name," he would say. "I don't see anything dramatically different. I would think that I am one of the major assets at ABC, and I would think that they merged, not because of me, but in looking over the assets they are getting, I imagine I am part of this deal."

A growing chorus of media voices picked up the story. The *New York Post* splashed it all over its late afternoon edition: "ABC Gobbled Up in $3.5B Takeover."

"To paraphrase Pogo, we have seen the news and it is us," Peter Jennings commented wryly at the start of his "World News Tonight" broadcast.

"When members of the Politburo are summoned back to town, you know it's not just to discuss ratings," White House correspondent Sam Donaldson quipped later in the week to *Newsweek*. "Clearly, someone had died."

On the day after St. Patrick's Day, few people in America knew who had died, or why, or what the story meant. The television pictures kept coming. The television sets stayed on. But before the ink was dry on the merger contract that Leonard Goldenson and Thomas Murphy had signed, a flood of money began pouring into the broadcasting industry.

When ABC's stock reopened for trading on the afternoon of March 18, the price shot up from 74¼ per share, where it had closed the previous Friday, to 115. The question on every senior-level executive's mind—those eighty who had been given restricted stock options, supposedly to encourage their job performance—was how much those options were worth *now*.

That afternoon, Michael Mallardi held a high-level meeting to discuss that very question. He was launching into a detailed staff explanation of the "golden parachute" provisions of the deal when he realized that not everyone would participate.

"Would everyone here *not* in the restricted stock plan please leave the room?" he abruptly commanded.

The amount of cash coming to those who *were* in the restricted stock plan was presented in black-and-white in the proxy statement that shareholders of both companies were sent before voting to approve the merger. On August 9, some 268,725 shares worth more than $32.5 million would be awarded to the fortunate eighty, like a reward not for effort but for being in the right place when the companies merged. Even before the merger, the price of an ABC share had quadrupled since 1981, when the stock plan was instituted—all the time the company itself was going down the tubes.

Beyond the first pool of glimmering network shares lay another rich handout. On January 6, 1986, when the Capital Cities buyout was scheduled to take effect, several hundred thousand shares, worth tens of millions of dollars, would be distributed to the same executives—minus the few unlucky ones who had lost their jobs in the interim. Capital Cities had guaranteed existing employee benefits for a minimum of three years after the transaction, and the payments on the restricted stock plan were part of the deal.

Goldenson and Murphy had broken a psychological barrier, standing an old idea—that the airwaves were public property, not to be bought or sold for private gain—on its head. Wall Street quickly noted that less than half the $3.5 billion price paid for ABC could be attributed to tangible assets. The rest, more than $2 billion, was "goodwill" (in the accountants' term), money that derived from the government license that the network held. The license was free.

233

Once ABC was sold, it was not so much a question of *whether* CBS and NBC would fall into the hands of new owners as when, for how much, and to whom. *"Après moi le déluge,"* Louis XV once said. In March 1985, Leonard Goldenson had opened the broadcasting industry sluice gates.

Hardly a week passed that spring and summer without news of another big deal. Rupert Murdoch paid $2 billion for John Kluge's Metromedia TV stations, combined them with Marvin Davis' Twentieth Century-Fox, and created the Fox Network.

The Tribune Company purchased KTLA-TV, an independent TV station in Los Angeles, for $510 million, eclipsing by $290 million the largest sum ever previously paid for a local TV outlet. As the money fever passed from broadcasting into related publishing, cable, and Madison Avenue businesses, no sector of the wider American communications industry was left untouched. They were all convulsed in a takeover frenzy.

The reaction was so immediate that less than twenty-four hours after Capital Cities and ABC announced their news, the three-man Wall Street investment boutique of Coniston Partners announced that it would wage a proxy fight against Storer Communications. Labeling itself the Committee for the Full Value of Storer Communications, the Coniston raiding party filed an FCC petition that eroded the last piece of the public-interest dam in Washington, which had protected broadcasters from hostile takeovers in the past. Mark Fowler allowed Coniston to take its case to Storer's shareholders without filing a transfer-of-ownership form, which would have caused public hearings and procedural delay. The shareholders owned Storer, not Storer management, the FCC reasoned. So the institutional investors who held Storer stock—many of them representing pension-fund money that belonged to middle-class employees who would subsequently be thrown out of their jobs by the takeover management—were allowed to vote on the takeover.

Storer's fate was ultimately decided by a mild-mannered "buy-side" analyst for Alliance Capital Management in New York named Ted Fitilis—who had recommended Storer shares to his firm's portfolio managers and clients before the Coniston proxy fight. Alliance Capital controlled $20 billion in institutional funds, and Fitilis controlled more than 12 percent of Storer. He held the swing vote in the Storer war.

Would he side with Peter Storer, the son of the company's founder, who had desperately joined forces with the "white knights" of Kohlberg, Kravis, and Roberts to maintain a semblance of control? Or would he side with Coniston Partners? He held blue proxy cards (Coniston) in one hand, and white proxy cards (Storer) in another.

Fitilis ultimately sided with Storer, voting the white cards, but the company's management still did not retain control. The proxy war had forced it to form an alliance with Kohlberg, Kravis, and Roberts, Wall Street's leading takeover team. Its assets were broken up and resold separately—the fate Leonard Goldenson had just managed to avoid at ABC.

After the Storer transaction, the FCC gave a green light to every hostile takeover petition that came before it, and friendly and unfriendly speculators rushed to close the gap between the broadcast industry's publicly traded and private buyout values.

On March 18, the same day that Capital Cities and ABC announced their deal, Ted Turner was giving a deposition in New York as part of CBS's lawsuit against Fairness in Media.

Under oath Turner admitted that he had consulted with Jesse Helms's group about possibly acting in concert against CBS. William Paley's proud network, the old Tiffany's of broadcasting, had progressed from a battle about ideology in the Westmoreland libel trial into the snake pit of high finance.

On April 18, Turner unveiled his own junk-bond offering of $5.4 billion for all outstanding CBS shares. After successfully parlaying two UHF-TV stations in Atlanta and Charlotte into WTBS and Cable News Network, Turner was determined to bag a network. He put no cash on the table, proposing instead that CBS's shareholders trade their equity in the company for his high-yield debt. Tom Wyman, terming Turner's bid "grossly inadequate," concocted an elaborate defensive strategy. He bought back $1 billion worth of CBS shares, and changed the company bylaws to limit the amount of debt that it could carry on its books. By these means CBS beat back the Turner bid on Wall Street and in the courts.

But Laurence Tisch, after being rebuffed by Goldenson in 1981, made his Trojan Horse move against CBS in August 1985. He promised Wyman he would help the network defend itself against political opportunists like Jesse Helms and upstart entrepreneurs like Turner. Piggybacking himself onto a short-term arbitrage opportunity in the CBS stock buyback plan, Tisch started buying shares. At Wyman's invitation he became the company's largest shareholder. But within a year Tisch had become the biggest opportunist of all, switching his passive investment to an active one and deposing the hapless Wyman. (Turner quenched his thirst for the big deal by rushing to the MGM film library; Las Vegas financier Kirk Kerkorian fleeced him in that $1.5 billion purchase.)

Two networks were down. There was only one to go. When the General Electric Company purchased RCA and NBC in December 1985, the hat trick was complete. The industry had come full circle. General Electric had given birth to RCA in 1919 and to NBC in 1926. Now it had swallowed them up.

14

Summertime Blues

On the evening of Friday, March 22, the old network logo outside Hard Rock was shrouded in brown manila paper. ABC's offices were closing for the weekend, and except for a few security guards the lobby was empty.

Was the network's symbol being replaced, one departing employee wanted to know? Would the initials "CCC/ABC" or "Capital Cities–ABC" be put in the old spot?

"It's just being cleaned," said the lobby security guard.

While Tom Murphy and Leonard Goldenson flew, side by side in a private plane, to Washington, D.C. to make the obligatory courtesy call on the FCC, the forbidding prospect of a top-to-bottom housecleaning spread through ABC headquarters.

At a broadcasting industry luncheon a few weeks later, Ben Hoberman, the president of ABC Radio, greeted Herb Granath, the president of ABC Video Enterprises. To a friendly "How are you?" Granath replied with a shaky, palms-down gesture.

"That pretty much describes all of ABC," commented Hoberman.

"Yup, and pretty soon it'll be replaced with another," Granath said. Hoberman drew a finger across his throat and smiled, and the other executives at the table broke into nervous laughter.

Everyone at ABC observed different coping rituals in the wake of the buyout agreement, but the level of anxiety was running so high that Goldenson, Pierce, Murphy, and Burke staged a closed-circuit meeting for all employees. David Brinkley, the famous newsman, moderated.

"Gentlemen," Brinkley began, speaking like a TV news anchor, "I think you will all agree that what has happened between Capital Cities and ABC is a piece of broadcasting history."

Brinkley turned to Leonard Goldenson. "Mr. Goldenson, how did it happen?"

Goldenson forthrightly described the gist of his discussions with Murphy and added that his main motivation for pursuing the sale of ABC had been to assure that the network would not be taken over by a hostile bidder, broken up, and resold. He gave no details of the deregulatory moves in Washington or the Wall Street activity that had caused him to agree to Murphy's friendly bid.

"Mr. Murphy, you must be able to add a bit to that," said Brinkley.

In courtly fashion, Murphy recalled his meeting with Fred Pierce in Phoenix three years before, when Pierce had just learned that he would be named ABC's president. Even then, Murphy recalled, Pierce had told him, "It might make sense for our two companies to get together."

Brinkley, turning to Pierce, asked, "So the first germ of this idea was yours?"

"I guess that's the way it started," Pierce replied ruefully. "I didn't realize it would wind up this way."

"Whoever thought it would come to this?" Pierce later echoed himself. "Who could have known things would end this way?"

In casual conversations with friends and colleagues throughout the spring, Pierce seemed bewildered to realize that ABC would no longer be his to run. But there was a nine-month waiting period between the announcement of the deal, on March 18, and January 1986, when it was scheduled to close. Until the FCC approved and Capital Cities actually paid the $3.5 billion, Pierce was still in charge. It did not take long for the double-talk to begin.

"We are pleased and proud to tell you," said the first post-merger letter to ABC employees, "that Capital Cities' management team shares our belief that [the key to] success in this business is respect for our employees. . . . We can assure you that employee benefits equally favorable in the aggregate as those currently provided by ABC will be continued."

The letter did not mention that employee benefits mattered only if the employees were on the job to collect them.

The press, meanwhile, was pointing out that Murphy's company had only twenty-four people, including secretaries, at its Villard Houses headquarters, while ABC had more than four hundred on its corporate staff. "Culture clash" was the new operative term. When Capital Cities and ABC shareholders both approved the merger, the takeover began to look like the Manchu invasion of China, with the small, highly efficient Capital Cities army poised across Fifth Avenue, waiting to impose itself on bloated, decadent ABC.

While many network employees worried about keeping their jobs, Pierce was trying to hire a new chief programmer. The prime-time schedule was miserably weak. In his last few months as president of ABC Entertainment, Lew Erlicht had cut himself loose from Thomopoulos and Pierce and begun to make a small start in rebuilding the schedule. He put Glenn Gordon Caron, who had coproduced a promising network pilot two years earlier, under contract. "Moonlighting," Caron's second effort, premiered with Bruce Willis and Cybill Shepherd during the spring. Two other series in development—the comedy "Growing Pains" and "MacGyver," one of the first shows produced by Henry Winkler under his big 1978 network production contract—also showed promise.

But the overall schedule was so feeble that Pierce reached back into the network's past to try to fix it. A new contract bringing

239

back Leonard Goldberg, ABC's chief programmer from 1966 to 1969, was virtually signed, sealed, and delivered in mid-April. The press release announcing the appointment was written. The plans collapsed at the last minute.

"ABC Fails to Lure Ex-Program Chief Back to Help Cure Ailing Program Schedule," declared the headline in the *Wall Street Journal*.

The reason for Goldberg's unwillingness to return to ABC went to the heart of broadcasting's problems in Hollywood. In 1957, Goldberg had joined ABC as a network rating clerk (Pierce's old job), but he had become a multimillionaire since he turned himself into a Hollywood independent producer. He fully appreciated the difference between working on salary as an employee and sharing in profits as a program supplier. Talent contracts were the norm in Hollywood, even among the studio management. The new deals that Diller and Eisner had signed at Twentieth Century-Fox and Disney linked their compensation to the box-office results of their movies and to growth in the studios' stock. At ABC Goldberg wanted his salary to be based on a similar scale of incentive and performance. If the ratings went up, he felt the chief programmer should get a percentage of the added profit. For Pierce this demand was unacceptable. Hollywood had priced itself out of network TV's range.

The network departed from its normal spring practice by holding its affiliate meeting in New York in May, and Pierce tried to make light of an awkward situation.

"We liked our affiliates so much that this year we decided to merge with one of them," he said in his opening remarks to the three-day gathering.

The top executives of Capital Cities did not attend the business portion of the meeting, since the soon-to-be network owner was no longer an "affiliate" in any real sense of the term. But Tom Murphy and Dan Burke watched closely all of ABC's business moves during the period before the takeover was finalized, and while Pierce was delivering his welcoming address to the rest of the gathering, Dan Burke stood in the rear balcony of the New York Hilton ballroom, listening. As soon as Pierce finished, Burke slipped away from the crowd.

Meanwhile, after months of planning, another network gala was in the works. Gary Pudney had organized an affiliates' celebration based on the ABC-TV special "Night of 1,000 Stars." The Radio City Music Hall in-house extravaganza was to climax the three-day meeting. Six thousand guests assembled in the cavernous hall to watch the four-hour show. The stars of "Dynasty" gave a fashion show. Jack Wagner of "General Hospital" sang a new tune, "All I Need." Lana Turner, who had appeared as the 1,000th guest star on "The Love Boat," sailed across the stage in a mock-ocean liner. Emmanuel Lewis of "Webster" delivered his patented act as a pint-sized star. Ted Koppel and Barbara Walters of ABC News performed a comedy routine. It was past 11 P.M. when the members of the audience, many of them network employees given tickets at the last minute, strolled up the red carpet from Radio City to the Hilton hotel, where a sumptuous buffet dinner awaited. New York City had closed down Avenue of the Americas. On a beautiful spring night, the network treated itself to a final fling.

When the first round of staff cutbacks, destined eventually to build into a wave of layoffs, was announced in mid-July, they were described as part of "an ongoing trimming process." The network public-relations staff waged a cold war in the press to reposition Fred Pierce as a cost-cutter. ABC's 2.5 percent work-force reduction, which was to be completed by Labor Day, involved 350 employees. Each department head had a quota, and department heads were allowed latitude in deciding exactly which employees to let go. With a Darwinian rigor, the company weeded out its weak and wounded employees, usually older middle managers who had not progressed far in their careers or had no powerful protector championing their cause. The severance terms were one week of pay for each year of service and $10,000 in salary. An employee earning $60,000, for instance, who had worked at ABC for fifteen years received a one-time payment of twenty-one weeks' salary. If the combination of an employee's age and years of service reached the "magic number" of 80, the employee got full pension benefits upon leaving. A sixty-year-old with twenty years of employment qualified; a fifty-five-year-old with twenty years did not.

The network shed its weak and ungainly members like a woman burning letters from old lovers. It was discarding a part of its institutional past, preparing for the marriage buyout. And just as the employees singled out for termination learned of their misfortune, the first chunk of restricted stock options came due, distributing more than $32.5 million among the favored eighty executives.

Where terminations were insufficient, the network used settlements to bury its secrets before Capital Cities arrived. Cash payments, increased pensions, and in some instances eligibility to receive the second installment of restricted stock were the digging tools. Employees signed separation agreements that legally constrained them from discussing the network's business after they had left the company, and this covered up the holes.

Most settlements worked so anonymously that no one outside ABC ever knew what was being covered up or by whom or for what reason. Two, however, took place publicly, in full view. The spectacles of Tony Thomopoulos and Cecily Coleman provided comic relief and intrigue that entertained network bystanders through the long hot summer.

Thomopoulos, who had married Cristina Ferrare, also gave every appearance of being interested in John DeLorean's money.

Ferrare had met DeLorean in 1973 at a party at the Gucci store in Beverly Hills. She was a twenty-three-year-old, recently divorced *Vogue* model, seeking to develop a career as an actress. DeLorean, twenty-five years her senior, had left a big job at General Motors and was going into business for himself. During the decade that they were married, Ferrare abandoned the world of modeling and acting. Her career was eclipsed by that of the more flamboyant and entrepreneurial DeLorean. After he founded the DeLorean Motor Company in Northern Ireland, however, DeLorean became enmeshed in a government "sting" operation, and ended up in an airport hotel room, a suitcase full of cocaine in his lap, saying, "It's better than gold. Gold weighs more than this, for God's sake."

During DeLorean's indictment and trial, Ferrare stood by his side in Los Angeles in the role of a faithful wife. All the while, she was using the publicity that attended his disgrace to showcase her beauty and revitalize her career. Ferrare still had her good looks, and in early 1984, when she met Thomopoulos at a party and asked him to dance, she used them to snare his attention. At the time, Thomopoulos was engaged to marry Candace Farrell, a beautiful executive in charge of advertising at ABC Motion Pictures. He broke off the engagement and began dating Ferrare.

Each week, as the government's case against DeLorean proceeded to trial, Ferrare received a fresh supply of dresses from a New York fashion designer. According to DeLorean, she spent two hours getting dressed and made up in order to look her impeccable best at her daily court appearances. By the end of the trial, she was almost as much the star of the proceedings as her husband. Her sculpted facial features began appearing in glossy magazines and on local TV stations across the country again.

In August 1984, when DeLorean was found not guilty, he stood up in the Los Angeles courtroom and exclaimed, "Praise the Lord!" (The flamboyant entrepreneur had been turned into a born-again Christian by his trial experience.) Ferrare told him that she was leaving him. She had been hired as the on-air hostess of "A.M. Los Angeles," she said, a morning show on KABC-TV, and she and Thomopoulos had leased a house in Hollywood together, starting September 1.

While ABC's programming disintegrated that fall and winter, Thomopoulos and Ferrare became a picture-book Hollywood couple. They were the perfect industry romance—the TV industry mogul and the classic beauty. Son of a Greek restaurant owner from the Bronx meets daughter of an Italian butcher from Cleveland.

The only problem was the Capital Cities takeover. Since Thomopoulos was not a member of ABC's board of directors, he had played no role in the discussions that led to the buyout. In fact he had been kept very much in the dark, and even served as an unwitting decoy for the deal. On March 12, just as Goldenson and Murphy were concluding their talks, Thomopoulos had announced a "reorganization" in his Broadcast Group to fix ABC's flagging ratings, without reference to the takeover deal.

After Ferrare filed for a divorce from DeLorean in California in October, she and Thomopoulos were married in a private April ceremony at the Palm Springs home of Wallis Annenberg. Wallis, the daughter of *TV Guide* billionaire Walter Annenberg, was a good friend of Gary Pudney, who had served as Thomopoulos' best man at the ceremony.

DeLorean's reputation was in tatters, but he still had an estate worth an estimated $20 million or more and in California the divorce statutes called for the equitable distribution of all marital property. Ferrare was legally entitled to half that sum. The only roadblock standing between her obtaining $10 million or more from her former husband—a settlement far richer than that received by any network executive in the Capital Cities buyout—was the prenuptial agreement that she had signed before her marriage to DeLorean in 1973. DeLorean, seeking to avoid any payment, had separately filed for divorce in New Jersey.

During the summer of 1985, while most network employees worried about where the next paycheck would come from, the three-ring circus among DeLorean, Ferrare, and Thomopoulos was broadcast in both states like a domestic squabble in "L.A. Law."

"She's not pregnant—she's just fat," the *New York Post* reported in May, making Thomopoulos' new bride a juicy item for the gossip columns. "The switchboard at L.A.'s KABC-TV was lighting up every morning with fans wanting to know. So many, that she finally went on the air and told her viewers, 'I'm not pregnant—I just got fat.' "

"She gained weight like crazy after the trial. She went through so much," Ferrare's manager explained. "When it was over, the pressure was relieved, and she started to eat."

Ferrare's chances for getting half of DeLorean's estate depended on her convincing the courts that he had taken advantage of her youth and inexperience when she signed the prenuptial agreement. But when the facts were put before Judge Olson, a retired judge selected mutually by both parties as the independent arbitrator in California, he ruled that Ferrare was not "a retarded, unsophisticated ninny from Peoria, Illinois, or Davenport, Iowa. Such people rarely get to a party at Gucci's in the first place. . . . Her previous marriage and divorce, her six or seven years of professional modeling experience and the inferences that can be drawn from this 'fast track' life all tend to negate the claims now made on her behalf."

Olson noted that Ferrare's application for divorce in California was invalid, since she had not yet fulfilled the state's residency requirements when the petition was filed. Until that requirement was fulfilled the Thomopoulos-Ferrare marriage was bigamous.

When the case moved to the rolling New Jersey countryside outside New York, where DeLorean owned a farm, Thomopoulos actively entered the divorce proceedings. Taking time off from the network, he brought his own attorney into the case. His entourage arrived daily in a network limousine to the rural county seat where the disposition of marital assets would be decided. Thomopoulos sat in the front row of the courtroom discussing legal strategy. He had opted out of ABC, and was apportioning his time in strict accordance with where he thought he had the greatest chance of getting rich.

In his ruling on the case, the New Jersey state judge said of Ferrare that "she was not a 'babe in the woods.' There was no fraud or misrepresentation committed by the husband [DeLorean].

245

He made it perfectly clear that he did not want her to receive any portion of the marital assets in his name."

So DeLorean kept his $20 million, and Thomopoulos and Ferrare had to be content with each other.

Cecily Coleman had better luck.

When her lawsuit went before Judge Barrington Parker in federal district court in Washington, the transfer of ABC's station licenses to Capital Cities was pending before the FCC. The discovery phase of Coleman's lawsuit and the Capital Cities merger negotiations had advanced along roughly parallel tracks. The network was still supporting Jim Abernathy after his dismissal—it could do little else since Everett Erlick and Peter Cusack were codefendants in the case. But Coleman's lawsuit also coincided with the near-revolt among the women producers and correspondents at the ABC News bureau in Washington. This had climaxed the previous February, when the news division gave a special luncheon for Barbara Walters to celebrate an award she was receiving. When American Women in Radio and Television cited Walters for being a "role model for so many broadcasters," Arledge invited all the top women in the division to New York, including overseas correspondents, to meet with the corporate brass and fete the "20/20" anchor. Responding to toasts from Pierce and Arledge, Walters described her many career breaks and added, obliquely referring to the resentment that many of the other women colleagues felt toward Kathleen Sullivan, ABC's only other woman anchor, "Kathleen is in a dangerous position. We must all support her."

Carole Simpson, a black correspondent, and several of her colleagues had come armed with computer printouts demonstrating with numerical efficiency the network's habit of discriminating against its female employees. When Simpson presented the salary and on-air assignment figures, Arledge's newest management paramour, who had previously dismissed the women's claims as being motivated by professional jealousy, remarked, "Isn't that terrible."

Arledge himself exclaimed, "A pattern!" After being called on the carpet by his own staff on the eve of the takeover, he could do little else. Kathleen Sullivan, the one exception to what was being discussed, remained silent throughout the meeting.

ABC News took steps to put its own house in order, promptly promoting a half-dozen women, raising salaries, and forming a management-sponsored women's counsel to monitor continuing improvements. The more activist women correspondents and producers never filed the class action lawsuit they had threatened.

But Coleman got her own settlement a few months later. With her lawsuit scheduled to go to trial at the end of June 1985, she had added to her legal team attorneys from the National Organization of Women (NOW), who toned down the confrontational Mark Lane. Dan Burke, the president of Capital Cities, was a member of NOW's board of directors and had been the featured speaker at its annual fund-raising dinner the year before, so the plaintiff had an indirect ally while the FCC was deciding whether to transfer ABC's TV licenses to the new owners. The only question was how much money Coleman's complaint was worth. In December 1984, before the takeover, she refused an offer of $250,000 to settle the case. Through the judge, Lane had gained access to the network's personnel files on similar cases, and on that basis had expanded her claim to $15 million, alleging that a "pattern" of sexual harassment existed at the network.

But on June 28, when the jury had been selected and the trial was scheduled to begin, there was still no settlement. Only when a Washington attorney named Al Kramer, with whom Tom Murphy had had dealings fifteen years before during the Capital Cities' acquisition of Triangle Broadcasting, swung into action as a go-between, did the two parties begin to seek common ground. The judge delayed the opening arguments until the following day at 2 P.M. At noon on June 29, Murphy arrived at ABC's New York headquarters for an upstairs meeting. At 2:15 the judge came out of his chambers in Washington, announced that the case had been settled, and dismissed the jury.

"ABC Harassment Case Is Settled for $500,000," the *Wash-*

ington Post reported the next day, disclosing the supposedly secret terms. The NOW attorney for Coleman called it "a big victory" for women's rights. Two thirds of the money went tax-free to Coleman, one-third to Mark Lane. Her settlement windfall was worth just about as much as the restricted stock options that Abernathy had been forced to forfeit when he was fired from ABC.

The network atmosphere after Labor Day was like the title of the 1960s song, "Eve of Destruction." The only stop left on the calendar before Capital Cities took over was the start of the fall TV season. Hurricane Gloria rode up the East Coast during Week 1, its dissipated eye making landfall on Long Island on September 27. The weekly Nielsen release arrived the following Tuesday like a barometer falling vertically. NBC had averaged a 19.3 rating, CBS 17.4, and ABC 14.2. It was the network's worst prime-time season start since 1962.

A TV network could rebound from one bad season if the ratings improved quickly, because advertising rates were adjusted after the fact. But ABC's ratings did not improve. Week after week, despite World Series broadcasts and a Brandon Stoddard miniseries about the Civil War called "North and South," the numbers remained mired in the basement. And for the first time in network TV history, Madison Avenue demand for Big Three advertising was shrinking. The increased competition from cable networks, syndicated programming, and independent TV stations had finally begun to drain away the network's life blood.

The beginning of the end came in one hectic week in mid-November. Tony Thomopoulos resigned first, citing "family considerations" and his desire to live full-time on the West Coast. "This was a life-style change," he told the *New York Times*, "an amicable parting."

Fred Pierce praised his colleague for making "significant contributions to our successes over the past twelve years," and announced a corporate restructuring of his own. Among his personnel changes, Lew Erlicht was demoted out of the chief programmer's job.

Goldenson then bequeathed a new chief programmer—Brandon Stoddard, his favorite—to the new Capital Cities arrivals. He summoned him to the thirty-ninth floor office to ask him to accept the post. Stoddard had always refused the same invitation when only Pierce had offered it in the past. A direct request from Goldenson was a different matter.

A few minutes after Stoddard, at the New York airport on his way back to Hollywood, called to accept, Goldenson dialed Tom Murphy at Villard House.

"Tom," he said, "I just wanted you to know: Fred and I have just spoken to Brandon about the job. He said I was very persuasive."

When the FCC, following a different timetable, gave the merger its official approval the next day, Pierce called two dozen remaining staffers together for a luncheon on the fortieth floor.

"Since a number of you were in town," he began, "I wanted to get you all together to discuss the management reorganization. As it happens, today the FCC has decided that our merger with Capital Cities is approved. There are six weeks before the agreement legally takes effect. The reorganization that has been announced, I feel, is doing a lot to the energy and vitality of our organization. The response from all quarters has been overwhelmingly positive."

Pierce canvassed the room, asking his staff to confirm the "overwhelmingly positive" response to the changes. "It was like Custer and the Indians," said one executive. Pierce was a beleaguered general, trying to rally the troops by having his lieutenants describe all the great deeds they would accomplish—"after we get them Indians."

Before the luncheon was over, Goldenson stepped into the dining room. To his credit, Pierce hailed the founder's arrival, raised his glass and said, "Leonard, if it weren't for you, many of us wouldn't be here today."

Goldenson, who had once bought a network himself, had few illusions about what it all meant. When the FCC's approval came through, he had called Tom Murphy and told him, "Tom, the candy store is yours."

Pierce would learn the meaning of this phrase on a bitterly cold day in early January. Clad in a camel's hair winter coat, wearing a grim, hollow look on his face, he walked from Hard Rock to Villard House—on the same path that Murphy had walked nine months earlier, but in reverse—carrying a small manila envelope tucked under one arm. It contained the terms of his resignation from ABC.

Epilogue

"The long months of preparation for the merger are over," Tom Murphy and Dan Burke told network employees on the day they took over ABC. "Today we become Capital Cities/ABC, Inc."

They added: "The economic environment in which we are operating will make the year ahead challenging and will require the best efforts of all of us."

Behind the bland art of corporate understatement one could discern an old children's rhyme: "Humpty Dumpty sat on a wall, Humpty Dumpty had a great fall. All the King's horses and all the King's men, couldn't put Humpty together again."

The takeover waters subsided slowly on Broadcasting Row between January 1986 and the end of the decade, and when they receded the Big Three networks were stranded like beached leviathans, disoriented mammals run aground. The skyscraper houses of ABC, NBC, and CBS were still standing. Three big companies still dominated American broadcasting. And the country's viewers—vegetating, entranced or amused—were still glued to their TV sets. In one respect, the most important from Wall Street's point of view, the networks were more impregnable than ever.

The vast umbrella of General Electric and the sizeable shareholdings of Laurence Tisch and Warren Buffett protected their new managers from any takeover activity from hostile bidders in the future.

But network broadcasting as it had been set up since the 1920s was dying.

As the new owners imposed a harsh new creed on the decrepit organisms they had acquired, Broadcasting Row was hit by a management neutron bomb. Financiers and deregulators had put a fresh twist on the wartime oxymoron: "To save the village we had to destroy it." Preserving the Big Three involved the destruction of the old network culture, the end of its patriarchal Jewish traditions, and the termination of massive numbers of citizen-employees. Of the new network owners only one—Laurence Tisch— was a Jew, and although religion and public service may have been one motivation for his controlling CBS, profit margins, not a *mitzvah*, were his overriding concern.

And the funny thing was, America's viewers were the beneficiary of the networks' demise. For every indicator of Big Three network weakness—Nielsen ratings and viewership down, revenues from cable and TV syndication up, Big Three advertising down—more and more new channels were opening up for the public to choose from. Every advertising dollar siphoned away from ABC, NBC, and CBS (more than $2 billion in 1989) ended up in the coffers of new national TV distribution outlets. In the more than 70 percent of American homes served by cable, the viewer could turn glassy-eyed while flipping across as many as forty different channels, instead of the usual three.

On the other hand, the blossoming of new channels did not improve television; it merely diluted the medium, adding opportunities for special-interest viewing while eroding existing programming formats and the few remaining programming standards of the old network order. And in the process, it demolished prospects for continued network profitability on anything like the scale of the past. Only NBC regularly recorded profits during the post-takeover period, thanks to high ratings from "The Cosby Show" and other prime-time programs put in place by Brandon Tartikoff, Fred Silverman's successor as chief programmer at NBC. CBS dipped into the red or hovered near break-even in successive years. In 1986, in the biggest financial reversal at a network ever, ABC took $70 million in losses—a $170 million shortfall from its profits the year before.

There was no prospect of imminent network relief, either. Beyond the ongoing revolution in national TV distribution wrought by satellites and cable loomed another, more long-term techno-logical threat—the twin developments of high-definition television and fiber optic transmission, which gave every indication of un-dercutting local TV station franchises, where ABC, NBC, and CBS still made money, in the 1990s.

ABC had climbed high and fallen fast in the decade before its takeover, and its landing was the rudest (and the least publicized) in the industry. As soon as Capital Cities officially took over in January 1986, Tom Murphy and Dan Burke began dismantling the old network and remolding it in their own image.

Casual drug use was the first perk to go. Less than one week into the takeover, employees were warned that their new bosses would not tolerate drug abuse on or off the premises. "Capital Cities/ABC Plans Campaign Against Illegal Drug Use on Its Prem-ises," declared one headline in the *Wall Street Journal*. "ABC Owner Going to Dogs—To Sniff Out Drugs," cracked the *New York Post*. Later mandatory drug testing was made part of the screening process for all new network employees.

Sexual harassment was another piece of the housecleaning. Even before the Capital Cities closing, the network unveiled a new policy on fair employment practices. "All operating units of the Company are required to . . . ensure that the company's prohibition against sexual harassment is strictly followed," announced the out-going management. "Harassment includes any unwelcome sexual advances, requests for sexual favors, and other verbal or physical conduct of a sexual nature. Sexual harassment becomes illegal when it is an explicit or implicit condition of employment, promotion, compensation or benefits, or interferes with employee performance."

Capital Cities later publicized the new policy by showing clips from its in-house training films on ABC News. It also made on-the-job sexual harassment an explicit programming theme on prime-time shows like "Hooperman." The implied moral lessons represented a 180-degree turn away from those of 1970s' series like "Charlie's Angels" and "Operation Petticoat."

The sudden change in the network climate caused an uproar at ABC News, the most autonomous (and pampered) division in the company. Producers and reporters learned of Capital Cities' doings from newswire copy, and some news personnel feared that the newcomers would invade sacrosanct First Amendment territory. Tom Murphy had to hold a full-dress meeting in one of ABC's uptown studios to assure the news division that he and Dan Burke had no such plans.

While making the proper reassurances, Capital Cities put out the word internally that it did not want ABC (unlike CBS) to wash its dirty linen in public, and the early months' crises passed like phantoms in the night. A firestorm of negative publicity greeted the network's decision to cancel "Amerika," a TV miniseries that had grown out of right-wing criticism to ABC's purportedly left-wing depiction of nuclear war in "The Day After." "Amerika" depicted a Soviet occupation of the United States, and the timing of its cancellation (which was based on the show being over budget) happened to coincide with ABC News' plans to send Peter Jennings to Moscow for a week-long series of live reports on the Soviet Congress. Again, right-wing critics rose up in arms, and Capital Cities' first major programming decision was to reinstate the show. When "Amerika" was broadcast in 1987, the network lost an estimated $20 million.

The most nagging problem in Hollywood was still the issue of program ownership of all entertainment shows. Here, too, Capital Cities ran into a buzz saw. The "industry negotiations" between the studios and the networks that were meant to resolve the financial interest and syndication rule dispute took a new twist when ABC's old management claimed the 6 percent "investment tax credit" on licensed TV shows. The network bore part of the programming risk, the argument went; it should be entitled to part of the tax deduction.

Hollywood's TV suppliers joined forces and filed a $1.5 billion lawsuit against Capital Cities/ABC in early 1986, charging the network with breach of contract. The lawsuit was warning to the new owners, a shot across the bow. The implied message was, "You won't solve your financial problems at our expense." Capital Cities characterized the Hollywood action as without merit, but it was the one to back down.

The next round of the cold war in Hollywood, scheduled to begin in 1990, would be the expiration of the consent decrees prohibiting ABC, NBC, and CBS from owning more than five hours of their weekly prime-time entertainment. The lifting of this restriction, which promised to tilt the balance of power back toward the networks for the first time since 1970, raised the possibility of another all-out lobbying session in Washington.

Most TV viewers (and most network employees too), unaware of these long-range industry trends, were preoccupied with the surface signals of a network in extremis: poor ratings, a new group of owners and managers, a disheartened group of soon-to-be-fired workers. Tom Murphy and Dan Burke maintained a low public profile while mapping their future strategy for ABC. They put an intelligent but eccentric ex-World War II paratrooper from their own Capital Cities ranks in Fred Pierce's old office. They gave no interviews, and issued few press releases. But the glimpses that insiders gave of the company's new direction left no doubt that the old network was gone forever.

"We don't pay as much attention to revenues here; we focus on costs," Dan Burke told a traumatized group of ABC officials who had gathered at Villard House to be inculcated with the new business philosophy.

"Don't buy anything new," Tom Murphy instructed the maintenance men. "Take it out of stock." He himself moved into temporary quarters in the thirty-ninth floor conference room with a personal computer and used furniture from the network storeroom.

A member of the old management team, anxious to make a favorable impression, promised John Sias, the new network head, "We're going to go through the department with a fine-tooth comb." Sias reportedly replied, "No fine-toothed comb. Use a meat ax."

The price of Capital Cities/ABC stock soared during the post-takeover period on the strength of the financial community's belief that Capital Cities would succeed in wringing profits from properties where the network's previous management had not. The paper value of Warren Buffett's 18 percent stake in the new company grew from $525 million to more than $1.3 billion in less than three years. But Wall Street's expression of confidence was contingent on massive layoffs. Murphy and Burke asked a "sunset committee" of inherited managers to recommend specific cutbacks, and 1,500 employees of every variety—secretaries, corporate clerks, budget planners, middle managers—were fired in the spring and summer of 1986, on top of the 350 let go the previous summer. Only network salesmen who produced revenue were exempt. Most of the terminated personnel were middle-aged employees in the middle of their careers. They reentered the job market a few months ahead of a flood of other network refugees from CBS and NBC.

Capital Cities did offer more generous severance terms than ABC had done near the end of Fred Pierce's presidency. Under the new regime, departing employees got two weeks of pay for every year of network service and $10,000 in salary, instead of just one. But it was a scant silver lining in the swollen dark cloud. To a TV reporter working for a Buffalo newspaper owned by Warren Buffett, Dan Burke candidly admitted, "I can't smile when I walk into work for fear of making somebody feel bad."

The layoffs and demotions produced a corporate version of "The Day After" at Hard Rock. There were crying jags in elevators, shrieks of pain behind closed office doors, and numbing grief. One employee was celebrating the forty-sixth anniversary of his starting day at the network when he got word that he had been fired. Another heard from the newswire in the hospitality suite of a New Orleans hotel, where he was attending an industry convention. One outplacement executive at the firm retained by Capital Cities to help those fired line up new work described the network's ex-employees as the bitterest group of individuals he had ever seen. The idea that ABC was a family, a permanent life-support system, died hard.

In the diaspora that followed, it was not clear who got the worst part of the bargain—the executives who stayed on, or those who departed, either voluntarily or by necessity. Everyone followed individual paths of self-preservation.

Among those who stayed, Michael P. Mallardi, the bedtime connoisseur of Machiavelli's *The Prince*, emerged as the power broker among the old guard. Mallardi knew the ins and outs of the network's faulty financial projections, and Capital Cities put him in charge of all the new company's local TV stations, with oversight responsibility for Video Enterprises (including ESPN, which was now highly profitable) too. Murphy and Burke had no desire to get directly involved in network layoffs; they left it to Mallardi's staff to oversee the details. Mallardi's willingness to play the enforcer in the new order made him an object of loathing to many former colleagues. But on Wall Street, he was described by *Fortune* as one of "America's Most Wanted Managers": "Broad-gauged, energetic. Keen financial sense, but not a cold-eyed bean counter. Experience in both entertainment and communications side of business. Strong people person, with a knack for getting along."

Roone Arledge got mixed reviews. Capital Cities stripped him of his sports presidency ("The executive producer of ABC Sports is Roone Arledge" was no longer broadcast at the end of network sports events) and Arledge participated directly in only one more big TV sports event—ABC's coverage of the 1988 Winter Olympics, for which he and Fred Pierce had negotiated a whopping $309 million rights fee. Madison Avenue advertisers, leery about underwriting an Olympics without Arledge's involvement, requested that he supervise production.

In an interview with Howard Cosell on a syndicated show called "Speaking of Everything" (Cosell left ABC in 1985), Arledge described what had occurred in network television. "I think that networks did not get to be networks just by being good bottom-line investments. They didn't get to be the institutions that they are in this country just by cost-cutting," Arledge said. "It's a little bit like a person who is hit by a truck or a car. You're lying bleeding in the street. . . . All three companies were. You need people to come in and save your life. But once you're revived, you need someone with dreams, and you need vision, and you need leadership."

The vitality of ABC News, where Arledge was still president, lent credence to the idea that he could provide vision and leadership for the future. By 1988, this once also-ran division outshone all its network rivals. Arledge once again displayed his showman's skills by hiring Diane Sawyer, the "60 Minutes" correspondent, from CBS. The ABC News anchor roster—Peter Jennings, Ted Koppel, David Brinkley, Sam Donaldson, and Barbara Walters— was already by far the most impressive in the business.

But when Cosell interviewed Arledge, shortly before the 1988 Winter Olympics, the two men sounded like an aging celebrity and a tired warrior whose day was past. Arledge, asked to describe the most interesting event he had witnessed in broadcasting, recalled Arturo Toscanini's last concert on NBC Radio in a way that was emblematic of his own career.

"I don't think I've ever seen anything as emotional and fulfilling," Arledge said. "I was one of about six or seven people who knew that it was his last concert at the time. . . . That little man, eighty-seven years old, conducted a Wagner concert, and in the middle of it he was overcome with emotion and lost control of the orchestra. And NBC, not realizing that it was one of the most momentous moments in the history of music, played a Brahms record in the middle of the live performance, so nobody should hear that it wasn't perfect."

The poignancy of a maestro losing control seemed to Arledge to represent the summing up of Toscanini's life and conducting career—"the opposition to Mussolini, the La Scala years, the New York Philharmonic and the New York Metropolitan, the love affairs he had with various sopranos, the debuts of the Puccini works." But Arledge might have described himself in the same terms. The maestro of live television had seen his own performance interrupted by the constraints that Capital Cities had placed on it. No one, not even Arledge, was allowed to lose control at the network now.

Among the other top-level executives who stayed at the network, Brandon Stoddard faced the hardest task of all. ABC's chief programmer, who had always been successful before, was personally identified with a dismal prime-time schedule for three years under Capital Cities. Fred Pierce, Tony Thomopoulos, and Lew Erlicht had left the programming development pipeline in a state that was almost beyond repair. The Hollywood creative community showed little residual good will toward the network. And most of the top staffers on the West Coast left to go into independent production at the end of the 1985–86 season. Stoddard had to rebuild the schedule from the bottom up.

The 1984–85 season passed with ABC at the bottom of the prime-time ratings. So did the 1985–86 season. And the 1986–87 season. Only in February 1988 did the network eke out a second-place finish in a sweeps period—and that was due to the Winter Olympics in Calgary (on which the network lost a reported $60 million) and to aging CBS shows as much to ABC's renewed strength. Stoddard began to turn the schedule around with shows like "Thirtysomething," "China Beach," and "The Wonder Years"—new prime-time series from young, unproven Hollywood producers who would not have been listened to seriously by network executives at Century City three years before. Aaron

Spelling's exclusivity deal with ABC expired, freeing up time periods for new shows. Then "Roseanne," a comedy starring Roseanne Barr, premiered. The first new series proposed by Marcia Carsey and Tom Werner at ABC since the network turned down "The Cosby Show" became network TV's top-rated hit.

Tom Murphy and Dan Burke rewarded Stoddard that same spring by spinning him off in an in-house production subsidiary for prime-time series which the network would jointly own—an appointment tied to the relaxation of program ownership limits in 1990.

"I'm smiling for the first time in a long time," Stoddard said, adding that his three-year stint as chief programmer had been like "serving time in prison."

Among the major players who left ABC voluntarily, none became more invisible more quickly than Everett H. Erlick, the takeover's *éminence grise*. Several months before Murphy and Burke took over, Erlick announced that he would be going into private law practice. He gave a parting interview in *Broadcasting*, which warmly portrayed him as a "confidant to Leonard Goldenson" and an "adviser and consenter to corporate strategy." "In retrospect: the Erlick years at ABC," the magazine titled the article, evoking a gratifying image of a TV statesman.

But after starting afresh as the senior partner in the new New York office of Arnold & Porter, a prestigious Washington law firm, Erlick had to adapt to professional life outside the network cocoon, and discovered that it was not as durable. His role had always been that of an industry insider, someone whom Mark Fowler, the outgoing FCC chairman, might call on the telephone and ask for advice. But Arnold & Porter's probable assumption was that Erlick would act as a "rainmaker"—a partner capable of bringing new business into the firm—and here was a new challenge. Wielding power at ABC, Erlick had been a feared man. Once he resigned, there was nothing left to fear. He left Arnold & Porter after one year.

Former network executives whose careers had gotten entangled in Erlick's legal machine continued separate lives and careers. Cecily Coleman moved with her husband into a home in Arlington, Virginia, worked part-time as a producer for public TV, and became the mother of a baby boy, Aaron. Jim Abernathy, financially and emotionally pressed after his unexplained firing, went into business for himself and quickly established himself as a New York public relations and Wall Street consultant. He and Coleman never spoke again.

After all the publicity about Pierce's "psychic" relationship with Beverlee Dean, Dean was still in a state of limbo, living in Encino with the hope of becoming a Hollywood producer. She stayed in contact with acquaintances who worked in network TV, but she was bitter about her experience at ABC. Dean gave up the practice of reading the handwriting of celebrity clients; the intuitive skills that she had once possessed in abundance seemed to have deserted her.

Mindy Naud, on the other hand, settled into a new life in Europe. While working on a movie called *Escape* in Italy, she met a film producer in the music mixing room, fell in love, and got married. Two children later she had her own company, Mindy Films S.R.L., and was producing movies abroad. Although Naud returned often to Hollywood for holidays with family and friends, she never auditioned for another role in network TV again.

The career of one person whose success Dean had predicted was still on an ascending track. Less than a week after announcing his resignation from ABC, Tony Thomopoulos landed on his feet in a new job as president and chief operating officer of United Artists. Jerry Weintraub, the studio's chairman, was the good friend who hired Thomopoulos; he was fired a few months later by Kirk Kerkorian, the studio's owner. But Thomopoulos survived the shakeup, and for three years continued to play an institutional role in the West Coast creative community—signing movie deals (including the one that financed the hit movie *Rain Man*), appearing at private screenings, maintaining Hollywood appearances. He appeared to have left the debacle of ABC entirely behind.

"Mr. Thomopoulos is in the movie business now and has nothing to say about television," his United Artists secretary replied in clipped, British tones to an inquiry about his days at the network.

Cristina Ferrare kept her job as the on-air hostess of KABC-TV's "AM Los Angeles," and also played a continuing role in local society. Every morning at 9, she provided an interview forum for a new set of publicity-hungry celebrity guests.

Hollywood displayed its sense of humor about the couple in oblique, inside jokes. In *Beverly Hills Cop II*, a Paramount movie that starred Eddie Murphy, the featured "bad guy" was a gun-running, drug-smuggling character named Thomopoulos. A staff lawyer at Paramount, when asked about the choice of names, replied that the studio could find more than one Thomopoulos in the telephone book.

Thomopoulos's contract at United Artists expired shortly before the studio was sold in 1989, and was not renewed. He tried briefly to run the studio with financing from an obscure, Monaco-based company. When the buyout failed, he signed on as an independent movie and TV producer at Columbia Pictures, another studio rumored to be up for sale.

Gary Pudney also enjoyed briefly enhanced powers directly after the takeover. In the revamped West Coast entertainment staff, he was named vice president for network specials and variety programming, and in that capacity began producing for broadcast viewers the same kind of entertainment shows that he was accustomed to putting together for in-house network galas. Among the up-and-coming celebrities featured in Pudney's special programs were Fawn Hall, Oliver North's shredding secretary, and Ronald Reagan, Jr., who traveled to Africa and visited tribesmen.

Pudney's extravagant West Coast style was so antithetical to the new management mores that Capital Cities was actively promoting in New York that his continued presence at the company was a mystery to many of his former colleagues. His social connections provided one possible answer. Walter Annenberg, the father of Wallis, one of Pudney's dearest Hollywood friends, owned

TV Guide, and TV insiders believed that Murphy and Burke, after buying Triangle Broadcasting from Walter Annenberg in 1970, harbored hopes of purchasing Triangle Publishing and *TV Guide* one day too.

In August 1988, a few weeks after Rupert Murdoch bought *TV Guide,* Gary Pudney was asked to leave ABC.

A few people had moved ahead of the industry by leaving the network ahead of the turmoil, and brought the good times along with them.

Elton Rule was one. After leaving ABC, he rejoined his old colleague I. Martin Pompadur, and the two men became the general partners of a Merrill, Lynch investment group that acquired local radio, TV, and cable outlets around the United States. Within three years, at ML Media Partners and a second holding company called Multivision, they had acquired a portfolio of more than $1.1 billion in media properties, with the avowed aim of reselling them later at a substantial capital gains, and their other investments were rapidly expanding.

In spacious offices at 2020 Avenue of the Stars, across from his old network offices on the West Coast, Rule kept in touch with many of his former colleagues, often dispensing advice and counsel to out-of-work friends. Perhaps because he had played no direct role in the sale of the network, he was strongly identified with the better qualities from its past. Rule expressed no regrets about his long career at ABC. He was making more money as a private businessman than he ever had inside a corporation. He and Goldenson continued to speak on the telephone every week or ten days.

Barry Diller and Michael Eisner, the most successful members of the generation of programmers weaned at ABC, had grown into *the* leading corporate players in the entertainment industry, inheriting the crown of Adolph Zukor and his movie studio heirs. Diller was Rupert Murdoch's on-the-spot executive at Fox Television, responsible for building a fourth TV network and running

Twentieth Century-Fox. Rupert Murdoch was the new father figure, as Leonard Goldenson and Charles Bluhdorn once had been, whom Diller had to please, but Diller yielded to no one else. He hired Leonard Goldberg, who had offered him his first network job more than twenty years earlier, to oversee Fox's movie production. (Goldberg resigned in early 1989.) To develop new shows for his network, he hired talented, unorthodox programmers in their twenties—spitting images of himself and Eisner in 1966. Diller was as rich as he was powerful. His 25 percent stake in the studio when it was sold to Murdoch had been converted into 1.2 percent of Murdoch's News Corp, Ltd—four million shares worth almost $80 million in 1989. This equity, plus $3 million in annual salary and five percent of Fox Television's pre-tax income, made him one of Hollywood's best-compensated executives.

The only person better compensated in Hollywood than Diller was Eisner. During his first four years as chairman of Walt Disney, Eisner quadrupled the publicly traded value of its assets. Still masking his shrewd commercial instincts behind a happy-go-lucky exterior, Eisner was growing fabulously wealthy on company stock options worth, in 1988, an estimated $132 million. A core of top production executives who had followed Eisner to Disney from Paramount churned out highly popular, if undistinguished movies, making the studio the top box-office performer in Hollywood. But it was the Disney theme parks, which Goldenson had been the first to subsidize, that were turning the company into an entertainment giant. The animation studio of *Cinderella* and *Snow White and the Seven Dwarfs* was expanding into Europe and Japan, turning Eisner into a real estate mogul and programming specialist. But to children watching TV, he was the friendly man who talked with cuddly animal characters while introducing the "Disney Sunday Movie."

Only Fred Pierce, once the network's most promising young executive, failed to live up to expectations. More than anyone else in the industry, he had risen with network television, gloried in its power, and fallen with its demise. Upon his resignation, Murphy and Burke bought Pierce out of his network contract at reportedly half of its value. He stayed on the board of directors, and had the "right to maintain an office at the headquarters of the corporation." But this now meant Villard House, not network headquarters. For the next three years, Pierce was out of sight and out of mind to most of his old network colleagues. He became an industry nonentity.

With a nest egg of more than $8 million from the takeover alone, Pierce relaxed for the first time in years. A former colleague met him at the Mallihouana Beach Club in Anguilla, a toney Caribbean resort, a few months after the buyout.

"What are you doing?" Pierce asked.

"I'm not working," his former colleague replied.

Pierce laughed. "Neither am I."

He occasionally returned to Hard Rock for a haircut from Vito or David, the fourth-floor barbers, and on one such visit took the elevator up to Goldenson's office suite. The old chairman received Pierce cordially, but they no longer had the network as a common business ground between them. When Pierce sought advice, he met with a stony response.

"I wouldn't know how to advise you on that," Goldenson said at the end of the meeting.

In 1989, Pierce cut the umbilical cord with the network and went into business for himself. He formed The Fred Pierce Company in New York, and tried to refashion himself as an independent producer of network programming. His first business partner in this new venture, oddly enough, was his old nemesis—Fred Silverman.

"I'm not rumpled any more," Silverman told *Forbes* during the 1988–89 season. Indeed, the former wunderkind of TV programming was now its graybeard prodigy. Silverman had five prime-time series, starring well-known actors from the 1970s like Andy Griffith, Tom Bosley, and Carroll O'Connor, on the air, mostly at NBC, where Brandon Tartikoff had willingly put his old boss and programming mentor back into business in a big way. As

Silverman's career rebounded (and Pierce's sagged), the "two Freds" finally buried the hatchet and went into business together. Silverman was already one of the most prolific independent producers of prime-time programming in Hollywood. The first project in his new joint venture company with Pierce was a late-night weekly variety program created to air on NBC's local TV stations after "Saturday Night Live." Pierce seemed destined to recover his professional legs through business dealings with former subordinates. In June 1989 he became an independent producer for Hollywood Pictures, the newest production arm of Michael Eisner's expanding Disney empire.

"Once you've built an empire, you don't want to see it disappear overnight," Goldenson said after selling ABC. "But you get a funny feeling in the pit of your stomach when you're no longer in power."

For Goldenson, the first few months after the takeover were the most difficult of all. Money and business had always been high on his list of priorities, and the more than $50 million that he received for his seat at the network table had to provide some satisfaction. But the thrill of gambling had always provided a higher pleasure—and after cashing in his chips, he now had to watch Tom Murphy roll anew with his old dice.

Goldenson did not retire easily. He visited his thirty-ninth floor office regularly, kept abreast of network programming news (most of it bad) and new business developments (most of it worse). As the chairman of the Capital Cities/ABC executive committee, he still had a major voice in the company's affairs. But while the dust was settling from the buyout, Murphy and Burke had little time to pay him any heed. One of Goldenson's old friends was overheard saying, "The executive committee meets once a year at 3 a.m."

Goldenson's compensations were now of a more subtle and enduring variety than money could buy. Not long after the takeover, *Fortune* put a picture of Tom Murphy on the cover with the headline: "Culture Shock Rattles the TV Networks." The same issue of the magazine featured Goldenson on the inside, along with past laureates like Andrew Carnegie, Thomas Edison, and Walt Disney, as an inductee in the U.S. Business Hall of Fame.

"A mild-mannered movie magnate bet on a failing TV network and won big," *Fortune* summed up Goldenson's career. He himself liked to compare his business success with that of Henry Kaiser, who built the Grand Coulee Dam and America's wartime merchant marine. Kaiser had been Goldenson's original sponsor for "Maverick," and he had always gambled big, taking on far larger and more daunting tasks than his experience and long odds seemed to permit.

Goldenson's gamble on Hollywood and network TV was over. He had placed his chips on the table before anyone, including himself, could know whether or not it would succeed. When retirement came and his industry was exploding with bigger and bigger deals, Goldenson self-deprecatingly but happily described his own achievement with the old showman's term "hokum"—the magical enthusiasm of a child watching movies or playing with trains. ABC's heyday, like that of the railroads, was over. There would never be another network with so many talented and deluded executives. But their delusion—the idea that America could be one nation, under God, united by TV—had built a network and been shared by millions. Sitting in the new office complex that Tom Murphy had built for ABC on the old West 66th Street riding stable site, Goldenson could look back on sixty years of Hollywood and broadcasting history, and know that he had done good. For the first time in his life, he could become a pure spectator.

Bibliography and Sources

The facts and quotations in *Beyond Control—ABC and the Fate of the Networks* come from three types of source material: (1) books, magazine and newspaper articles, and industry data banks; (2) interviews conducted by the author; and (3) the author's direct acquaintance with the characters presented in the narrative.

All quotations, whether derived from books, from interview sources, or from personal experience, reflect actual conversations and meetings. The person who speaks was not in all cases the source. Some conversations were reported by third parties.

The following bibliography contains most of the written material used in preparing the text. Because some interviewees requested anonymity, the list of sources is partial. For background research, the author wishes to thank especially Mark Wanamaker of the Bison Archives, Jim Poteet and Leslie Slocum of the now-defunct Television Information Office, and the staff of the Television Bureau of Advertising.

BOOKS

Adams, Charles F. and Henry, *Chapters of Erie*. J. R. Osgood, 1871.
Barnouw, Erik, *The Golden Web: A History of Broadcasting in the United States* (Vol. II, 1933–53). New York: Oxford University Press, 1968.

——— A Tower of Babel: A History of Broadcasting in the United States (Vol. 1, to 1933). New York: Oxford University Press, 1966.

——— Tube of Plenty: The Evolution of American Television, rev. ed. New York: Oxford University Press, 1982.

Bilby, Kenneth, The General: David Sarnoff and the Rise of the Communications Industry. New York: Harper & Row, 1986.

Boyer, Peter, Who Killed CBS? The Undoing of America's Number One News Network. New York: Random House, 1984.

Brown, Les, Television: The Business Behind the Box. New York: Harcourt, Brace, Jovanovich, 1971.

Cowan, Geoffrey, See No Evil: The Backstage Battle over Sex and Violence on Television. New York: Simon & Schuster, 1979.

DeLorean, John Z., with Ted Schwartz, DeLorean. Grand Rapids, Mich.: Zondervan, 1985.

Gabler, Neal, An Empire of Their Own: How the Jews Invented Hollywood. New York: Crown, 1988.

Gitlin, Todd, Inside Prime Time. New York: Pantheon Books, 1985.

Jones, Landon, Great Expectations, America and the Baby Boom Generation. New York: Ballantine, 1981.

Jowett, Garth, Film: The Democratic Art, a Social History of Moviegoing in America. Boston: Little, Brown, 1976.

McCraw, Thomas K., Prophets of Regulation. Cambridge, Mass.: Belknap Press, 1984.

McNeil, Alex, Total Television: A Comprehensive Guide to Programming from 1948 to the Present. New York: Penguin Books, 1984.

Moldea, Dan E., Dark Victory: Ronald Reagan, MCA, and the Mob. New York: Viking, 1986.

Morison, Samuel Eliot, Henry Steele Commager, and William E. Leuchtenberg, The Growth of the American Republic. New York: Oxford University Press, 1969.

Paley, William S., As It Happened: A Memoir. Garden City, N.Y.: Doubleday, 1979.

Quinlan, Sterling, Inside ABC: American Broadcasting Company's Rise to Power. New York: Hastings House, 1979.

Sklar, Robert, Movie-Made America: A Social History of American Movies. New York: Random House, 1975.

Sterling, Christopher H., and John M. Kittross, Stay Tuned, A Concise History of American Broadcasting. Belmont, Calif.: Wadsworth, 1978.

Train, John, The Money Masters. New York: Perennial Library, 1987.

Wharton, Edith, The House of Mirth. New York: Charles Scribner's Sons, 1905.

Magazine/Newspaper Articles

"ABC Entertainment President Stoddard Resigns to Head New In-House Venture," *Wall Street Journal*, March 22, 1989.

"ABC News Under the Gun: A Long Talk with Roone Arledge," *New York*, August 15, 1983.

"ABC on Silverman's Quitting," *New York Times*, February 22, 1978.

"ABC's Fred Pierce: The Most Powerful Man in Television," *New York*, October 10, 1977.

"ABC's Leonard Goldenson: A Shrewd Strategy for Staying on Top," *Forbes*, July 19, 1982.

"ABC Newswomen's Gripes," *New York Daily News*, January 23, 1986.

"ABC Under Inquiry for Alleged Irregularities in Fees," *New York Times*, August 17, 1980.

"ABC Upping Pudney to Set New Trend," *The Hollywood Reporter*, April 17, 1986.

"ABC Will Proceed with 'Amerika'," *New York Times*, January 23, 1986.

"America's Most-Wanted Managers," *Fortune*, February 3, 1986.

"American Broadcasting Companies, Inc.," First Boston Research, August 22, 1984.

"Amid Inquiry, Aides of ABC Tell of Gaps in Fiscal Power," *New York Times*, August 18, 1980.

"Anthony Thomopoulos," *New York*, September 18, 1978.

"The Apprenticeship of Frank Yablans," *New York*, September 23, 1974.

Article on Fred Silverman's ABC Departure, *Fortune*, February 27, 1978.

"At a Ripe 25, 'Hospital' Is Healthy," *New York Times*, April 2, 1988.

"Barry Diller: A Profile," *Broadcasting*, September 25, 1972.

"Baseball Gets Billion-Dollar TV Deal," *New York Times*, April 8, 1983.

"Bonanza at the Top of Disney," *New York Times*, August 29, 1987.

"Capital Cities & ABC," *Broadcasting*, March 25, 1985.

"Capital Cities Assumes Command at ABC," *Electronic Media*, January 6, 1986.

"Capital Cities' Capital Coup," *Fortune*, April 15, 1985.

"The Capital Man of Capital Cities," *Television*, March 1965.

"A Case of Intrigue," *Los Angeles Times*, December 12, 1982.

"Communications Conglomerate to Test Employees for Drug Use," *New York Times*, January 12, 1986.

"Culture Shock Rattles the TV Networks," *Fortune*, April 14, 1986.

"For Roone, It's a Wider World," *New York Daily News*, January 28, 1986.

"For 25 Cents, Every Moviegoer Was Royalty," *New York Times*, January 24, 1989.

271

"Fred Pierce: A Profile," *Broadcasting*, January 20, 1975.

"Glamor Galore at ABC Gala," *New York Post*, June 9, 1985.

"Hearings Before the Subcommittee on Communications on S. 1707," 98th Congress, November 2 and 4.

"Hollywood's Cocaine Connection," *TV Guide*, February 28, 1981.

"Hollywood's Hottest Independent: An Interview with Stephen J. Cannell," *View*, March 1985.

"Hollywood's Hottest Stars," *New York*, July 30, 1984.

"How Paramount Keeps Churning out Winners," *Business Week*, June 11, 1984.

"In Dispute: Producers' Suit Could Hurt ABC Shows for Fall Season," *Electronic Media*, March 10, 1986.

"In Retrospect: The Erlick Years at ABC," *Broadcasting*, December 2, 1985.

"Intelligencer," *New York*, August 10, 1984.

"The Intense Talks Behind ABC Deal," *New York Times*, March 20, 1985.

"It's a Good Marriage That Uses Wife's Name," *USA Today*, March 29, 1985.

"John Sias, Executive Clown, Just Got Serious," *Channels*, July/August, 1986.

"Looking Out for No. 1," *American Film*, September 1979.

"Lost Bearings," *Forbes*, August 13, 1984.

"Luring Ad Dollars from Network TV," *Washington Journalism Review*, October 1986.

"The Man Re-animating Disney," *New York Times Magazine*, December 29, 1985.

"Meanwhile, Back at ABC," *Los Angeles Herald Examiner*, March 19, 1985.

"1985: A Year Like No Other for the Fifth Estate," *Broadcasting*, December 30, 1985.

"Plaintiff's Trial Brief in the matter of DeLorean v. DeLorean," Ruling by Judge Imbriani, Superior Court of New Jersey, Chancery Division—Family Part, Somerset County, Docket No. 09378-85.

"The Psychic Who Came in from the Cold," *Los Angeles Times*, *Calendar* magazine, March 15, 1981.

"Q & A: Fred Pierce, ABC Chief Discusses Ratings Dilemma, Impending Merger," *Electronic Media*, September 30, 1985.

"Roone!" *Broadcasting*, December 2, 1985.

"Roone Arledge: ABC News Sports a New Leader," *Washington Post*, May 3, 1977.

"SEC Insider Trading Inquiry File re: Capital Cities Communications, Inc. and American Broadcasting Co. Inc., merger."

"Silverman Superstar," *Newsweek*, January 30, 1978.

"Son of Hollywood's Hottest Stars," *New York*, October 8, 1984.

"A Star Is Born," *Business Week*, April 1, 1985.

"Super Television: The Promise—and High Risks—of High Definition TV," *Business Week*, January 30, 1989.

"Ted Turner: Back from the Brink," *Fortune*, July 7, 1986.

"Tony Thomopoulos, Right-Hand Man to Fred Pierce, Named to Succeed Fred Silverman," *Broadcasting*, February 6, 1978.

"Too Much Gold in the Parachute?" *New York Times*, January 26, 1986.

"TV Industry Has Fun with ABC's Psychic," *Los Angeles Times*, March 22, 1981.

"TV Sports Money Machine Falters," *New York Times Magazine*, January 26, 1986.

"The Upward Mobility of ABC's Fred Pierce," *Broadcasting*, November 13, 1978.

"Winning Diane: How ABC's Roone Arledge Snatched Her Away from CBS," *New York*, March 13, 1989.

INTERVIEW SOURCES

Seymour Amlen, Missy Attridge, David Aylward, Erik Barnouw, Bob Beck, Seth Baker, Richard Beesemyer, Charlene Bergman, Kathy Bonk, Emma Bowen, Peter Boyer, Bob Boyett, Bill Breen, Daniel Brenner, Dean Burch, Richard Burns, Herb Cahan, Jack Callahan, Mark Carliner, Nancy Carter, Deborah Caulfield, Tom Chisman, Arthur Cohen, Barry Cole, Michael Collyer, Barbara Corday, David Crook, Peter Cusack, Michael Dann, Beverlee Dean, John DeLorean, Dennis Doty, Mitch Drobner, Everett Erlick, Ted Fitilis, Rita Flynn, Theresa Fulbert, Barbara Gallagher, Mickey Gardner, Charles Garry, Ivan Goff, Henry Geller, Leonard Goldberg, Leonard Goldenson, James Fletcher Goodman, Merrill Grant, Kathryn Harris, Jack Hausman, James Hay, J. William Hayes, Tom Herwitz, Steven Heyer, Leonard Hill, Bernard Hollander, Arnold Huberman, David Johnson, Freeman Jones, Jordan Kerner, Bob King, Al Kramer, Phil Kriegler, John Lazarus, J. William Lilley, Richard MacDonald, James Maher, David Markey, Harry Marks, Paul Masterson, Richard Merkle, Steve Mills, John Mitchell, Ellis Moore, Earle K. Moore, Melinda Naud, Randy Nichols, Richard O'Leary, Norma Pace, Everett C. Parker, Alan Pearce, Frederick Pierce, I. Martin

Pompadur, John Rockwell, Thomas Rogers, Alan Ross, George Reeves, Lee Rich, Bud Rukeyser, Elton Rule, Edgar Scherick, Andrew Schwartzman, Shaun Sheehan, Simon B. Siegel, Bob Shanks, Charles Smith, Dale Snape, Geoffrey Stern, John Trombadore, Edwin Vane, Shug Villa, Charles Ward, Susan Watson, Joan Wechsler, Jerry Zucker, Eugene Zukor, Jr.

Index

Aaron Spelling Productions, 146; *see also* Spelling, Aaron

ABC (American Broadcasting Company):
audience demographics orientation at, 67, 70, 149, 167; back-end deals, 130, 149, 190; as beneficiary of government regulation, 109–10; buyout offers (1965), 51; Capital Cities merger proposals, 160, 199, 214, 217–18, 221–25; chairmanship, 4, 68, 127–29, 136, 142, 159, 163, 231; conflict-of-interest cases at, 126, 140–42; consent decree on prime-time entertainment ownership (to 1990), 117, 255, 260; conversion to color technology of, 51–52; corporate sex and promiscuity at, 84–85, 195–98, 200; distribution handicap of, 46, 51, 95–96, 112, 113; drug use charges at, 218, 253; early TV, 38–41, 43–46, 109, 164; employee benefits programs at, 127, 164, 227, 233, 239; and FCC deregulation attempt, 174, 180, 183; formed from NBC Blue Network, 29, 37, 109; growing dichotomy between network and corporate faction, 127, 134–35; headquarters of, 3–4, 51, 52, 267; insider promotion vs. outsider hiring at, 123; ITT merger proposal, 51–52, 65, 109, 156, 221; layoffs, post-takeover, 241–42, 256–57; local affiliates of, 46, 53, 56, 70, 95–96, 103, 113–14, 115, 160, 214, 217, 240–41; local station ownership, 38–39, 83, 198, 257; merger with United Paramount Theatres, 39–41, 47, 109, 209; new-technologies ventures of, 152–55, 157, 158, 187–90 (*see also* ESPN; TeleFirst; Video Enterprises); 1978–79 revenues, 119; nonbroadcasting businesses, 124, 127, 134–35; Number One network, 5–6, 9–10, 12, 51, 80–81, 82–83, 87, 89, 94–97, 119; profits, 83, 119, 156, 210, 253; profit projection for 1985–90, 219; profit reversal, 252–53; programming, 9, 44–46, 47–52, 62–63, 70–71, 73–74, 77–81, 87, 96–97, 119, 129, 133, 143, 158, 165–72, 185–87, 190–92, 211–12, 239–40, 259–60; programming staff, 59–64, 73–75, 80, 88–89, 94, 98–104, 129–30, 149, 239–

275

Huntington Williams was educated at Groton School and Yale. He received a doctorate from Oxford, where he was a Marshall Scholar and wrote *Rousseau and Romantic Autobiography* (Oxford University Press, 1983). From 1981 to 1985 he worked as an editor and corporate speechwriter at ABC. Born in Baltimore and raised in North Carolina, he lives in New York.